The Mareva Injunction and Anton
Practice and Precedents

LAMB CHAMBERS

LAMB
CHAMBERS

Lamb Building, Elm Court, Temple,
London EC4Y 7AS
020 7797 8300
Fax: 020 7797 8308; DX: 418 London
E-mail: info@lambchambers.co.uk
URL: www.lambchambers.co.uk
Out of hours telephone: 020 8590 6104/
8878 6889

Chambers of Christopher Gardner QC
Clerk: John Kelly; Administrator: Miss
Linda Spanner

Gardner, Christopher QC 1968†	**Miles,** Napier 1989
Priest, Julian QC 1954	**Meakin,** Timothy 1989
Leeming, Ian QC 1970†	**Stuart,** James 1990
Sharp, Alastair 1968†	**Gatty,** Daniel 1990
McNeile, Anthony 1970	**Majumdar,** Shantanu 1992
West, Mark 1973†	**Blaker,** Gary 1993
di Mambro, David 1973	**Haggerty,** Elizabeth 1994
Carey, Jeremy 1974†	**Happe,** Dominic 1993
Connerty, Anthony 1974	**Jones,** Rhiannon 1993
Shaw, Stephen 1975	**Hayes,** Richard 1995
Allston, Anthony 1975	**Richards,** Dr Jonathan 1995
Stewart, Paul 1975	**Frith,** Timothy 1996
Brilliant, Simon 1976	**Prand,** Annette 1995
Caun, Lawrence 1977	**Stagi,** Alexandra 1997
Emerson, Paul 1984	**Ellis,** Dr Peter 1997
Williams, Simon 1984	**Daley,** Howard 1997
Ough, Dr Richard 1985	**Wille,** Andrew 1998
Blackwood, Clive 1986	**Watkins,** Guy 1999

Lamb Chambers
Lamb Building, Elm Court, Temple,
London EC4Y 7AS, ☎ 020 7797 8300
✉ info@lambchambers.co.uk
Call Date: July 1985, Inner Temple
Qualifications: [MA Law, MBBS, MSc, in
Management, FCIArb , MRCS , LRCP,
Chartered Arbitrator]
✉ ough@ough.com

*The Mareva Injunction and Anton Piller
Order.*

Lamb Chambers is accredited by the Law
Society for CPD. A list of seminars which
chambers is willing to undertake and a list
of articles and publications produced by
chambers is available at the Lamb Chambers website. Enquiries in respect of seminars on any other subjects in which Lamb
Chambers practises are welcome.

The Mareva Injunction and Anton Piller Order

Practice and Precedents

Second Edition

Richard N Ough
MA (Law), MB, BS, Dip Law, MRCS, LRCP, LMCC, ACIArb
Barrister

William Flenley
MA (Oxon), LLM, BCL
Barrister

Consultant Editor
John N Adams, LLB
Barrister, Professor of Commercial Law, University of Kent
Director, Common Law Institute of Intellectual Property

Butterworths
London, Dublin, Edinburgh
1993

United Kingdom	Butterworth & Co (Publishers) Ltd, 88 Kingsway, LONDON WC2B 6AB and 4 Hill Street, EDINBURGH EH2 3JZ
Australia	Butterworths, SYDNEY, MELBOURNE, BRISBANE, ADELAIDE, PERTH, CANBERRA and HOBART
Belgium	Butterworth & Co (Publishers) Ltd, BRUSSELS
Canada	Butterworths Canada Ltd, TORONTO and VANCOUVER
Ireland	Butterworth (Ireland) Ltd, DUBLIN
Malaysia	Malayan Law Journal Sdn Bhd, KUALA LUMPUR
New Zealand	Butterworths of New Zealand Ltd, WELLINGTON and AUCKLAND
Puerto Rico	Equity de Puerto Rico, Inc, HATO REY
Singapore	Butterworths Asia, SINGAPORE
USA	Butterworth Legal Publishers, AUSTIN, Texas; BOSTON, Massachusetts; CLEARWATER, Florida (D & S Publishers); ORFORD, New Hampshire (Equity Publishing); ST PAUL, Minnesota; and SEATTLE, Washington

A CIP Catalogue record for this book is available from the British Library

First edition 1987

ISBN 0 406 11647 4

Typeset by Doublestruck Ltd, London
Printed and bound in Great Britain by Mackays of Chatham plc, Chatham, Kent

To Geoffrey, Elizabeth and Thomas Ough
and David Flenley

Foreword

When I began practice at the Bar, neither the Mareva injunction nor the Anton Piller order had been conceived. When I left the Bar, the latter was only four years old and the former had yet to be born.

Now, applications for such injunctions or orders form a major part of the interlocutory business of the courts. The expansion of trade, the ease with which assets can be transferred both in and out of the jurisdiction and the temptation to spirit away evidence have made the two remedies essential weapons in the armoury of the court to protect both assets and evidence pending trial.

Inevitably, the infant remedies developed quickly and, since the first edition of this book, there have been a number of important decisions. The second edition brings the work up to date so that it is a comprehensive practitioner's guide to the principles currently governing the grant of the two remedies. It will, I am sure, be invaluable to all practising in the civil courts.

I commend the authors on the scope and clarity of their work.

Taylor C.J.

Lord Taylor of Gosforth
Lord Chief Justice of England

June 1993

Preface to the second edition

Since the first edition of this book, six years ago, the world of Anton Piller orders has been transformed by the decisions in *Lock International plc v Beswick* [1989] 1 WLR 1268 and *Universal Thermosensors Ltd v Hibben* [1992] 1 WLR 840. A new type of Mareva injunction, the 'worldwide Mareva', has been invented and refined. Parties seeking to apply for either order must now take the greatest care to ensure that they comply with the obligation to make full and frank disclosure, and with the other obligations imposed upon them so as to protect the defendant.

The purpose of this book is to provide a clear and practical guide through an otherwise rather technical maze. In addition to synopses, this edition contains at the start of Chapter 9 and Chapter 10 quick summaries for solicitors who either wish to apply for one of the orders, or are approached by a client who has just been served with one and requires quick advice.

We should like to thank Lord Taylor of Gosforth CJ for most kindly agreeing to write the Foreword.

In addition, we should like to thank those who have taken considerable time and effort to read and make invaluable comments on the manuscript: Francis Bacon, Harold Burnett QC, Marija Danilunas, Nicholas Davidson QC, Susanna Fischer, Tom Leech, Alison Ough, Michael Pooles, James Wadsworth QC, Laurie West-Knights and Roger Wyand. We owe a particular debt of gratitude to Julian Picton and Clare Price.

The consulting editor Professor Adams has provided practical help at all stages.

We have also benefited from a seminar at the Common Law Institute of Intellectual Property, chaired by Mr Stephen Stewart QC CBE, on the reform of the Anton Piller jurisdiction. Any errors which remain are our own.

The book could not have been written without the help of our clerk, Stephen Smith, who provided the time in which to write. Finally, we thank everyone at Butterworths, whose patience has been supreme.

We have attempted to state the law as at 11 May 1993.

William Flenley & Richard Ough
4 Paper Buildings
Temple, EC4

11 May 1993

Preface to the first edition

The Mareva injunction and the Anton Piller order are properly called the nuclear weapons of the law. They are more than that – there is no four-minute warning. They can be used tactically or strategically.

Their very nature, and the speed with which they can be deployed, is daunting. This may deter some practitioners from relying on them. It should not do so.

All those for whom prompt protection of legal rights is vital, whether this be in the English High Court or county court or in another jurisdiction in which these orders have been followed, should find this work helpful. Practitioners who do not familiarise themselves with the procedures set out in this book may well be in peril.

A pragmatic approach is taken in this book. A synopsis enables the practitioner to determine rapidly whether an order is applicable to a particular case, and also whether there are grounds for variation or discharge of an order, once granted. The synopsis is cross-referenced both to precedents and the body of the book. Numerous examples from the cases are included as illustrations.

I wish to thank Mr John Adams for initiating, encouraging and contributing to this project and introducing me to Butterworths. I am also indebted to the editorial staff of Butterworths for their great assistance in the preparation of this book. My gratitude is due to Mr W R Heeler of Chancery Chambers, Royal Courts of Justice, for providing me with the Chancery Division notes and precedents which have been incorporated to assist practitioners in this rapidly developing and technical area of the law. I am also indebted to Mr Richard Slowe for the precedent laid out in Appendix L (the *ne exeat regno* writ from *AL Nankel for Contracting and Trading Ltd v Lowe* [1986] QB 235).

I wish also to express my thanks to Mr John Hopkins of Downing College, Cambridge and the City University, whose stimulating teaching first interested me in these orders, and Mr Lionel Zysman of the City University, tutor for my MA on the Anton Piller order, from which this book evolved. I acknowledge the encouragement of my former pupil master, Mr Roger Wyand, who permitted me to write both an MA dissertation and part of this book during pupillage. I am grateful to His Honour Judge Robert Taylor, Mr Robert Owen, Miss Helen Kavanagh and Miss Margaret Bowron who kindly read and made detailed comments on the manuscript and the Mr Gilbert Gray, QC for his tangible and intangible contributions. My debt to the learning of friends and colleagues is considerable, but none of my intellectual creditors can be blamed for errors, the responsibility for which is mine alone. I also wish to thank Miss Sharon Beattie, Miss Susan Smith and also Miss M C O'Regan, librarian, for her assistance. Lastly, I wish to thank Miss Elaine Herring, who assisted me enormously with drafts.

Richard Ough
4 Paper Buildings, Temple, London
and 2 Park Square, Leeds

March 1987

Contents

PART II: THE PLAINTIFF'S APPLICATION

PART IV: QUICK SUMMARIES, SYNOPSES AND PRECEDENTS

Table of statutes

References in this Table are to paragraph numbers and Appendices. Paragraph numbers and Appendices printed in bold type indicate where the Act is set out in part or in full.

Table of cases

PART I

The nature of the orders

CHAPTER 1
Introduction

1.0 The Mareva injunction and Anton Piller order are interlocutory court orders. They are usually made ex parte and before proceedings have been commenced, but may be made at any stage of the proceedings.[1] The orders may be granted by the High Court; county court proceedings, other than those in the Patents County Court, must be transferred to the High Court for the application to be made.[2] The names 'Anton Piller' and 'Mareva' derive from early cases in the Court of Appeal which confirmed the jurisdiction to grant the orders.[3]

---

1 In matrimonial cases, Anton Piller orders may be granted during the course of the proceedings. They may also be granted in aid of execution. But generally they are made before proceedings have been commenced. See Chapter 3.
2 See **5.6**.
3 *Anton Piller KG v Manufacturing Processes Ltd* [1976] Ch 55; *Mareva Compania Naviera SA v International Bulkcarriers SA* [1975] 2 Lloyd's Rep 509.

1.1 The Mareva injunction is essentially a 'freezing' order. It temporarily freezes assets of a defendant or potential defendant which may be required to satisfy a judgment or potential judgment in the plaintiff's favour. This is to prevent the defendant from frustrating the potential judgment by disposing of his assets within the jurisdiction, or removing them from it. The Mareva injunction is not, however, intended to give plaintiffs security for their anticipated judgments, and so it cannot interfere with the rights of the defendant's secured creditors.

1.2 The Anton Piller order is a form of discovery which, under the circumstances discussed below, permits search of the defendant's premises and seizure of items or documents found there which might form evidence in the plaintiff's action or proposed action against that defendant. The search is made by solicitors. The judge may order that it be the plaintiff's solicitors, supervised by an independent solicitor who has experience of the workings of Anton Piller orders;[1] alternatively the order may provide that it be only the plaintiff's solicitors. If evidence of a type specified in the order is found, then the plaintiff's solicitors may remove it for limited periods for copying or photographing.[2] The rationale of the order is that, if it is not granted, the defendant may destroy the evidence or documents before the trial, and thus evade justice.

1 *Universal Thermosensors Ltd v Hibben* [1992] 1 WLR 840 per Sir Donald Nicholls V-C at 861. See Chapter 7.
2 The draft order issued with judicial approval now provides that the plaintiff's solicitors shall return the originals of all documents obtained as a result of the order within two working days. Also, where ownership of any article obtained as a result of the order is disputed, the article must be given up to solicitors for the defendant within two working days, as long as those solicitors provide an undertaking to retain the article in safe custody until trial. See 11.2.

1.3   The Mareva injunction and Anton Piller order are orders which, although ancillary to the main action, often have a decisive effect on the case. In *Bank Mellat v Nikpour*[1] Sir John Donaldson MR stated:

> '[the Mareva injunction] is in effect, together with the Anton Piller order, one of the law's two "nuclear" weapons.'

1 [1985] FSR 87 at 92. See also *Columbia Picture Industries Inc v Robinson* [1986] 3 All ER 338 at 356 concerning the 'traumatic effect' of an Anton Piller order.

1.4   Anton Piller orders and Mareva injunctions may be granted in the same order.[1] The court may also grant other ancillary orders at the same time, for example: orders that the defendant swear an affidavit stating the whereabouts of his assets; for cross-examination of the defendant on such affidavit; for delivery up of the plaintiff's personal property; or restraining the defendant from damaging his own assets or from leaving the jurisdiction.[2]

1 *A J Bekhor & Co Ltd v Bilton* [1981] QB 923.
2 See Chapter 4.

1.5   Because Anton Piller orders and Mareva injunctions are normally granted ex parte, the defendant has no opportunity to address the court on whether the order should be made. At first sight, this flies in the face of the principle that the court must hear both sides of a dispute. It is also dangerous, as the court may act without knowledge of arguments which might properly be made on behalf of the defendant. For these reasons, various obligations are imposed upon the plaintiff who makes the ex parte application. He must give full and frank disclosure of any points which the defendant might fairly raise if he were present to oppose the application; he must undertake to compensate the defendant in damages if the court decides that he ought to pay any; and he must undertake to serve the evidence on the defendant as soon as reasonably practicable and to notify the defendant of his right to apply to have the order set aside. Mareva injunctions must also contain provisions for the protection of third parties such as banks. Anton Piller orders must include undertakings by the plaintiff's solicitors: for instance they must undertake to return originals of all documents obtained as a result of the order within two working days.

1.6 During the 1970s and 1980s the grant of Mareva injunctions and Anton Piller orders became relatively common. In 1977 Lord Hailsham of St Marylebone described the Mareva injunction as being 'extremely popular'[1] and by 1978 the Anton Piller was 'in daily use'.[2] In *Siporex Trade SA v Comdel Commodities Ltd*[3] Bingham J stated:

'The advent of the Mareva injunction has, as is notorious, led to [ex parte] applications [for injunctive relief] becoming common-place, hundreds being made each year and relatively few refused.'

1 *Siskina (Cargo Owners) v Distos Compania Naviera SA* [1977] 3 WLR 818 at 829.
2 *Ex Parte Island Records Ltd* [1978] Ch 122 at 133 per Lord Denning MR and see the comments of Goulding J in *Protector Alarms Ltd v Maxim Alarms Ltd* [1978] FSR 442 at 443.
3 [1986] 2 Lloyd's Rep 428.

1.7 RECENT DEVELOPMENTS: ANTON PILLER ORDERS

Since the first edition of this book, there has been no reduction in the number of reported cases concerning Mareva injunctions and Anton Piller orders. Further, there can be no doubt that both remain extremely useful weapons in the legal armoury. A newspaper report on 9 May 1993[1] stated that a large computer company had suspected wrongful activity involving its confidential information by the subsidiary of a competitor for two years. But, according to the report, it was only when the company's solicitors obtained and executed an Anton Piller order that the suspicions could be confirmed.

1 *Independent on Sunday*, Business Supplement, p 6.

1.8 But, at least as far as Anton Piller orders are concerned, the emphasis in the reported cases has been increasingly upon improving the safeguards for the defendant. The courts have underlined the importance of a strict interpretation of the requirements placed upon the plaintiff.[1] The reason was expressed by Scott J in *Columbia Picture Industries Inc v Robinson*:[2]

> 'It has to be accepted that a common, perhaps the usual, effect of the Anton Piller order is to close down the business which, on the applicants' evidence, is being carried out in violation of their rights . . .
>
> What is to be said of the Anton Piller procedure which, on a regular and institutionalised basis, is depriving citizens of their property and closing down their businesses by orders made ex parte, on applications of which they know nothing and at which they cannot be heard, by orders which they are forced, on pain of committal, to obey, even if wrongly made ?'

1   *Lock International plc v Beswick* [1989] 1 WLR 1268 per Hoffmann J.
2   [1986] 3 WLR 542 at 567–568.

1.9   In *Universal Thermosensors Ltd v Hibben*,[1] Sir Donald Nicholls V-C has recently introduced a number of new requirements on solicitors who serve Anton Piller orders. The outcome of that case shows the importance to solicitors of following such guidelines. It appeared that there had been serious irregularities in the execution of the order by the plaintiff's solicitors.[2] The defendants sued the solicitors personally. The solicitors, who apologised to the court, settled by paying a total of £34,000 plus costs on an indemnity basis to the various defendants. This case shows the dangers for solicitors and counsel in applying for Anton Piller orders without the most thorough preparation and consideration of the authorities. No lawyer should now apply for such order without very careful consideration of and compliance with the various safeguards for the defendant. It is plain that such applications may still be appropriate, for instance in cases of blatant fraud.[3] But the pendulum has swung firmly against the ready grant of Anton Piller orders.

1   [1992] 1 WLR 840 at 860–861. See Appendix J, and **7.3**.
2   Ibid at 849D.
3   Ibid at 861G.

1.10   In addition, the recent case of *Tate Access Floors Inc v Boswell*[1] suggests that, outside the area of intellectual property law, Anton Piller orders should be granted only in relation to property which is undoubtedly the plaintiff's, if there is a danger of a conspiracy charge against the defendant. This is due to the privilege against self-incrimination.[2]

1 [1991] Ch 512.
2 See **4.3**, especially **4.3.7**.

1.11 RECENT DEVELOPMENTS: MAREVA INJUNCTIONS

The recent cases on Mareva injunctions, unlike those on Anton Piller orders, are not all concerned with narrowing the circumstances in which the order will be granted. For example, since the first edition, the courts have developed a new body of law on 'worldwide' Mareva injunctions, which attempt to freeze assets held abroad.[1] Further, the courts have, in some circumstances, been willing effectively to pierce the corporate veil, to prevent individuals escaping the effect of Mareva injunctions by use of companies which they wholly control.[2] Third, Mareva injunctions may now be granted in support of statutory causes of action.[3]

1 See **2.20**.
2 See **2.2.11**.
3 See **2.2.7**.

1.12 But there has also been development of the protections for defendants. There has been considerable guidance from the Court of Appeal on the consequences of plaintiffs failing to give full and frank disclosure.[1] The courts have begun to apply stricter scrutiny to plaintiffs' claims that the defendant is a crook, who will dissipate his assets to frustrate judgment,[2] and to plaintiffs' claims about the strength of their own case.[3] Further, the recent case of *Polly Peck International plc v Nadir (No 2)*[4] underlines the importance of carefully considering the avoidance of damage to the business of the defendant.

1 See **8.6.1**.
2 See per Sir Peter Pain in *O'Regan v Iambic Productions Ltd* [1989] NLJR 1378.
3 *Polly Peck International plc v Nadir (No 2)* [1992] 4 All ER 769.
4 Ibid.

1.12 THE PRACTITIONER'S POSITION

From the practitioner's point of view, most cases in which a Mareva injunction or Anton Piller order is granted are likely to settle. It must strengthen the plaintiff's bargaining position to obtain and, at the inter partes hearing, keep a Mareva injunction. An Anton Piller order may be the only way to obtain vital information to show that the plaintiff's case is justified. On the other hand, to obtain the order at the ex parte hearing but lose it at the inter partes hearing may be positively detrimental, not least in costs. From the plaintiff's point of view, the law has now developed to a stage where, save in the most exceptionally urgent cases, it is better to spend extra time preparing the application so as to ensure that one has complied with the numerous obligations of the plaintiff than to rush to court with a risk that one has not considered the application fully. But from the defendant's point of view, there are considerable opportunities to seek to have the order discharged at the ex parte hearing due to some defect in the plaintiff's preparation or case.

CHAPTER 2

The Mareva injunction

2.0 FUNDAMENTAL PRINCIPLE OF THE MAREVA INJUNCTION

2.0.1 Since its introduction in 1975,[1] the Mareva injunction has become a well-established feature of civil litigation. No civil practitioner should be unfamiliar with its use. It has now been extended to include orders of 'worldwide' effect,[2] and to cover assets of all varieties. But the fundamental principle of the jurisdiction remains essentially as Lord Denning MR stated it in the original *Mareva* case:

> 'If it appears that [a] debt is due and owing – and there is a danger that the debtor may dispose of his assets so as to defeat it before judgment – the Court has jurisdiction in a proper case to grant an interlocutory judgment so as to prevent him disposing of those assets.'[3]

Seventeen years later, in 1992, this principle was reiterated by Lord Denning's successor, Lord Donaldson of Lymington MR:[4]

> 'So far as it lies in their power, the courts will not permit the course of justice to be frustrated by a defendant taking action, the purpose of which is to render nugatory or less effective any judgment or order which the plaintiff may thereafter obtain.'

His Lordship made clear, however, that the Mareva jurisdiction was distinct from other types of interlocutory injunction in that it was not subject to the principles in *American Cyanamid Co v Ethicon Ltd*,[5] which are relevant to the latter.

---

1   *Mareva Compania Naviera SA v International Bulkcarriers SA, The Mareva* [1980] 1 All ER 213, CA.
2   See **2.20**.
3   Above, at 215.

4   *Polly Peck International plc v Nadir (No 2)* [1992] 4 All ER 769 at 785, CA.
5   [1975] AC 396.

2.0.2   The statutory basis of the Mareva jurisdiction is now s 37 of the Supreme Court Act 1981.[1] A Mareva injunction may be granted in respect of a dispute which is to be referred to or is in the course of domestic arbitration,[2] and probably also in support of foreign arbitration proceedings.[3]

1   Appendix A.
2   See s 12(6)(f) and (h) of the Arbitration Act 1950 and *The Rena K* [1979] 1 All ER 397.
3   Cf *Channel Tunnel Group Ltd v Balfour Beatty Construction Ltd* [1993] 2 WLR 262; below, **2.20.15**.

2.0.3   The fundamental principle of the Mareva jurisdiction has now been held to apply where the plaintiff can demonstrate that:

(a) he has a good arguable case;

(b) the defendant has assets within the jurisdiction and there is a serious risk that, if not restrained by injunction, he will either remove his assets from the jurisdiction or dissipate them within it, so as to frustrate any judgment which the applicant might subsequently obtain.

A party may apply for a Mareva injunction after trial as well as before.[1] These two requirements, together with the procedure governing applications, are considered in Chapter 5.

1   *Orwell Steel (Erection and Fabrication) Ltd v Asphalt and Tarmac (UK) Ltd* [1984] 1 WLR 1097.

2.0.4   The fundamental principle of the Mareva jurisdiction is tempered by the court's desire to ensure that the injunction does not unduly prejudice either defendants or third parties, such as banks. In part, this is achieved by requiring the plaintiff to give various undertakings to the court, and to give full and frank disclosure of any flaws in his case to the court granting the order. These points are dealt with in Chapter 6. Further, the court will impose limits on the order to protect the defendant. These are discussed in this chapter, as are the position of and safeguards for third parties and, in particular, banks. Also discussed in this chapter are the requirements that the plaintiff have a cause of action against the defendant, the scope of assets to which the injunction will attach, and the jurisdiction to grant 'worldwide' Mareva injunctions.

2.1 SCOPE OF THE INJUNCTION

2.1.1 The assets to which the injunction attaches may be tangible or intangible, realty or personalty. In addition to bank accounts and choses in action, they include chattels such as motor vehicles, jewellery, objets d'art and other valuables.[1] Where moneys are held in a bank account in foreign currency, the bank may convert sufficient sums into the currency stated in the order to meet the requirements of the order. The conversion may be made at the bank's current rate of exchange. The converted sum should then be held subject to the order.[2]

1 *CBS UK Ltd v Lambert* [1983] Ch 37.
2 *Z Ltd v AZ and AA-LL* [1982] 2 WLR 288 at 314 per Kerr LJ.

2.1.2 The injunction may apply to real property. In relation to unregistered land, a pre-judgment Mareva injunction cannot be registered as a land charge because it is not an order made 'for the purpose of enforcing a judgment'.[1] In relation to registered land, the test for whether the Land Registry will permit a caution to be lodged is different.[2] For instance, s 54(1) of the Land Registration Act 1925 states that:

> 'Any person interested . . . as a judgment creditor, *or otherwise howsoever*, in any land or charge registered in the name of any other person, may lodge a caution with the registrar . . .'

It is at least arguable that this provision is sufficiently wide to permit the registration of a caution in favour of a party holding a Mareva injunction, but in practice the Land Registry is sometimes chary about such registration.

1 *Stockler v Fourways Estates Ltd* [1984] 1 WLR 25.
2 Land Registration Act 1925, ss 53–55.

2.1.3 Unless the plaintiff seeks a worldwide Mareva injunction,[1] there must be some grounds to show that the defendant has assets within the jurisdiction.[2] The injunction will apply to assets which are acquired after it has been granted, but before the eventual execution of any judgment obtained in the action.[3]

1 See **2.20**.
2 *Third Chandris Shipping Corpn v Unimarine SA* [1979] QB 645 per Lord Denning MR at 668.
3 *TDK Tape Distributor (UK) Ltd v Videochoice Ltd* [1986] 1 WLR 141 at 145.

2.1.4 In general, the assets must be in the legal or beneficial ownership of the defendant, although the court may be willing to infer ownership in an exceptional case where there is a strong evidential basis for the inference, and it is necessary to do so to protect the plaintiff.[1] The court should not extend an injunction to cover assets which appear on their face to belong to a third party unless it has good reason to suppose that in truth the assets belong to the defendant. If the injunction is extended to cover these assets, the order should contain an undertaking in damages to protect the third party, and the third party should be served with a copy of the order. Where either the defendant or a third party asserts that assets covered by the injunction are not the defendant's, the court may remove them from the scope of the injunction if it accepts the assertion. It is not, however, bound to accept the assertion without more. It may choose to do so; on the other hand, it may choose to determine the question of ownership as a preliminary issue. These principles are stated in the judgment of Lloyd LJ in *SCF Finance Co Ltd v Masri*.[2]

1   *The Theotokis* [1983] 2 Lloyd's Rep 204. See now *TSB Private Bank International SA v Chabra* [1992] 1 WLR 231; **2.2.11**.
2   [1985] 1 WLR 876 at 884, CA. The order does not apply to joint accounts unless it is so drafted. *Z Ltd v AZ and AA-LL* [1982] 2 WLR 288 at 299 and 312 per Kerr LJ.

2.1.5 As to what the injunction prevents the defendant doing, the words 'otherwise dealing with' include disposing of, selling, pledging or charging an asset, whether a chattel or a chose in action.[1] In *Canadian Imperial Bank of Commerce v Bhattessa*,[2] a Mareva injunction restrained the defendant, inter alia, from causing or permitting any of his assets within the jurisdiction from being 'sold, charged, disposed of or otherwise dealt with, save insofar as the value of his assets within the jurisdiction exceeded [a stated sum]'. The defendant borrowed money to acquire assets which he then charged to a third party. Harman J held that he had breached the order and was in contempt of court unless, the burden of proof being upon him, he could show that the value of his assets within the jurisdiction exceeded the stated sum. He fined the defendant £10,000.

1   *CBS UK Ltd v Lambert* [1983] Ch 37.
2   (1991) Times, 10 September.

2.2   NEED FOR AND NATURE OF CAUSE OF ACTION

2.2.1 Does the plaintiff need to have a cause of action subsisting at the time when he applies for the injunction? Although Lord

Denning MR suggested in 1983 that he did not,[1] it is now clear that he does. In the *Veracruz*,[2] the Court of Appeal confirmed that the law is as stated by Lord Diplock in *The Siskina*:[3]

'A right to obtain an interlocutory injunction is not a cause of action. It cannot stand on its own. It is dependent on there being a pre-existing cause of action against the defendant arising out of an invasion, actual or threatened, by him of a legal or equitable right of the plaintiff for the enforcement of which the defendant is amenable to the jurisdiction of the court. The right to obtain an interlocutory injunction is merely ancillary and incidental to the pre-existing cause of action.'

1 See *Chief Constable of Kent v V* [1983] QB 34.
2 *Veracruz Transportation Inc v V C Shipping Co Inc and Den Norske Bank A/S, The Veracruz I [1992] 1 Lloyd's Rep 353, CA. See also* Zucker v Tyndall Holdings plc *[1992] 1 WLR 1127, CA.*
3 *Siskina (Cargo Owners) v Distos Compania Naviera SA* [1979] AC 210 at 256, HL.

2.2.2 'Threatened invasion of a legal right'

Some difficulties have arisen over precisely what Lord Diplock meant by the phrase 'threatened invasion of a legal right'. There is usually no difficulty in showing that there has been an 'actual invasion of a legal right'. But what happens if there is reason to believe that the defendant will, for instance, breach his contractual obligations with the defendant, but has not yet done so? Does this count as a 'threatened' invasion of a legal right, so that a Mareva injunction may be granted?

2.2.3 In The *Veracruz*,[1] the plaintiffs had agreed to purchase the defendants' cruise ship. Under the terms of the agreement, the defendants were obliged to undertake substantial repairs before delivering the vessel to the plaintiffs. Before they had taken delivery, the plaintiffs suspected that the repairs had not been properly carried out. They were bound to pay the purchase moneys on delivery. They sought a Mareva injunction over the purchase moneys, once they came into the hands of the defendants. The application was made partly on the basis that the repairs had been done deficiently. Hobhouse J held that, in so far as the plaintiffs could show a good arguable case for damages for defects in the vessel when it was received, he had jurisdiction to grant a Mareva injunction. The Court of Appeal reversed his decision. Quoting the dictum of Lord Diplock in the *Siskina*,[2] Beldam LJ held that no cause of action arose until the vessel was delivered. The cause of action had to exist at the time when the application for the Mareva injunction was made, otherwise the court had no jurisdiction to grant it. Accordingly, no Mareva injunction could be granted before the vessel was delivered because, until that time, there was no cause of action.

1   Above.
2   Above.

2.2.4 Further, the Court of Appeal in *The Veracruz* decided not to follow the decision of Saville J in *A v B*.[1] The latter case had also concerned a contract to buy a ship, where, before delivery, the plaintiff purchasers suspected that, on delivery, the ship would not be in the condition required by the contract. Saville J held that he could, before the time for delivery, grant a Mareva injunction which would come into effect at the moment when the vessel was delivered. The basis of his decision was that, when the vessel was delivered, the cause of action would arise. But Beldam LJ in the *The Veracruz* stated that this approach was incorrect: the cause of action had to have arisen at the time when the application for the Mareva injunction was made.[1]

1   [1989] 2 Lloyd's Rep 423. See also per Bingham J in *Siporex Trade SA v Comdel Commodities Ltd* [1986] 2 Lloyd's Rep 428 at 436.

2.2.5 The question still remained, however, of the nature of the 'threat' to which Lord Diplock was referring, when he spoke of a 'threatened invasion of a legal right'. More light was cast on this in *Zucker v Tyndall Holdings plc*.[1] Staughton LJ[2] held that there was a 'threatened invasion of a legal right', sufficient to ground an interlocutory injunction, if there was a threat to break a contractual obligation which was 'presently performable'. In other words, a Mareva injunction could be granted if, at the time of the application, the defendant was threatening to break a contractual obligation which he ought to be performing at that time. But, said Staughton LJ, the authorities[3] showed that a threat to break a contractual obligation which was due to be performed later could not be a ground for an interlocutory injunction. This gives a clear answer to the question of what counts as a 'threatened invasion of a legal right'. Unfortunately the precise ratio of the case is unclear, as none of the judges stated that he agreed with any of the others, but Neill LJ appeared to adopt similar reasoning.[4]

1   [1992] 1 WLR 1127, CA.
2   Ibid at 1136.
3   Eg *The Veracruz* (above).
4   See [1992] 1 WLR at 1135A–1135B.

2.2.6 Dillon LJ, with whom Neill LJ also agreed, decided *Zucker* on alternative grounds. His judgment suggests that the English court will not grant a Mareva injunction in support of foreign proceedings if it is unclear whether the plaintiff has a good cause of action in those proceedings, and where a foreign court has not yet decided whether he does. The case concerned an agreement governed by Swiss law, which the Swiss courts had jurisdiction to determine. Dillon LJ stated:[1]

'The Mareva relief is sought in aid of the plaintiffs' claim for [a] money payment. But the jurisdiction of the court to award the money payment depends on Swiss law and the Swiss courts and the English court has no jurisdiction to award it, nor is it asked to. Therefore the claim for Mareva relief, in aid of the claim for money payment, must be premature until the Swiss court has made its determination. Therefore, as in the *Ninemia* case [[1984] 1 All ER 398], the application for Mareva relief is premature.'

This reasoning does not apply in relation to cases proceeding in member states of the European Community,[2] where the enactment of s 25 of the Civil Jurisdiction and Judgments Act 1982 has reversed the effect of *The Siskina*.[3]

1 Ibid at 1137E.
2 See per Kerr LJ in *Babanaft International Co SA v Bassatne* [1990] Ch 13 at 30F, and **2.20.15**.
3 Above.

2.2.7 Statutory cause of action

It was decided in *Securities and Investments Board v Pantell SA*[1] that the court has jurisdiction to grant a Mareva injunction to a plaintiff who has no common law right of action, but instead has a right of action which has been expressly conferred by statute. The right of action was to sue for sums of money. This applies even though the plaintiff him/herself will not receive the proceeds of the action. Sir Nicolas Browne-Wilkinson V-C stated:[2]

'. . . in my judgment the statutory right of action for the benefit of investors conferred on the SIB by section 6 [of the Financial Services Act 1986] is as much a right of action as any normal right of action in common law. It follows that in my judgment the SIB is as much entitled to apply for protection by way of Mareva relief on behalf of the investors

adversely affected by a breach of the Act as would an ordinary
private individual be entitled to in an ordinary action.'

1   [1990] Ch 426.
2   Ibid at 431H.

2.2.8   Matrimonial proceedings

In matrimonial cases it will usually be preferable for the parties to rely
upon s 37(2)(a) of the Matrimonial Causes Act 1973 to restrain
dissipation of the other party's assets. This provision is directly
designed for matrimonial cases. The district judge of the county court
has jurisdiction to grant the order, and the procedure is almost bound
to be cheaper than applying for a Mareva injunction.

2.2.9   It is clear, however, that Mareva injunctions may be granted in
matrimonial cases, in particular where assets outside the jurisdiction
are concerned.[1] But the injunction should never be granted to extend
over all a party's assets, because, except in wholly unusual
circumstances, there is never a likelihood that one party would be
awarded all the other party's assets at the ancillary relief hearing.[2]

1   See *Ghoth v Ghoth* [1992] 2 All ER 920, CA.
2   Ibid.

2.2.10   Miscellaneous cases

The court has jurisdiction to grant a Mareva injunction in support of
any order it makes for costs, including an order for costs in an
interlocutory hearing. This applies even if the sum owing under the
costs order has not been quantified by taxation or agreement.[1] The
court has a similar jurisdiction in relation to a judgment for damages
to be assessed.[2] But if the party seeking the injunction overestimates
the sum likely to be recovered, and in consequence obtains an
injunction which restrains more assets than were in fact necessary,
then he is likely to be liable to the other party on the undertaking in
damages for any loss which this causes.[3] Third, the court has
jurisdiction to grant a Mareva injunction where there is a dispute
which is to be referred to, or is in the course of, arbitration.[4]

1   *Jet West Ltd v Haddican* [1992] 1 WLR 487, CA.
2   Ibid at 490E.
3   Ibid at 491E.
4   See *The Rena K* [1979] 1 All ER 397 and Arbitration Act 1950, s 12.

2.2.11 No cause of action against one of two defendants

There appears to be at least one exception to the principle that no Mareva injunction may be granted over the assets of a party against whom the applicant has no cause of action. In *TSB Private Bank International SA v Chabra*,[1] the plaintiffs had a good arguable case against Mr Chabra, who had fled to India and refused to disclose his address there. Further, the plaintiffs had a good arguable case that assets, apparently vested in a company, were beneficially held by Mr Chabra and that the company was 'nothing more than the alter ego of Mr Chabra'.[2] If no injunction were made against the company, there was a real risk that the company would dispose of its assets so as to defeat the plaintiff's chance of satisfying any judgment against Mr Chabra. Mummery J held that he had jurisdiction to grant a Mareva injunction against the company, even although the plaintiffs admitted that they had no cause of action against it. He said:[3]

> 'There is one defendant, Mr Chabra, against whom the plaintiff undoubtedly has a good cause of action: the claim on the guarantee . . . The claim for an injunction to restrain disposal of assets by Mr Chabra is ancillary and incidental to that cause of action. In my judgment, the claim to a similar injunction against the company is also ancillary and incidental to the claim against Mr Chabra and the court has power to grant such an injunction in an appropriate case. It does not follow that, because the court has no jurisdiction to grant a Mareva injunction against the company, if it were the sole defendant, the court has no jurisdiction to grant an injunction against the company as ancillary to, or incidental, to the cause of action against Mr Chabra: see for example, *Vereker v Choi* [1985] 4 NSWLR 277 at 283. I agree that such a course is an exceptional one, but I do not accept that it is one that the court has no jurisdiction to take.'

His Lordship was willing to exercise the jurisdiction partly because Mr Chabra was abroad so that, if a Mareva injunction were granted against him alone, it might prove unenforceable. This case is in line with the case of *Atlas Maritime Co SA v Avalon Maritime Ltd, The Coral Rose (No 3)*,[4] which shows a similar toughening of approach against defendants who seek to hide behind the corporate veil.

The *Chabra* case was applied in *Aiglon Ltd v Gau Shan Co Ltd*.[5] Hirst J held that the applicant (A) had a good arguable case against B. It appeared that B had made it impossible for itself to meet A's claim, by transferring its assets to C. This meant that an injunction against B alone would not protect A from the risk of being unable to enforce against B.

Hence Hirst J was willing to grant a Mareva injunction against C as well, without the need for A to show that it had a cause of action against C.

1   [1992] 1 WLR 231.
2   Ibid at 239F.
3   Ibid at 241–242.
4   [1991] 1 WLR 917. See below, **2.6**.
5   [1993] 1 Lloyd's Rep 164 at 170.

2.2.12   Causes of action in two different countries

Felixstowe Dock & Railway Co v United States Lines Inc[1] was a case involving simultaneous foreign proceedings. The English court was asked to discharge a Mareva injunction on the basis that a court in the United States had already granted a 'restraining order', in Chapter 11 bankruptcy proceedings. The restraining order purported to stay all claims against the defendants both inside and outside the United States. Hirst J applied conflict of laws principles. He held that the existence of the restraining order was only one factor, albeit a substantial factor, in the exercise of his discretion whether to continue the English Mareva injunction. On the facts, he decided to continue it. Accordingly, where a foreign court purports to stay proceedings in England, this will not necessarily succeed or lead to the discharge of a Mareva injunction granted by the English court. Reference must be made to the principles of conflict of laws, which are beyond the scope of this book.[2]

1   [1989] QB 360.
2   See Dicey & Morris on the *Conflict of Law* (ed Collins) (11th edn, 1987).

2.2.13   Different considerations apply where a Mareva injunction has been obtained in English proceedings, but those proceedings have been left dormant while the plaintiffs prosecute their claim in another jurisdiction. Normally, leaving the English proceedings dormant would be likely to result in the discharge of the English Mareva.[1] But this will not be the case where the plaintiff has actively prosecuted his case in the foreign jurisdiction.[2]

1   See **5.8.2**.
2   *House of Spring Gardens Ltd v Waite* [1984] FSR 277.

2.3   SAFEGUARDS FOR THE DEFENDANT

2.3.1   In this section are discussed various provisos which, save in exceptional circumstances, must be inserted in the order for the protection of the defendant. They are in addition to various undertakings which the plaintiff must give which are considered in Chapter 6. The rationale of the provisos was recently re-stated by Lord Donaldson of Lymington MR in *Polly Peck International plc v Nadir (No 2):*[1]

'. . . It is not the purpose of a Mareva injunction to prevent a defendant acting as he would have acted in the absence of a claim against him. Whilst a defendant who is a natural person can and should be enjoined from indulging in a spending spree undertaken with the intention of dissipating or reducing his assets before the day of judgment, he cannot be required to reduce his ordinary standard of living with a view to putting by sums to satisfy a judgment which may or may not be given in the future. Equally no defendant, whether a natural or a juridical person, can be enjoined in terms which will prevent him from carrying on his business in the ordinary way or from meeting his debts or other obligations as they come due prior to judgment being given in the action.'

The provisos permit the defendant access to sums to meet his ordinary living expenses, his ordinary business expenses and the reasonable legal costs of the action. Further, the injunction must not extend beyond the likely value of the plaintiff's claim. The provisos appear in the order as follows:

'Notwithstanding paragraph 1 hereof, the Defendants shall be entitled to draw and expend from a bank account or other source the identity of which shall first be notified by them to the Plaintiffs' solicitors:

(a) A sum not exceeding £.... per week for ordinary living expenses;

[(b) A sum not exceeding £.... per week for ordinary business expenses]

[(c) A sum not exceeding £.... per week for reasonable legal expenses]

(d) Such further sum or sums, if any, as the Plaintiffs' solicitors may from time to time agree in writing.'

These provisos will each be considered in turn.

1 [1992] 4 All ER 769 at 785.

2.4   THE 'ORDINARY LIVING EXPENSES' PROVISO

2.4.1   In determining reasonable living expenses the court considers the defendant's wealth and ordinary standard of living. Wealthy defendants have high living expenses. *PCW (Underwriting Agencies) Ltd v Dixon*[1] concerned a wealthy Lloyd's underwriter: the Court of Appeal decided that a Mareva injunction should allow the defendant sufficient funds:

(a) to meet his reasonable living expenses, not exceeding a specified amount of £1,000 per week;

(b) to pay his outstanding accounts, not exceeding £27,500; and

(c) to pay his solicitors on account the costs of the action, not exceeding £50,000 in addition to £20,000 already paid.

1   [1983] 2 All ER 697.

2.5   THE 'ORDINARY BUSINESS EXPENSES' PROVISO

2.5.1   Similarly, a defendant should be allowed to apply his assets to pay his ordinary business debts in the same way as he would if not restrained by injunction.[1] It is likely to be immaterial that the payments may be contractually illegal.[2] As was recently re-emphasised in *Polly Peck International plc v Nadir(No 2)*,[3] the injunction should not prevent a man from continuing his lawful business. It is also to the plaintiff's advantage that the defendant continues his business, as the business represents an asset which could go towards satisfying any judgment given to the plaintiff. But the same criteria apply to ordinary business expenses as to ordinary living expenses: ordinary living expenses do not include, for example, 'the purchase of a Rolls-Royce or the equivalent in legal terms of the private employment of a Queen's Counsel to defend you against a serious criminal charge'.[4]

1   See *Iraqi Ministry of Defence v Arcepey Shipping Co SA* [1981] QB 65; *PCW (Underwriting Agencies) Ltd v Dixon* [1983] 2 All ER 158 and *Avant Petroleum v Gatoil Overseas Inc* [1986] 2 Lloyd's Rep 236.
2   *Iraqi Ministry of Defence v Arcepey Shipping Co SA* [1981] QB 65.
3   [1992] 4 All ER 769, CA. See further discussion of this case in Chapter 5.
4   *TDK Tape Distributor (UK) Ltd v Videochoice Ltd* [1986] 1 WLR 141 per Skinner J at 146.

2.5.2   It has been suggested that the *Polly Peck* case marks a more liberal approach to the position of the defendant, and may make it harder for plaintiffs to obtain Mareva injunctions.[1]

1 Zuckerman, 'Mareva and Interlocutory Injunctions Disentangled' [1992] 108 LQR 559. See further **5.13**.

2.6 THE 'LEGAL EXPENSES' PROVISO

2.6.1 The court will not restrict the defendant from reasonably defending the action in which the Mareva injunction is granted or challenging the injunction itself. By this proviso the court permits the defendant to expend either a specific or a reasonable sum on legal expenses for that purpose. The legal expenses proviso was considered further in *Atlas Maritime Co SA v Avalon Maritime Ltd, The Coral Rose (No 3)*.[1] The defendant company was wholly owned and controlled by a third party called Marc Rich. The defendant's only asset had been a ship. The plaintiff's claim was for damages for breach of a contract to sell it. The plaintiff obtained a Mareva injunction to the value of US$7.5m, subsequently reduced to $3m, over the ship. The defendant sold the ship for over $10m. It kept the $3m subject of the Mareva. It paid the remaining $7m or so to Marc Rich. The effect of this was to leave the defendant unable to pay its legal expenses to defend the proceedings. The defendant applied to have sums released from the Mareva injunction in order to pay its legal expenses. The Court of Appeal refused the application. Following the Court of Appeal's earlier decision in the same proceedings,[2] the court was entitled to 'lift up or look behind' the corporate veil, without actually 'piercing' it. Lord Donaldson of Lymington MR said:[3]

'[The legal expenses] proviso only applies in cases in which the operation of the injunction would impede the person enjoined from defending himself against the claim.'

He added:[4]

'In exercising the equitable Mareva jurisdiction, the court should . . . not limit its consideration to funds to which the party concerned has a legal right, if there are reasonable grounds for believing that it can obtain money otherwise.'

The evidence showed that the finances of the defendant were entirely controlled by Marc Rich. His Lordship was satisfied that Marc Rich would make funds available to the defendant to enable it to fund the proceedings, unless Marc Rich and the defendant thought the proceedings not worth defending. Accordingly, the defendant would suffer no prejudice from a refusal to vary the Mareva order: it would be able to obtain funds to defend the proceedings from a third party.

1   [1991] 1 WLR 917, CA.
2   *Atlas Maritime Co SA v Avalon Maritime Ltd, The Coral Rose* [1991] 1 Lloyd's Rep 563, CA.
3   *Atlas Maritime Co SA v Avalon Maritime Ltd (No 3)* [1991] 1 WLR 917 at 926, CA.
4   Ibid at 927B.

2.6.2   This case shows that where a defendant is in reality controlled by another, the court will not be prepared to release sums from the Mareva injunction for legal expenses, when in fact the defendant could obtain them from the party which controls it. But the principle quoted above from the judgment of Lord Donaldson of Lymington MR could and arguably should go further: it may be that the court will not allow the removal of funds for legal expenses if it is satisfied that the defendant could obtain funding of his legal expenses from third parties.[1]

1   Cf *M V Yorke Motors v Edwards* [1982] 1 WLR 444. See also *TSB Private Bank International SA v Chabra* [1991] 1 WLR 231, at **2.2.11** above.

2.7   THE MAXIMUM SUM PROVISO

2.7.1   *'Save in so far as the unencumbered value of those assets exceeds £....'*
The purpose of this proviso is that the order should freeze the defendant's assets only up to the level which the plaintiff is reasonably likely to recover on his claim.[1] If the plaintiff estimates his claim at a level higher than it turns out to be worth, then he may be liable to the defendant for any loss which the defendant has suffered due to the injunction extending further than the true extent of the plaintiff's claim.[2] The liability arises from the plaintiff's undertaking in damages.[3] Accordingly, the plaintiff should take care not to overestimate his claim.

1   See *Z v AZ and AA-LL* [1982] 2 WLR 288 per Lord Denning MR at 298.
2   See *Jet West Ltd v Haddican* [1992] 1 WLR 487 at 491, per Lord Donaldson of Lymington MR. Cf *Guiness Peat Aviation (Belgium) NV v Hispania Lineas Aereas SA* [1992] 1 Lloyd's Rep 190, and **2.10** below.
3   See Chapter 6.

2.7.2   It appears that the maximum sum to which the injunction is limited may include an amount in respect of the plaintiff's costs. In *Charles Church Developments plc v Cronin*,[1] the plaintiff's claim was for damages for infringement of copyright. These were likely to reach

£17,000, including interest. But the plaintiff had an alternative remedy for an account of the profits which the defendants had made as a result of their improper use of the copyright. They showed that they had a reasonable prospect of recovering £30,000. Mr Edward Nugee QC, sitting as a deputy High Court Judge, granted a Mareva injunction limited to £35,000. This comprised £30,000 for the account of profits and £5,000 in respect of the plaintiff's costs.

1   [1990] FSR 1.

2.8   BANK AS A DEFENDANT

The recent case of *Polly Peck International plc v Nadir (No 2)*[1] establishes that the court will rarely grant a Mareva injunction where the defendant is a bank. For further discussion see **5.13** below.

1   [1992] 4 All ER 769, CA.

2.9   DUTIES OF AND SAFEGUARDS FOR THIRD PARTIES, INCLUDING BANKS

2.9.1   Duties of third parties

'. . . it is an essential aspect of the jurisdiction to grant Mareva types of injunction that the position of innocent third parties should be fully protected . . .'[1]

Mareva injunctions will frequently affect third parties. For instance, if the defendant has a bank account, the injunction ought to apply to it. The bank at which the account is held will have to be notified of the injunction so that it may prevent the defendant from removing funds from the account, other than in ways permitted by the provisos in the injunction (discussed in this section and the last section). The same applies to other financial institutions where the defendant holds assets.

1   *Project Development Co Ltd SA v KMK Securities Ltd* [1982] 1 WLR 1470 per Parker J at 1471C.

2.9.2   What does the law require of these third parties? The sanction against a third party who assists in breach of the order is an application for contempt of court.[1] If the third party has no notice of the order, it cannot be in contempt of court for allowing the defendant to remove assets, even if the third party knew that the defendant might remove them from the jurisdiction or dissipate them: until the third party knows of the order, it cannot be blamed for failing to support it.[2]

1 See eg per Nourse LJ in *Bank Mellat v Kazmi* [1989] QB 541 at 547.
2 Ibid.

2.9.3   What is the position once the third party has notice of the order? In *Z Ltd v A-Z and AA-LL*,[1] Lord Denning MR had suggested that whenever an asset was subject to a Mareva injunction, a third party who held the asset ought not to dispose of it at all. But this view was not accepted by Sir John Donaldson MR in *Law Society v Shanks*.[2] In his view, handing to a defendant an asset which belonged to him did not amount to assisting in dissipation or disposal, unless there were special circumstances

> 'where it is known that the sole purpose of requiring the asset to be handed over to the defendant is to facilitate a dissipation of that asset . . .'

The draft Mareva order now incorporates, after the various provisos,[3] the condition:

> 'Provided, however, that nothing in sub-paragraph (a), (b), (c) or (d) of this paragraph shall impose any obligation on any third party to enquire into the purpose or purposes for which any sum or sums drawn by the Defendants thereunder are in fact required or used.'

1 [1982] QB 588 at 574.
2 (1987) 131 Sol Jo 1626, 18 Fam Law 206, CA.
3 See **2.3ff**, and **11.1**.

2.9.4   In *Bank Mellat v Kazmi*,[1] Nourse LJ accepted that Sir John Donaldson's view represented the correct approach:

> 'I respectfully agree that mere notice of a Mareva injunction cannot render it a contempt of court for a third party to make over an asset to the defendant direct. Otherwise it might be impossible, for example, for a debtor with notice to pay over to the defendant even the most trivial sum without seeking the directions of the court. A distinction must be drawn between notice of the injunction on the one hand and notice of a probability that the asset will be disposed of or dealt with in

breach of it on the other. It is only in the latter case that the third party can be guilty of contempt of court.'

1 Above. Cf the 'Spycatcher' litigation: *Attorney-General v Newspaper Publishing plc* [1988] Ch 333.

2.9.5 It is not entirely clear what constitutes 'notice of a probability that the asset will be disposed of or dealt with in breach of the order'.[1] Nourse LJ stated that 'no general test' could be formulated for the circumstances in which this would apply.[2] He did not, however, agree with Sir John Donaldson's view that such circumstances would be rare.[3] In the *Bank Mellat* case,[4] the plaintiff had obtained a judgment against the defendant for £96,000, most of which remained unpaid, and a Mareva injunction. The third party, the Department of Health and Social Services, owed the defendant £8,480. The defendant indicated that, if the money could not be paid to him directly, he wished to withdraw his claim for it from the Department. The court found that the defendant was determined to prevent the £8,400 getting into the hands of the plaintiff. That was sufficient for the court to hold that there was a probability that the money would be disposed of in breach of the injunction. Accordingly, on the application of the third party, the court ordered the third party to pay the money to the defendant's bank account, which was subject to the Mareva.

1 *Bank Mellat v Kazmi* [1989] 1 QB 541.
2 Ibid.
3 In *Shanks* (1987) 131 Sol Jo 1626, 18 Fam Law 206, CA.
4 Above.

2.9.6 On the other hand, in the *Shanks* case,[1] the court held that assets which a third party held should be paid directly to the defendant. The plaintiff had a judgment debt and a Mareva injunction against the defendant. The defendant retired and became entitled to a pension; in addition his employers wished to pay him a gratuity. But the employers refused to make either payment to him, on the basis that to do so would amount to assisting the defendant to dissipate his assets in breach of the order. The injunction was in any event defective in that it made no provision for the defendant's reasonable living expenses. As mentioned above, the court rejected the notion that simply rendering to the defendant an asset which was his amounted to dissipation. In the absence of evidence of special circumstances, to the effect that the defendant intended to dispose of the assets, the order did not prevent the employers from paying the defendant his pension and gratuity. It is submitted that this is a case where the injunction was being used as an aid to enforcement. A preferable course might have been to consider an attachment order against the employer, or a garnishee order against the account into which the pension was paid.

1   (1987) 131 Sol Jo 1626, 18 Fam Law 206, CA.

2.9.7   There are some transactions which must be carried out regardless of the Mareva injunction, for instance, the honouring of letters of credit (see **2.16** below). But this does not apply to ordinary cheques. If a bank refuses to honour a cheque, it should be careful to put a correct statement on the cheque of the reason for its return. A misleading statement may be damaging to the reputation of the defendant and libellous, in which case the defendant may sue the bank for libel.[1] For instance, the returned cheque should not carry an endorsement which suggests that the defendant has been found liable if in fact the injunction is granted before judgment so that it is not based upon a judgment. It may turn out that the defendant is not liable in the action.

1   See *Gatley on Libel and Slander* (8th edn, 1981) at para 56. Lloyds Bank recently agreed to pay 'substantial sums' to the owners of a slaughterhouse whose cheques it had mistakenly 'bounced'. Counsel for Lloyds told Drake J that the sum was being paid to compensate the customers for the damage and embarrassment they had suffered. See page 1 of *The Times*, 21 July 1992.

2.9.8   The defendant may have a joint bank account with a third party, such as his wife. The court has discretion to order the freezing of the account notwithstanding the third party's claim.[1]

1   *SCF Finance Co Ltd v Masri* [1985] 1 WLR 876. See **2.1.4**.

2.10   UNDERTAKINGS AND PROVISOS TO PROTECT THIRD PARTIES

2.10.1   Undertaking to pay reasonable costs

The order must contain undertakings and provisos for the protection of third parties. First, there is the undertaking to pay reasonable costs of the third party caused by or in complying with the order:[1]

'(a) to indemnify any third party in respect of any costs, expenses, fees or liabilities reasonably incurred, from the time when this order first adversely affected such third party, as a result of the making of this order;

(b) to pay the reasonable costs incurred by any third party to whom notice of this order has been given, in ascertaining whether any assets to which this order applies are within their control and in complying with this order and to indemnify any such person against all liabilities which may flow from such compliance.'

This undertaking will include, for example, the costs of a bank in searching through its records to discover whether the defendant has an account at any of its branches. Plaintiffs should beware that banks' charges for this work may be high. The undertaking will also indemnify the third party in respect of any liability to which it is exposed by seeking to ensure that the order is obeyed. Paragraph (a) of the undertaking has been added to take account of the comments of Webster J in the *Guiness Peat Aviation* case, and is appropriate where the plaintiff seeks interim delivery up of the defendant's assets: see next paragraph.

1 *Searose Ltd v Seatrain (UK) Ltd* [1981] 1 Lloyd's Rep 556. See also *Clipper Maritime Co Ltd v Mineralimportexport* [1981] 1 WLR 1262 and *Z Ltd v A-Z and AA-LL* [1982] QB 558.

2.10.2 In *Guiness Peat Aviation (Belgium) NV v Hispania Lineas Aereas SA*,[1] Webster J considered the effect of an undertaking

'to indemnify any person . . . to whom notice of this order is given against any costs, expenses, fees or liabilities reasonably incurred in complying with or seeking to comply with the terms of this order.'

He held that the undertaking covered costs which innocent third parties incurred in complying with the order, but not losses which the order itself caused them. The plaintiffs had obtained a Mareva injunction and an order that the defendants give interim delivery up of an aircraft. The defendants had chartered the aircraft to a third party, Pandora. The plaintiffs attended at Teesside airport and took control of the aircraft. Pandora had to make alternative arrangements to fly their passengers to Majorca and suffered losses of over £12,000. Webster J held that these losses were caused by the *grant* of the order, not by *complying with it*. Accordingly, they were not covered by the undertaking quoted above. He added, however, that when obtaining the order for interim delivery up,[2] the plaintiffs should have given an undertaking

'. . . to indemnify Pandora against any costs, expenses, fees or liabilities reasonably incurred as a result of the making of the order; . . . in terms which indemnified Pandora not simply against costs and liabilities incurred from the time at which they should have been notified of the order, or the time at which they would have applied for its discharge or variation, but from the time at which it first adversely affected them.'[3]

As this undertaking had not been given or required, Webster J could not award damages for loss based upon it. But he indicated another way in which the plaintiffs would have to compensate Pandora. The plaintiffs had failed to notify Pandora of its rights to apply to vary the order. Webster J indicated that this was almost certainly in contempt of court: it was in breach of an undertaking to do so. He said that if formal application had been made to commit the plaintiffs for contempt, he would have made no order as long as the plaintiffs agreed to compensate Pandora for all losses caused to Pandora as a result of the making of the order for interim delivery up. In this way, Pandora would have been compensated by a different means.

1 [1992] 1 Lloyd's Rep 190.
2 See Chapter 4.
3 See [1992] Lloyd's Rep at 196.

2.10.3 If a third party makes an application to the court for a variation of the injunction, and succeeds, then it is likely that the plaintiff will be ordered, under this undertaking, to pay the third party's costs.[1] Will the costs be ordered to be taxed on the standard basis or on the indemnity basis?[2] In *Project Development Co Ltd SA v KMK Securities Ltd*,[3] Parker J held that the correct order was that costs should be taxed on the solicitor and own client basis, with a direction that nothwithstanding the terms of the rules, the burden of establishing the reasonableness of incurring the costs, and the reasonableness of the amount, should be upon the third party. This case was decided before the change in the bases of taxation. It is not entirely clear how it should now be applied. The solicitor and own client basis of taxation has now been replaced by the indemnity basis of taxation. Accordingly, the editors of the *Supreme Court Practice 1993* suggest that the proper order is that the costs should be taxed on the indemnity basis, but with a direction that, notwithstanding the terms of RSC Ord 62, r 12(2), the third party must establish that his costs were reasonably incurred and were reasonable in amount.[4] The difficulty is that this order is almost indistinguishable from an order that the costs should be taxed on the standard basis.[5] One might therefore think it more straightforward simply to order taxation on the standard basis. It is suggested that the law may need clarification on this point.[6]

1 *Project Development Co Ltd SA v KMK Securities Ltd* [1982] 1 WLR 1470.
2 The bases of taxation are defined by RSC Ord 62, r 12.
3 See note 1.
4 See note 29/1/22 at Volume 1, p 521.
5 See Flenley, 'Winner Takes All?' [1992] 89 LS Gaz No 34 at 25.
6 The question was referred to by Harman J in *Capital Cameras Ltd v Harold Lines Ltd* [1991] 1 WLR 54 at 58. He accepted counsel's submission about the proper form of the order, following *Project Development* (above). Unfortunately the report does not say what counsel's submission was.

2.11 UNDERTAKINGS TO SERVE THIRD PARTIES AND TO NOTIFY THEM OF RIGHT TO APPLY FOR VARIATION OF ORDER

2.11.1 In order to ensure that third parties give effect to the order, the plaintiff will seek to notify them of its terms as soon as possible. Once he has given a third party notice, he must then abide by the following undertaking:

'To serve a copy of this order upon any third party to whom the plaintiff has given notice of this order.'

2.11.2 There is a further undertaking for the protection of the third party. The plaintiff must undertake

'to notify and inform any third parties (if any) affected by this order of their right to apply to this Court for this order to be varied or discharged in so far as this order affects such third parties.'

The meaning of this undertaking was considered in the *Guinness Peat Aviation* case.[1] The plaintiffs' solicitors did not notify the third parties, Pandora, of their right to apply to vary the order, before they executed it. Executing the order meant that the plaintiffs' solicitors took control of the aircraft in issue, so that Pandora could not use it in accordance with its agreement with the defendants. The plaintiffs' solicitors said that they had thought that, in order to comply with this undertaking, they were not required to notify third parties of their right to vary the order until they had formally served the third parties with the order. Webster J rejected that view. The plaintiffs should have notified Pandora of their rights to vary the order even before they had formally served Pandora with the order.[2]

1 Above.
2 See [1992] Lloyd's Rep at 195.

2.12   PROVISO TO PERMIT BANKS TO EXERCISE RIGHT OF SET-OFF

2.12.1   In addition, the order should contain a proviso to the following effect:

> 'Nothing in this order shall prevent any bank from exercising any rights of set-off it may have in respect of facilities afforded by a bank prior to the date of this order.'

This proviso benefits only banks. Its basis is similar to that underlying the 'ordinary business expenses proviso':[1] see *Oceanica Castelana Armadora SA v Mineralimportexport*.[2] A Mareva injunction had been obtained against the defendant with a maximum sum proviso of $2,190,060. Before the grant of the injunction the defendant had deposited a sum with a bank which in turn had issued loans which were still outstanding to the defendant. Referring to the ordinary business expenses proviso, Lloyd J said:[3]

> 'If the defendant can thus, in a suitable case, draw on his bank account to pay his ordinary creditors, notwithstanding a Mareva injunction, why should he not be free to pay his bank? Why should the bank be in a worse position than other ordinary creditors just because it is the bank which holds the funds in question?'

Lloyd J added[4] that such a set-off may be claimed even though the sum frozen consequently falls below the amount specified in the 'maximum sum' proviso.[5] If the order does not contain this proviso then the bank may apply to the court to vary it to include such proviso, and the plaintiff is likely to be ordered to pay its costs of so doing.[6]

1   Above.
2   [1983] 1 WLR 1294.
3   Ibid at 1300.
4   Ibid at 1301.
5   Above.
6   *Project Development Co Ltd SA v KMK Securities Ltd* (above).

2.12.2   Although this proviso does apply only to banks, the principle that the injunction should not interfere with payment of debts already owed to third parties is of wider application. It should apply to any debt owed to a third party.[1]

1   See **2.18**.

2.13   OTHER ORDERS INVOLVING BANKS AND THIRD PARTIES

2.13.1   The court may grant orders for discovery against banks. In addition, it may grant an interlocutory injunction preventing the defendant from disposing of his assets, including for instance the contents of a bank account, pending trial. This type of injunction may be granted in support of a tracing claim where the assets have been converted into different property. Orders of these types are discussed in Chapter 4. See also paragraph **2.16** below.

2.14   SPECIFIC TYPES OF FINANCIAL INSTRUMENT

2.14.1   There is authority on how some specific types of financial instrument should be treated, where the plaintiff seeks a Mareva injunction. It is not within the scope of this book to explain the nature of each of these types of instrument.[1]

1   For letters of credit see further Schmitthoff's *Export Trade* (9th edn, 1990).

2.15   BILLS OF EXCHANGE

2.15.1   A bill of exchange is essentially a cheque. Where a bill of exchange has been dishonoured and the holder has obtained judgment for the value of the bill, the court does have jurisdiction to grant a Mareva injunction to freeze the proceeds of the bill. But the court will exercise this power only if the party due to pay the judgment can clearly satisfy the usual requirements for a Mareva.[1] Accordingly, the party due to pay on the bill must show that he has a good arguable counterclaim, and that there is a real risk of removal or dissipation of assets which is likely to leave his counterclaim unsatisfied.

1   *Montecchi v Shimco (UK) Ltd, Navone v Same* [1979] 1 WLR 1180.

2.16   Injunction to restrain a third party bank from making payment on a letter of credit, performance bond or documentary collection

2.16.1   Letters of credit are essentially guarantees by banks to pay sums of money. Performance bonds are similar: again, they are designed to be guarantees that a bank will make payment to the payee in the event of default by the principal debtor. In general, the purpose of these facilities is that they are designed to be guarantees of payment, regardless of arguments by the party providing them, and so the courts are generally unwilling to interfere with that purpose and prevent payment.

2.16.2   The court does have jurisdiction to grant an injunction, not against the defendant, but against a third party bank directly, restraining it from making payment on a letter of credit or a performance bond. But the court will almost never exercise this power: the plaintiff must first show clear and strong evidence of fraud on the part of the payee of the letter of credit or bond, whom he must also sue. The rationale for this rule was explained by Sir John Donaldson MR in *Bolvinter Oil SA v Chase Manhattan Bank*:[1]

> 'Before leaving this appeal, we should like to add a word about the circumstances in which an ex parte injunction should be issued which prohibits a bank from paying under an irrevocable letter of credit or a performance bond or guarantee. The unique value of such a letter, bond or guarantee is that the beneficiary can be completely satisfied that whatever disputes may thereafter arise between him and the bank's customer in relation to the performance or indeed existence of the underlying contract, the bank is personally undertaking to pay him provided that the specified conditions are met. In requesting his bank to issue such a letter, bond or guarantee, the customer is seeking to take advantage of this characteristic. If, save in the most exceptional cases, he is to be allowed to derogate from the bank's personal and irrevocable under-taking, given be it again noted at his request, by obtaining an injunction restraining the bank from honouring that under-taking, he will undermine what is the bank's greatest asset, however large and rich it may be, namely its reputation for financial and contractual probity. Furthermore, if this happens at all frequently, the value of all irrevocable letters of credit and performance bonds and guarantees will be undermined.
>
> Judges who are asked, often at short notice and ex parte, to issue an injunction restraining payment by a bank under an irrevocable letter of credit or performance bond or guarantee should ask whether there is any challenge to the validity of the letter, bond or guarantee itself. If there is not or if the challenging is not substantial, prima facie no injunction should be granted and the bank should be left free to honour its contractual obligation, although restrictions may well be

imposed upon the freedom of the beneficiary to deal with the money after he has received it. The wholly exceptional case where an injunction may be granted is where it is proved that the bank knows that any demand for payment already made or which may thereafter be made will clearly be fraudulent. But the evidence must be clear, both as to the fact of fraud and as to the bank's knowledge. It would certainly not normally be sufficient that this rests upon the uncorroborated statement of the customer, for irreparable damage can be done to a bank's credit in the relatively brief time which must elapse between the granting of such an application and an application by the bank to have it discharged.'

1 *Bolvinter Oil SA v Chase Manhattan Bank* [1984] 1 WLR 392, CA. See also *Discount Records Ltd v Barclays Bank Ltd* [1975] 1 WLR 315 per Megarry J; *Edward Owen Engineering v Barclays Bank International Ltd* [1978] QB 159.

2.16.3 Further, in *Lewis & Peat (Produce) Ltd v Almatu Properties Ltd*,[1] the Court of Appeal stated that the same principles applied to documentary collections. Parker LJ added that it was of the first importance that routine banking transactions of this type should not be subject to interference by the Mareva jurisdiction unless there were exceptionally strong reasons to do so.

1 (1992) Times, 14 May.

2.17 SECURED DEBTS

2.17.1 A Mareva injunction cannot prevent the exercise of the rights of a creditor who has security provided by an agreement such as a mortgage or debenture. The rights of the secured creditor take priority. This was established in *Cretanor Maritime Co Ltd v Irish Marine Management Ltd*,[1] and applied in *Capital Cameras Ltd v Harold Lines Ltd*.[2] When the creditor's rights in respect of the property crystallise, he or it is entitled to apply to the court for either variation or discharge of the injunction, depending on which is necessary to give effect to the terms of the agreement under which he has the security. If and when the application succeeds, the court will order the party subject to the Mareva to pay his costs of the application.[3]

1 [1978] 1 WLR 966, CA.
2 [1991] 1 WLR 54.
3 Ibid. For the scale of taxation of the costs, see the discussion above at **2.10.3**.

2.17.2   Accordingly, where a party's solicitors held its funds in their client account, but had a lien over those funds in respect of their unpaid fees, the court declined to grant a Mareva over the funds. The solicitors' liens were clearly paramount to the claim by a judg-ment debtor against the solicitors' client, and so the judgment debtor could not show any reasonable prospect of recovering them in an action.[1]

1   *Prekookeanska Plovidba v LNT Lines Srl* [1988] 3 All ER 897.

2.18   UNSECURED DEBTS

2.18.1   The injunction should contain a proviso permitting the defendant to meet his ordinary business expenses and living expenses. This will permit payment of ordinary expenses which had already fallen due at the time when the injunction was granted.[1] The rights of a third party over assets subject to a Mareva injunction were considered in *Galaxia Maritime SA v Mineralimportexport*.[2] Kerr LJ stated:[3]

'But where the effect of service [of the injunction] must lead to interference with the performance of a contract between the third party and the defendant which relates specifically to the assets in question, the right of a third party in relation to his contract must clearly prevail over the plaintiff's desire to secure the defendant's assets for himself against the day of judgment.'

1   See *Iraqi Ministry of Defence v Arcepey Shipping Co SA* [1981] QB 65; *PCW Underwriting Agencies v Dixon* [1983] 2 All ER 158. If necessary the court will vary the injunction to allow such payments to be made. But this should not be necessary if the correct provisos were included in the injunction initially granted.
2   [1982] 1 WLR 539.
3   Ibid at 542.

2.18.2   In *Iraqi Ministry of Defence v Arcepey Shipping Co SA*[1] third parties sought variation of a Mareva injunction to enable the defendants' assets to be used to repay a loan which the third parties had made to the defendants. The plaintiffs claimed that the loan was an illegal contract and should not be enforced by the court. Robert Goff J stated:[2]

'It does not make commercial sense that a party claiming unliquidated damages should, without himself proceeding to judgment, prevent the defendant from using his assets to satisfy his debts as they fall due and be put in the position of having to allow his creditors to proceed to judgment with consequent loss of credit and of commercial standing . . . The [third parties] are seeking to recover a debt which the plaintiffs say is illegal and void as a moneylending transaction . . . No doubt the court will not enforce, directly or indirectly, an illegal contract; but by lifting the Mareva injunction in the present case to enable the defendants to repay to the [third parties] the loan they have received would not be to enforce the transaction, even indirectly. A reputable businessman who has received a loan from another person is likely to regard it as dishonourable, if not dishonest, not to repay that loan, even if the enforcement of that loan is technically illegal by virtue of the Moneylenders Acts. All the [third parties] are asking is that the defendants should be free to repay such a loan if they think fit to do so, not that the loan transaction should be enforced.'

1   [1981] QB 65 per Robert Goff J at 72.
2   Ibid at 486. See also *A v B (X Intervening)* [1983] 2 Lloyd's Rep 532, a case concerning ordinary living expenses.

2.19   STATE IMMUNITY

2.19.1   Where it applies, the doctrine of sovereign immunity provides a complete defence to civil proceedings in English law.[1] This includes a complete defence to an application for a Mareva injunction. Accordingly, if a state seeks the discharge of a Mareva injunction on the basis that it is immune to the jurisdiction of United Kingdom courts, this issue must be definitely determined at the outset. The court may not continue the injunction until trial on the basis that the plaintiff has a 'good arguable case',[2] because, if the state is indeed immune, then there is no jurisdiction to continue the injunction. If the issue arises, parties must be given an opportunity to prepare themselves properly to deal with the issue fully at the outset, rather than having to prepare as one would for an ordinary interlocutory application.[3]

1   See 18 Halsbury's Laws (4th edn) para 1548.
2   See Chapter 5.
3   Per Saville J in *A Company Ltd v Republic of X* (1990) Times, 9 April.

2.19.2   The scope of sovereign immunity has been greatly reduced by the State Immunity Act 1978[1] ('the 1978 Act'). Exegesis of the 1978 Act is not within the scope of this book, although the following short comments may be made. Sections 3–11 deal with the extent of immunity from suit for various types of action, such as commercial transactions, contracts of employment, and personal injury. Then ss 12 and 13 deal with procedural immunities. By s 13(2), there can be no injunction granted against a state unless the case comes within either sub-s 13(3) or sub-s 13(4). Subsection 13(4) allows execution, in some circumstances, against property of the state which is currently being used for commercial purposes. It is unclear whether such 'execution' could include a post-judgment Mareva injunction.

1   Appendix B.

2.19.3   Subsection 13(3) allows an injunction to be granted against a state

'. . . with the written consent of the State concerned; and any such consent (which may be contained in a prior agreement) may be expressed so as to apply to a limited extent or generally; but a provision merely submitting to the juris- diction of the courts is not to be regarded as a consent for the purposes of this subsection.'

In *A Company Ltd v Republic of X*,[1] a state entered into an agreement containing a clause waiving:

'. . . whatever defence it may have of sovereign immunity for itself or its property (present or subsequently acquired).'

Saville J held that the agreement was a commercial agreement which was intended to put the state on the same footing as a private individual.[2] Accordingly, it constituted a waiver within the meaning of s 13(3) of the 1978 Act. But the 1978 Act did not affect immunities conferred by the Diplomatic Privileges Act 1964 ('the 1964 Act'). The 1964 Act prevented a state's diplomatic premises, their contents, and means of transport from being made the subject of a Mareva injunction. In Saville J's view the privileges under the 1964 Act could be waived, but only where the state had given its consent directly to the court; a mere inter partes agreement could not waive the privileges, and so the agreement did not affect them.

1   (1990) Times, 9 April.
2   Cf *Trendtex Trading Corpn v Central Bank of Nigeria* [1977] 1 Lloyd's Rep 581, CA, decided on the common law before the 1978 Act came into effect.

2.20 WORLDWIDE MAREVA INJUNCTIONS

2.20.1 In the summer of 1988, the Court of Appeal extended the Mareva jurisdiction to include orders regulating the behaviour of parties in foreign jurisdictions. This was done in a trio of cases heard within weeks of one another: *Babanaft International Co SA v Bassatne*,[1] *Republic of Haiti v Duvalier*,[2] and *Derby & Co Ltd v Weldon (No 1)*.[3] Since then, the principles have been further refined.[4] It is important to state at the outset, however, that each of these three leading cases concerned a claim for £10million or more. In each case, the court stressed that, although it had jurisdiction to make the order granted, the granting of such orders must not come to be regarded as the norm. The application for the order in England, and the steps necessary to try to enforce it abroad, are bound to be very expensive. This sort of order should be considered only in exceptional cases where large sums are at stake, so that one can justify the risk of incurring considerable costs.

1 [1990] Ch 13.
2 [1990] 1 QB 202.
3 [1990] Ch 48.
4 See below.

2.20.2 How can the English court purport to control what happens outside its jurisdiction? This was the central objection to the making of 'worldwide' Mareva orders. In theory, someone who knows of an order of the English court and knowingly assists in breaching it is in contempt of the English court which made the order. So a foreign bank which knew of the English court's 'worldwide Mareva' but allowed moneys to be withdrawn by the defendant from a bank account in another country might be in contempt of court in England, even although no order had been made by its home court. The courts held that this would be an unacceptable result:

> 'It would be wrong for an English court, by making an order in respect of overseas assets against a defendant amenable to its jurisdiction, to impose or attempt to impose obligations on persons not before the court in respect of acts to be done by them abroad regarding property outside the jurisdiction. That, self-evidently, would be for the English court to claim an altogether exorbitant, extraterritorial jurisdiction.'[1]

1 Per Nicholls LJ in the *Babanaft* case [1990] Ch 13 at 44B.

2.20.3 The 'Babanaft proviso'

For this reason, the English court cannot grant a Mareva injunction over foreign assets in precisely the same terms as it would over assets within England and Wales.[1] The court's solution was to insert a proviso to the order, now known as the 'Babanaft proviso' because of the case in which it was introduced. The 'Babanaft proviso' was reconsidered in subsequent cases. The version of the proviso which should now be used is that which was set out by Lord Donaldson of Lymington MR in *Derby & Co Ltd v Weldon (Nos 3 and 4)*.[1] It reads as follows:

> 'Provided that, in so far as this order purports to have any extraterritorial effect, no person shall be affected thereby or concerned with the terms thereof until it shall be declared enforceable or be enforced by a foreign court and then it shall only affect them to the extent of such declaration or enforcement unless they are: (a) a person to whom this order is addressed or an officer of or an agent appointed by a power of attorney of such a person or (b) persons who are subject to the jurisdiction of this court and (i) have been given written notice of this order at their residence or place of business within the jurisdiction, and (ii) are able to prevent acts or omissions outside the jurisdiction of this court which assist in the breach of the terms of this order.'

1   [1990] Ch 65 at 84D–84E.

2.20.4   The proviso involves a division of parties who might be affected by the order into essentially three categories:

(a) the defendant, or other party to proceedings in which the order is granted;

(b) persons who are subject to the jurisdiction of the English court, have been given notice of the order, and are able to prevent breaches of the order outside England and Wales;

(c) other persons, for instance, foreign nationals or institutions not subject to the jurisdiction of the English court, or persons who are subject to the jurisdiction of the English court but have not been notified.

The effect of the proviso upon each of the three categories of person will be considered in turn.

The defendant

2.20.5   So far as the defendant's activities within the jurisdiction are concerned, these are governed by the domestic Mareva which will normally be granted at the same time.[1] What about the defendant's activities outside England and Wales? So far as Marevas are concerned, it now appears that, as long as the defendant is properly a party to proceedings brought in England, the English court has jurisdiction to order the defendant to do anything outside England & Wales which it would be able to order him to do inside England & Wales:

> 'The jurisdiction of the court to grant a Mareva injunction against a person depends not on territorial jurisdiction of the English court over assets within its jurisdiction, but on the unlimited jurisdiction of the English court in personam against any person, whether an individual or a corporation, who is, under English procedure, properly made a party to proceedings pending before the English court.'[2]

So the English court has the jurisdiction, for example, to order someone who is properly joined as a defendant to transfer assets from one foreign jurisdiction to another, if this will prevent him from taking action to render any future judgment or award of the court unsatisfied.[3] But this discretion should be exercised with great care.[4] The effect of this is that the first question is whether a party is properly joined to proceedings in England. This depends on the rules of court. If a party needs to be served outside the jurisdiction, see RSC Order 11, which should be carefully considered.

1   Although the court has jurisdiction to grant a worldwide Mareva against a person who is properly a party to litigation in England, even if such person does not have any assets in England and Wales. See *Derby & Co Ltd v Weldon (Nos 3 and 4)* [1990] Ch 65, CA.
2   *Derby & Co Ltd v Weldon (No 6)* [1990] 1 WLR 1139, CA, per Dillon LJ at 1149.
3   Ibid.
4   Ibid.

2.20.6   This deals with the theoretical problem of conflict of laws, as far as the defendant himself is concerned. But what is the practical use of an order which, if the defendant is abroad and has few assets in England, may be unenforceable against him? What practical step can be taken to force the defendant to comply with the order or punish him if he does not? If the plaintiff could find and serve him, he might consider contempt proceedings, but this may be impossible. Alternatively, he can ask the court to strike out the defence, leaving him with a judgment in default.[1] But he then needs to enforce the judgment, presumably abroad. This is why it is said that the order is 'binding only on the conscience of the defendant'.[2] In practice, there may often be little point in applying for a worldwide Mareva injunction unless the plaintiff is also prepared to countenance proceedings in the foreign jurisdictions where it is believed the defendant's assets are.

1   *Derby & Co Ltd v Weldon (No 6)* [1990] 1 WLR 1139, CA, per Dillon LJ at 1149.
2   Per Nicholls LJ in the *Babanaft* case, [1990] Ch 13 at 44.

Third parties who are bound to obey the order

2.20.7   Lord Donaldson MR's second category of person is persons who are subject to the jurisdiction of the English court, who have been given written notice of the order at their residence or place of business within the jurisdiction, and who are able to prevent acts or omissions outside England and Wales which assist in breaching the order. It should be noted that this applies to all 'persons', both natural persons and legal persons such as corporations. Partnerships such as solicitors' firms will also be covered. Once the English office of, say, an international bank has been notified, the bank is bound, as far as the English court is concerned, not to assist in the breach of the order. Presumably the sanction for disobedience of the English court's order by the bank's foreign offices would be contempt proceedings in England.

Third parties who are not bound to obey the order

2.20.8   Any third parties who do not come within the preceding category are not bound to obey the order unless or until there is an order of the foreign court which has jurisdiction over them. Even then, they are bound only to the extent that the foreign court orders. Accordingly, any third party over which the English court does not have jurisdiction, will not be bound unless there is a further application to its home court, and that home court grants an order in support of the English Mareva.[1] The proviso makes clear that the English court does not claim jurisdiction over such persons. So the plaintiff will need to make a further application in the foreign jurisdiction where he believes the defendant's assets are. He will need to consider whether such country has a procedure equivalent to the Mareva jurisdiction, and whether it is likely to exercise it in support of the order of the English court. But before he makes the application in the foreign court, he may have to apply to the English court for leave to bring such application.[2]

1 So far as countries in the European Community are concerned, cf the discussion below of the Civil Jurisdiction and Judgments Act 1982.
2 See **2.20.13** below.

Worldwide Mareva injunctions in support of English proceedings: requirements common to both pre- and post-judgment applications

2.20.9 The court has jurisdiction to grant a worldwide Mareva in support of proceedings brought in England, both before[1] and after judgment.[2] All such orders must contain a 'Babanaft proviso'. In addition, the following requirements are common to both pre- and post-judgment applications. The plaintiff must have a good arguable case on the merits. He must show that there are insufficient assets in England to meet his judgment, that the defendant has foreign assets, and that there is a real risk of disposal of those so as to frustrate enforcement of the plaintiff's judgment if he obtains one.[3] Even then, the court will rarely make such a worldwide Mareva injunction.[4] But, as Kerr LJ[5] said in a passage which has been cited in other cases:

'. . . some situations . . . cry out – as a matter of justice to the plaintiffs – for disclosure orders and Mareva type injunctions covering foreign assets of defendants even before judgment.'

1 *Derby & Co Ltd v Weldon (No 1)* [1990] Ch 48.
2 *Babanaft International Co SA v Bassatne* [1990] Ch 13.
3 *Derby & Co Ltd v Weldon (No 1)* [1990] Ch 48 per Parker LJ at 56.
4 See dicta of all judges in *Babanaft* and in *Derby & Co Ltd v Weldon (No 1)* above.
5 *Babanaft*, above, at 33D–33E. Cited by Staughton LJ in *Republic of Haiti v Duvalier* [1990] 1 QB 202 at 217.

2.20.10 What sort of case does cry out in this way? In *Babanaft*, the plaintiffs had obtained judgment for US$15 million. The trial judge found that the defendants were likely to take 'any step open to them to frustrate or delay execution of the judgment'. They were international oil traders whose business was carried out through a large number of companies incorporated in jurisdictions such as Panama and Liberia where it was difficult for outsiders to obtain any information about the ownership or assets of the company. The plaintiffs were likely to face 'considerable difficulties' in ascertaining the extent of the defendants' assets and enforcing judgment.[1]

1 See *Babanaft*, above, at 23.

2.20.11 Another case which cried out for worldwide Mareva relief was *Republic of Haiti v Duvalier*.[1] The claim was for US$120million. The

Republic of Haiti claimed that its former President and his family had embezzled these assets. There was a good arguable case. The defendants actually admitted that they had been moving their assets around the world in an attempt to escape the efforts of the plaintiff to freeze them. Staughton LJ stated: 'As the judge said, if ever there was a case for the exercise of the court's powers, this must be it.'[2] In *Derby & Co Ltd v Weldon (No 1)*,[3] the claim was for £25million. The defendants included a Panamanian and a Luxembourg company. The trial judge had found that the plaintiffs had a 'highly arguable' case, and that there was a 'high risk' that the defendants would dissipate their assets, as they were 'well used to moving funds worldwide'.[4] To sum up, this sort of order appears to be appropriate only where large sums are involved and there is evidence that the defendants are used to moving assets around the world through sophisticated means so that enforcement of the judgment or orders would cause considerable difficulty.

1   [1990 1 QB 202.
2   Ibid at 217A.
3   [1990] Ch 48.
4   Ibid at 54. See also *Aiglon Ltd v Gau Shan Co Ltd* [1993] 1 Lloyd's Rep 164, at **2.20.12**.

2.20.12   Applications after judgment in England

The court is likely to be more willing to grant a worldwide Mareva after judgment, as the plaintiff has proved his case.[1] At this stage, the plaintiff will also have the opportunity to apply to foreign courts for help in enforcing his judgment debt. Accordingly, the function of the Mareva is likely to be as

> '. . . a temporary "holding" injunction against the judgment debtor, requiring him not to move or deal with his assets without giving to the judgment creditor the few days' notice which is the minimum reasonably required to enable the judgment creditor to invoke any assistance which the local court may afford to him in respect of his judgment debt.'[2]

In *Aiglon Ltd v Gau Shan Co Ltd*,[3] arbitrators had made an award in the defendants' favour worth in the region of £1million. Proceedings were brought in the English courts relating to the award. Hirst J found that there was a good arguable case that the joint managers of both plaintiffs, based in Geneva, had been transferring assets between the plaintiffs in order to defeat the defendants' arbitration award against the first plaintiffs. In those circumstances, Hirst J stated that the case for a worldwide Mareva injunction against the plaintiffs became 'overwhelming'. Although the sum in issue was around £1million, this is significantly less than the sums involved in the cases referred to in **2.20.11** above.

1 *Babanaft*, above. But the injunction should be limited in time. See per Staughton LJ in *Republic of Haiti v Duvalier* [1990] 1 QB 202 at 214H.
2 *Babanaft*, above, per Nicholls LJ at 43.
3 [1993] 1 Lloyd's Rep 164. See also discussion at **2.2.11**. We are grateful to Graham Dunning, junior counsel for the plaintiffs, for indicating the monetary value of the claim. This does not appear in the report.

Applications before judgment in England

2.20.13 The court is generally unwilling to grant a worldwide Mareva injunction before judgment, as the plaintiff has not proved his case. But it is not necessary for the plaintiff to prove, before judgment, that the defendant is dishonest.[1] The court will require two additional undertakings for the protection of the defendant. First, the plaintiff must undertake not to make any application to a foreign court to enforce the order without first obtaining the leave of the English court. This is to prevent the plaintiff from seeking to obtain, abroad, interlocutory orders which will go further than a Mareva, and give the plaintiff pre-judgment security.[2] It also prevents undue oppression of the defendant by the bringing of numerous proceedings in various jurisdictions.[3]

1 *Derby & Co Ltd v Weldon (No 1)* [1990] Ch 48, especially per Nicholls LJ at 61C.
2 Ibid, per Nicholls LJ at 59.
3 Ibid, per May LJ at 55.

2.20.14 The second undertaking relates to information which the plaintiff obtains pursuant to an order for discovery made together with the Mareva (see Chapter 4). The plaintiff must undertake not to use such information in proceedings abroad against the defendant, without leave of the English court. Again, the purpose is to prevent oppression of the defendants by the use of such information to bring numerous sets of proceedings around the world.[1]

1 Ibid, per Nicholls LJ at 60.

Applications in support of foreign proceedings

2.20.15 There is jurisdiction to grant a Mareva injunction in England over assets situated in England and Wales, in support of some foreign proceedings including in some cases arbitration proceedings.[1] Which foreign proceedings may be assisted in this way? This depends on the principles of conflict of laws, which are beyond the scope of this book.[2] Suffice it to say that possibly the most important provision in that regard is s 25 of the Civil Jurisdiction and Judgments Act 1982.[3] Subject to certain excepted areas,[4] that section gives the High Court of England and Wales power to grant interim relief where proceedings have been or are to be commenced in one of the other member states of the European Community, or indeed another part of the United Kingdom. The interim relief which the court may grant under the Act includes a 'domestic' Mareva injunction,[5] that is, one which covers assets within England and Wales. Further, in the recent case of *Channel Tunnel Group Ltd v Balfour Beatty Construction Ltd*,[6] the House of Lords held that the court has power under s 37(1) of the Supreme Court Act 1981 to grant an interlocutory injunction in support of foreign arbitration proceedings. It seems likely that the court must also have power to grant a Mareva injunction in support of such proceedings, pursuant to s 37(3) of the Supreme Court Act 1981.

1   See *Alltrans Inc v Interdom Holdings Ltd* [1991] 4 All ER 458, especially at 466A; *Rosseel NV v Oriental Commercial Shipping (UK) Ltd* [1990] 1 WLR 1387, CA.
2   See Dicey & Morris on the *Conflict of Law* (ed Collins) (11th edn, 1987).
3   Appendix C.
4   See Schedule 1 to the Act, in Appendix C.
5   See note 1.
6   [1993] 2 WLR 262.

2.20.16   Can the English court grant a worldwide Mareva injunction in support of proceedings which are principally being litigated elsewhere? The case of *Republic of Haiti v Duvalier*[1] is authority for the proposition that the court has jurisdiction to do so, at least as far as proceedings in other European Community countries are concerned. But in the later case of *Rosseel NV v Oriental Commercial Shipping (UK) Ltd*, Lord Donaldson of Lymington MR said:[2]

'. . . where [the English court] is merely being asked under a convention or an Act of Parliament to enforce in support of another jurisdiction, whether in arbitration or litigation, it seems to me that, save in an exceptional case, it should stop short of making orders which extend beyond its own territorial jurisdiction.

I say that because, if you take a hypothetical case of rights being determined in state A and assets being found in states B to M, you would find a very large number of subsidiary jurisdictions – in the sense that they were merely being asked to enforce the rights determined by another jurisdiction – making criss-crossing long arm jurisdictional orders and, indeed resentment by the nations concerned at the interference with their jurisdictions.'

His Lordship, with whom Parker LJ agreed, went on to distinguish the *Duvalier* case: it was an exceptional case, first because of the size of the claim, and second because part of the alleged operation was being undertaken by an English solicitor. Without such exceptional circumstances the court would not make a worldwide Mareva order in support of proceedings in another jurisdiction. If any court is to make such order, it should be the court which is determining the litigation.

1   [1990] 1 QB 202, CA.
2   [1990] 1 WLR 1387 at 1389.

2.20.17   For the position where an English Mareva has been granted, but the court of a foreign state not a member of the European Community makes a worldwide order which purports to govern the parties in England, see *Felixstowe Dock & Railway Co v United States Lines Inc.*[1]

1   [1989] 2 WLR 109; above **2.2.12**.

2.20.18   Procedure

The plaintiff seeking a worldwide Mareva injunction should prepare a skeleton argument, to be delivered to the court with the papers, setting out the precise grounds on which it is said (i) that a Mareva injunction should be granted and (ii) that the injunction should be of worldwide effect. Further, the papers in such application should be delivered to the court in sufficient time for the judge to be able to read and digest them.[1]

1   *ALG Inc v Uganda Airlines Corpn* (1992) Times, 31 July. See further Chapter 5, and, for cases in the Commercial Court, paragraph 3.4 of the Guide to Commercial Court Practice at page 1242 of the *Supreme Court Practice 1993*.

CHAPTER 3

The Anton Piller order

3.1 NATURE OF THE ANTON PILLER JURISDICTION

3.1.1 The Anton Piller order permits the plaintiff to demand entry to the defendant's premises, business or residential, to search them, and to remove for a short time documents or other items which might form evidence in his action or proposed action against the defendant. Generally the order will provide that it must be served by an independent solicitor in the company of the plaintiff's solicitor. The plaintiff's solicitor then executes the order, supervised by the independent solicitor. Alternatively the order may provide for service and execution by the plaintiff's own solicitor without supervision.

3.1.2 This chapter discusses the scope of the order. Further, there has been a series of substantial changes in the Anton Piller jurisdiction since 1986. Those changes are discussed below in **3.8** and **3.9**. Chapter 5 considers the procedure for obtaining an Anton Piller order, and what the plaintiff's evidence must show. Chapter 6 deals with the safeguards for the defendant. The position of the defendant who is served with an Anton Piller order is considered in Chapter 7.

3.1.3 The order's name is derived from an early case, *Anton Piller KG v Manufacturing Processes Ltd.*[1] The purpose of the order is to prevent a defendant interfering with discovery and frustrating trial, by destroying documents or evidence, such as copies of the plaintiff's products, which might show his wrongdoing.

There are three principal areas of law in which the order is used:

> 'They are, first, the infringement of rights in intellectual property, such as trade marks, copyright and trade secrets; secondly, anti-competition cases brought by ex-employers against ex-employees; and thirdly, matrimonial proceedings where it is thought that a spouse has failed to make truthful

disclosure of his or her assets. There is a notable difference between the practice in the first two classes and the third. In the first two there is likely to be a pre-emptive strike, the application being made upon the issue of the writ and before it is served. In the third class [an Anton Piller] order is likely to be made as a last resort, when other measures are thought not to have resulted in truthful disclosure.'[2]

This list is not exhaustive, and the order may be granted in other types of case. But doubt has now been thrown on whether Anton Piller orders should be granted in any case not involving intellectual property, by the development of the doctrine of self-incrimination – see **4.3.7**.

1 [1976] Ch 55, CA.
2 See 'Anton Piller Orders – A Consultation Paper' (the Lord Chancellor's Department, November 1992) at para 1.9. The paper was written by a committee of distinguished judges with experience of Anton Piller orders. Its contents do not, of course, have the technical status of judicial authority.

3.1.4 If such evidence is found, then it may be removed by the plaintiff's solicitors. The plaintiff's solicitors then have two working days in which to copy and return to the defendant's solicitors any documents and any other articles the ownership of which is disputed. The defendant's solicitors must undertake to keep them in safe custody until trial. There may then follow an inter partes hearing at which the plaintiff applies for inspection of the articles seized and the defendant may put forward objections to such disclosure.

3.1.5 The Anton Piller order may be granted at any stage in an action from before the issue of the writ until after judgment, when it may be granted in aid of execution. It may be granted in all the divisions of the High Court and in the Court of Appeal. It may be granted in the Patents County Court, but not in any other county court. Cases within the jurisdiction of the county court should be transferred to the High Court for such application.[1]

1 See **5.6**.

3.1.6 The facts of the *Anton Piller* case[1] itself provide an example of the use of the order. The plaintiff company was a German manufacturer of electric motors and generators which had designed a frequency converter for the particular purpose of supplying power to computers produced by IBM. The defendants, an English company and their two directors, were the United Kingdom agents of the plaintiffs. The plaintiffs claimed that the defendants were in secret communication with other German manufacturers and were passing to them confidential information about the plaintiffs' power units and details of a new converter, the disclosure of which could be most damaging to the plaintiffs. To prevent the destruction by the defendants of documents in their possession relating to the plaintiffs' machines or designs, the plaintiffs applied ex parte in the Chancery Division for an injunction that the defendants permit the plaintiffs to enter the defendants' premises to inspect all such documents and to remove them into the custody of the plaintiffs' solicitors and for an interim injunction to restrain the defendants from infringing their copyrights and disclosing confidential information.

Brightman J granted the interim injunction, but refused to order inspection or removal of documents. He stated:[2]

'. . . it seems to me that an order on the lines sought might become an instrument of oppression, particularly in a case where a plaintiff of big standing and deep pocket is ranged against a small man who is alleged on the evidence of one side only to have infringed the plaintiff's rights.'

The plaintiffs' appeal was heard in chambers with judgments given later in open court. The Court of Appeal (Lord Denning MR, Ormrod LJ and Shaw LJ) allowed the appeal, laying down preconditions and safeguards which have been followed and extended in subsequent Anton Piller cases.

1   [1976] Ch 55.
2   Ibid at 60.

3.2   CRITICISM OF THE ANTON PILLER JURISDICTION

3.2.1   The Anton Piller order has been the subject of cogent criticism.[1] It undoubtedly subjects the defendant, against whom nothing may have been proved, to the possibility of having all his business papers and materials removed without any warning. If he declines to permit the plaintiff entry, he faces the risk of imprisonment for contempt of court.[2] In the 1980s, the European Court of Human Rights indicated that it was satisfied with the various safeguards which the English courts had developed in the operation of the order.[3] But the English courts themselves have become less sanguine.[4] Their reaction to criticism was to introduce new safeguards and to strengthen existing ones.

1 See Laddie and Dockray 'Piller Problems' (1990) 106 LQR 601.
2 See Chapter 8.
3 *Chappell v United Kingdom* [1989] FSR 617.
4 See below, especially at **3.8**.

3.3 EXTENSION BEYOND THE SUBJECT MATTER OF THE ACTION

3.3.1 Subject to difficulties with self-incrimination (**4.3.7**), the use of the Anton Piller order now extends beyond the subject matter of an intellectual property action to the search for and seizure of evidential material which is relevant to any action or proposed action.

3.3.2 *Yousif v Salama*[1] concerned moneys due under an agency agreement. The plaintiff sought an Anton Piller order in the Queen's Bench Division in respect of an office file and a desk diary which he claimed were essential evidence (although not the subject matter of the action) and which he feared the first defendant might destroy. The Court of Appeal, by a majority, granted the order. Lord Denning MR stated:[2]

'It seems to me that that would be an aid to justice. It would be preserving the evidence in the case. Under RSC Order 29, rule 2 there is a far-reaching power for preserving documents which are the subject matter of the action. These files here are not the subject matter of the action. But they are the best possible evidence to prove the plaintiff's case. There is a genuine fear that if the plaintiff waits till after the application is heard, the first defendant may destroy the documents before the date of the hearing. This is the sort of danger which the Anton Piller order is designed to prevent.'

Brightman LJ, concurring, stated:[3]

'If essential documents are at risk, then it seems to me that this court ought to permit the plaintiff to take such steps as are necessary to preserve them.'

Donaldson LJ accepted in principle the existence of the Anton Piller jurisdiction while dissenting on the exercise of the court's discretion in that particular case.

1 [1980] 1 WLR 1540.
2 Ibid at 1542.
3 Ibid at 1544.

3.4   MATRIMONIAL LAW

3.4.1   A similar order was made in *Emanuel v Emanuel.*[1] In
proceedings for ancillary relief brought by a wife following divorce,
the court ordered the husband to transfer to her two properties which
he owned and to make certain periodical payments. The husband did
not comply with the order. One of the properties was sold by the
husband before the hearing of the wife's claim for financial provision,
despite an undertaking not to do so given by the husband to Sheldon J.
The husband had, in addition, transferred the other property to his
sister, the second respondent. The husband was committed to prison
for six weeks for contempt of court. An ex parte application was made
by the wife for an order to permit her solicitor to enter the premises
occupied by the husband for the purpose of inspection and removal for
copying of documents relating to the husband's income and capital and
to the sale of the two properties, and for a similar order in respect of
premises occupied by the second respondent. Granting the orders,
Wood J held that where a party to divorce proceedings sought, by an
Anton Piller order, documents which were not themselves the subject
matter of the proceedings, the Family Division had jurisdiction to
grant the order if the applicant had a strong prima facie case that the
relevant documents were essential for his case and were at serious risk
of being removed or destroyed. He stated:[2]

> 'The husband is clearly ready to flout the authority of the
> court and to mislead it if he thinks that it is to his advantage
> to do so. The normal process of law is liable to be rendered
> nugatory. I have no doubt that justice in the present matter
> cannot be achieved without making the present order, and
> that there is a grave danger that evidence will be removed and
> destroyed. I cannot think that real harm will be caused to the
> husband from making the order, as the only documents
> sought are those which he ought properly to produce and,
> indeed, ought to have produced in the past. I am quite
> satisfied that the wife has a strong prima facie case to the
> effect that relevant documentation has not been produced in
> the past and is most unlikely to be produced in the future
> without the present order. Such essential documents are at
> risk.'

An order was granted in similar circumstances in *K v K.*[3]

1   [1982] 1 WLR 669.
2   Ibid at 676.
3   [1982] 13 Fam Law 46; see also *Kepa v Kepa* (1982) 4 FLR 515.

3.4.2   It should be noted, however, that the county court does not have jurisdiction to grant an Anton Piller order. Applications in cases proceeding in the county court should be transferred to the High Court for the application to be made. See Chapter 5.

3.5   USE OF THE ANTON PILLER ORDER TO ASSIST IN EXECUTION OF JUDGMENT

3.5.1   An Anton Piller order may be granted to assist in the execution of judgment. In *Distributori Automatici Italia SpA v Holford General Trading Co Ltd*[1] the plaintiffs, an Italian company which distributed bar refrigerators for use in hotels and restaurants in the United Kingdom, obtained judgment for the recovery of £67,433.53 against the defendants. The second defendant was the plaintiffs' exclusive agent in the United Kingdom and the second defendant's rights as agent were exercised through the first defendant company. An order was made requiring the second defendant to produce documents relating to the defendants' assets and liabilities. The second defendant claimed that he was unable to comply with the order because his office had been repossessed. The plaintiffs discovered, however, that he had later been to the office and removed two briefcases which the plaintiffs believed contained the relevant documents. The plaintiffs moved ex parte for an Anton Piller order for the production of documents relating to the assets of the defendants or to matters in question in the action and for a Mareva injunction.

It was held by Leggatt J,[2] applying *Orwell Steel (Erection and Fabrication) Ltd v Asphalt and Tarmac (UK) Ltd*[3] in which a Mareva injunction was granted by Farquharson J in similar circumstances, that it had been established that the court had jurisdiction to grant an Anton Piller order where there was strong prima facie evidence that documents were essential for a plaintiff's case and that there was a serious risk that they might be removed or destroyed. He added:[3]

> 'Where there is a real risk of justice being thwarted by a defendant intent on rendering any judgment nugatory, the need for an Anton Piller order may be even greater in aid of execution than of judgment. In my judgment the Court has jurisdiction to make an Anton Piller order for the purpose of eliciting documents which are essential to execution and which would otherwise be unjustly denied to the judgment creditor.'

1   [1985] 1 WLR 1066.

2   Ibid.
3   [1984] 1 WLR 1097.
4   [1985] 1 WLR 1066 at 1073.

3.6   'WORLDWIDE ANTON PILLER ORDERS'

3.6.1   Can and will the English court grant Anton Piller orders in relation to premises which are outside the jurisdiction of England and Wales? A similar question has been considered by the courts in the context of Mareva injunctions: see **2.20**. As far as Anton Piller orders are concerned, however, there are fewer cases, and they pre-date the 'worldwide Mareva' cases. Nevertheless, it is submitted that the court will apply similar principles when considering an extra-territorial Anton Piller order as when considering an extra-territorial Mareva injunction.

3.6.2   In the context of Marevas, it has been held that the court has *jurisdiction* to grant a worldwide Mareva against any defendant who is, under English rules of procedure, properly made a party to the proceedings.[1] In other words, the question of whether the English court has jurisdiction over a party depends on whether, under English procedure, that party can properly be made a party to English proceedings. Once it is established that the English court does have jurisdiction over a party, it may even order that party to transfer assets from one foreign country to another, if this will prevent him from taking action to render any future judgment or award of the court unsatisfied. But although the court does have jurisdiction to make such order, it will exercise its discretion to do so with great care.[2]

1   *Derby & Co v Weldon (No 6)* [1990] 1 WLR 1139, CA.
2   Ibid.

3.6.3   The cases concerning the grant of Anton Piller orders over premises outside England and Wales show a similar approach: the court has jurisdiction only if the defendant is properly joined as a party, under English rules of procedure. In *Altertext Inc v Advanced Data Communications Ltd*,[1] Scott J considered that an ex parte Anton Piller order in relation to premises abroad should be granted only if the court was convinced that it had jurisdiction over the defendant. He said:[2]

'The point is rather, I think, one of discretion. The court is not, in my view, justified in acting on an assumed jurisdiction in order to make against a foreign defendant in respect of foreign premises a mandatory order required to be executed before the foreign defendant has had a chance of contesting the jurisdiction . . . Anton Piller orders to be executed in respect of foreign premises ought not be granted, in my view, except against defendants over whom the courts have unquestionable jurisdiction.'

1 [1985] 1 WLR 457.
2 Ibid at 463.

3.6.4 In the earlier case of *Cook Industries Inc v Galliher*[1] the court had exercised its discretion to order the defendant to permit a flat in Paris to be searched by a French advocate who was also an English barrister. But in that case the defendant had had the opportunity to contest both jurisdiction and the exercise of discretion to grant the order, because the order had been made at an inter partes hearing at which the defendant had been represented by counsel. Numerous points were taken on jurisdiction, but Templeman J rejected these. He held that the court did have jurisdiction over the defendants. He then decided to exercise his discretion to grant the order sought. It is important to note that the order sought was more limited than an ordinary Anton Piller order: it was an order that the defendant should disclose the contents of the flat, and that he should permit the French advocate to enter and inspect the contents of the flat. The order contained no provision for removing items from the flat and it was not made ex parte. Further, the action against one defendant was based upon enforcing a judgment debt of US$2.5m which had been obtained against him on the basis of fraud. It is submitted that all these features make *Galliher* an exceptional case. It is doubtful whether the court would grant an Anton Piller order in the normal form in relation to foreign premises in the absence of these special features.[2]

1 [1979] Ch 439.
2 Further, it has been suggested on the basis of *Denilauler v Snc Couchet Frères* [1990] ECR 1553 at 1570, ECJ that it is inappropriate to apply in English courts for relief of the Anton Piller type when the order is to be executed in other member states of the EEC. See Gee *Mareva Injunctions and Anton Piller Orders* (2nd edn, 1990) at p 39.

3.6.5 The court will not exercise its discretion to grant an ex parte Anton Piller order in relation to premises in Scotland, even if it is certain it has jurisdiction. The plaintiff should apply instead to the Court of Session.[1] This is because the court respects the comity of other parts of the United Kingdom.

1 *Protector Alarms Ltd v Maxim Alarms Ltd* [1978] FSR 442.

3.6.6   It is suggested that even if the court were to make a 'worldwide Anton Piller order', or any similar order, the aid of foreign lawyers should be engaged to ensure that the domestic law of the foreign country is not breached by the execution of the order.

3.7   THE ROVING ANTON PILLER ORDER: CLASS INJUNCTIONS

3.7.1   RSC Order 15, r 12(2) provides, inter alia, that on application of the plaintiff the court may appoint any one of the defendants to represent all, or all except one or more of those persons in the proceedings. This is a representative action. RSC Order 15, r 12 also provides that the persons who are represented and the persons representing them should have the same interest in the proceedings.[1]

1   *Markt & Co Ltd v Knight SS Co Ltd* [1910] 2 KB 1021, CA; also *Roche v Sherrington* [1982] 1 WLR 599.

3.7.2   *EMI Records Ltd v Khudhail*[1] is authority for the proposition that the court has jurisdiction to grant an Anton Piller order against a representative class of persons, as long as they have sufficient identity of interest, and the other requirements of the Anton Piller order are fulfilled. The case concerned a group of street traders. The evidence suggested that they all sold illegally copied cassette tapes bearing the brand name 'Oak Records'. Sir John Donaldson MR held that the group had sufficient identity of interest for the grant of the injunction, because they all sold illegal copies from the same source, they must all know some of the other members of the group, and they all had a common interest in hiding the origin of the source of the tapes. The secrecy of the defendant's organisation was such that the plaintiffs had been quite unable to find out anything about the source of the goods or about the group.

1   [1985] FSR 36, CA. For further discussion see the note by the plaintiffs' counsel, Peter Prescott 'Class Injunctions' (1986) 2 EIPR 58.

3.8   RECENT DEVELOPMENTS

3.8.1   By 1986, Anton Piller orders were regularly being granted in all divisions of the High Court. But the case of *Columbia Picture Industries*

Inc v Robinson[1] was the first involving an Anton Piller order to come on for full trial. The hundreds of previous Anton Piller cases had all settled. The case gave Scott J the opportunity to consider the development and operation of Anton Piller orders. He delivered a devastating critique. He observed that a common and perhaps usual effect of Anton Piller orders was to close down the defendant's business.[2] He went on:

'What is to be said of the Anton Piller procedure which, on a regular and institutionalised basis, is depriving citizens of their property and closing down their businesses by orders made ex parte, on applications of which they know nothing and at which they cannot be heard, by orders which they are forced, on pain of committal, to obey, even if wrongly made?'

1   [1987] Ch 38.
2   Ibid at 73–74.

3.8.2   Scott J's judgment was endorsed by Hoffmann J in *Lock International plc v Beswick*[1] who stated:

'As Scott J pointed out, [Anton Piller orders] potentially involve serious inroads on principles which bulk large in rhetoric of English liberty, such as the presumption of innocence, the right not to be condemned unheard, protection against arbitrary searches and seizures, the sanctity of the home. My common experience of the evident surprise of counsel when I have refused applications leads me to endorse Scott J's observation, at p 76:

"the practice of the court has allowed the balance to swing much too far in favour of plaintiffs and that Anton Piller orders have been too readily granted and with insufficient safeguards for respondents." '

1   [1989] 1 WLR 1268 at 1279.

3.8.3   More recently, both those views were endorsed by Sir Donald Nicholls V-C in *Universal Thermosensors Ltd v Hibben*[1] who said:

'The Anton Piller procedure lends itself all too readily to abuse. This has been highlighted more than once: see the powerful judgments of Scott J in *Columbia Picture Industries Inc v Robinson* [above] and of Hoffmann J in *Lock International plc v Beswick* [above]. My impression is that these warning signals have been heeded, and that Anton Piller orders are, rightly, made much more sparingly than previously.'

1   [1992] 1 WLR 840 at 859–860.

3.9   SUMMARY OF RECENT DEVELOPMENTS

3.9.1   This trio of cases has shown a clear emphasis of the rights of the defendant, first by underlining the original safeguards required when Anton Piller orders were first developed, and second by adding some new ones. The cases show: a stricter scrutiny of the evidence produced by the plaintiff (Chapter 5); emphasis upon less draconian orders which the court may grant (Chapter 5); further developments of the undertakings which the plaintiff must give before the order is granted (Chapter 6); new safeguards for the defendant in the execution of the order (Chapter 7); and elucidation of when and to what extent the plaintiff or his or its solicitors may be liable to the defendant for non-disclosure at the ex parte application or errors in execution of the order (Chapter 8).

3.9.2   In particular, it appears that exemplary damages may be granted against the plaintiff or his solicitors for wrongful or oppressive execution of the order.[1] In addition, the power to grant the order has been removed from the county court (Chapter 5), and many of the new safeguards mentioned in the *Universal Thermosensors* case have been incorporated into a new draft order, recently issued by the Chancery Division with judicial approval (Chapter 11).

1   See per Scott J in *Columbia Picture Industries Inc v Robinson* [1987] Ch 38 at 87.

3.9.3   Finally, the full ramifications of the rule against self-incrimination have become apparent. The effect of the case of *Tate Access Floors Inc v Boswell*[1] appears to be that, outside the area of intellectual property law, Anton Piller orders should never be granted if the plaintiff's evidence suggests that the defendant might be liable on a conspiracy charge. There may be an exception if the order relates only to the plaintiff's own property. This is discussed in Chapter 4.[2]

1   [1991] Ch 512.
2   See **4.3.7**.

CHAPTER 4

Ancillary and other orders

4.0 The court may in the same order grant both a Mareva injunction and an Anton Piller order. In addition, the court may grant a number of ancillary orders or provisions.[1] In this chapter, the first section considers orders for discovery. Wide-ranging developments of the rule against self-incrimination are considered in **4.3**. The rest of the chapter considers orders:

– for the cross-examination of the defendant (**4.5**);

– for the delivery up of the plaintiff or defendant's chattels (**4.6**);

– restraining disposal of items subject to tracing claims (**4.7**);

– restraining the defendant from damaging his own assets (**4.8**);

– restraining the defendant from leaving the jurisdiction (**4.9**);

– Norwich Pharmacal orders (**4.11**);

and various other orders.

1   See generally *A J Bekhor & Co Ltd v Bilton* [1981] QB 923 at 940 with respect to the court's power to make orders ancillary to the Mareva injunction under s 45 of the Supreme Court of Judicature (Consolidation) Act 1925, the predecessor to s 37 of the Supreme Court Act 1981. See also *House of Spring Gardens Ltd v Waite* [1985] FSR 173, CA.

4.1   DISCOVERY

4.1.1   Mareva injunctions

A Mareva injunction may be granted together with an order that the defendant disclose the full value and whereabouts of his assets, and that he make and file an affidavit verifying this information.[1] Such order is plainly ancillary to the Mareva injunction itself. It is important to ensure that such order does not go further, however, and seek pre-action discovery on issues relevant to trial but not to enforcement of the Mareva injunction.[2]

1   See *A v C* [1981] 2 WLR 629; *AJ Bekhor & Co Ltd v Bilton* [1981] QB 923; *Z Ltd v A-Z* [1982] 2 WLR 288; *CBS (UK) Ltd v Lambert* [1983] Ch 37, CA.
2   See *AJ Bekhor*, above.

4.1.2   The principle that an order for discovery linked to a Mareva injunction is ancillary to the Mareva injunction appears to apply equally to worldwide Mareva injunctions.[1] Accordingly, a court which is prepared to grant a worldwide Mareva injunction is also likely to grant an order that the defendant disclose the whereabouts of his assets both inside and outside the jurisdiction of England and Wales.[2] The order may be accompanied by an undertaking by the plaintiffs not to use any information obtained under the disclosure to launch proceedings abroad without leave.[3]

1   See Chapter 2 for worldwide Mareva injunctions.
2   *Babanaft International Co SA v Bassatne* [1990] 1 Ch 13 per Kerr LJ at 28 and 37; *Derby & Co Ltd v Weldon* [1990] 1 Ch 48 per Nicholls LJ at 59–60; *Derby & Co Ltd v Weldon (Nos 3 and 4)* [1990] 1 Ch 65 per Neill LJ at 94–95.
3   *Derby & Co Ltd v Weldon* [1990] 1 Ch 48 per Nicholls LJ at 60A.

4.1.3   Anton Piller orders

Anton Piller orders often include an order for disclosure. This may be a wide-ranging order including, for example, an order that the defendant disclose the names and addresses (and telephone numbers) of the suppliers of counterfeit goods.[1] But such orders may now be held to be in breach of the defendant's privilege against self-incrimination: see **4.3** below. The jurisdiction of the court extends in a proper case to making an interlocutory order for disclosure of information about the operation of foreign companies and trusts.[2] The court may also make an order for the administration of interrogatories against the defendant.[3]

1   See *EMI Ltd v Sarwar and Haidar* [1977] FSR 146. Although *Wilmot Breeden Ltd v Woodcock Ltd* [1981] FSR 15 suggests that a strong case is required before discovery of the names of suppliers and customers is granted ex parte, a provision to this effect is now contained in the standard version of the Anton Piller order issued by the Chancery Division with judicial approval. See precedent 2A in Chapter 11.
2   *X Bank v G* (1985) Times, 13 April, CA.
3   *AJ Bekhor & Co Ltd v Bilton* [1981] QB 923.

4.2 DISCOVERY BY A THIRD PARTY BANK

4.2.1 The court has power to order a bank not party to the proceedings to disclose the state of the account of a customer, and documents relating to the account, where the plaintiff's claim against the customer is a tracing claim. See *Bankers Trust Co v Shapira*,[1] which concerned the alleged embezzlement of £5million. But in that case the Court of Appeal held that to justify such an order, the evidence of fraud against the customer had to be very strong. The plaintiff was required to give an undertaking in damages to the bank, to pay the bank's expenses of making the discovery and to use the documents disclosed solely for the purpose of tracing the money.

1   [1980] 3 All ER 353, CA.

4.2.2   Three points arise on this case. First, the power of the court to restrain a third party bank from dealing with moneys of the defendant's which are the subject of a tracing claim by the plaintiff was further considered in *Polly Peck International plc v Nadir (No 2)*.[1] This is dealt with in **4.7** below.

1   [1992] 4 All ER 769, CA.

4.2.3   Second, the *Shapira* case should now be read in light of the courts' subsequent development of the doctrine against self-incrimination, which is discussed in the next section. In *Shapira*, Lord Denning MR said that the order should be granted only

> 'when there is good ground for thinking the money in the bank is the plaintiff's money, for instance when the customer has got the money by fraud, or other wrongdoing, and paid it into his account at the bank.'[1]

If the defendant has got the money by fraud then it appears that the doctrine against self-incrimination might apply. It could be argued that that doctrine is irrelevant where it is a third party bank, rather than the defendant himself, who is ordered to provide the material. But this reasoning appears to have been rejected in the analogous case of orders under the Bankers' Books Evidence Act 1879,[2] so it is doubtful whether it is correct here.

1   Above, at 357.
2   See note 38/13/4 in the *Supreme Court Practice 1993*, volume 1 at page 655.

4.2.4   Third, it is possible that the *Shapira* case does remain good law on the basis that it is a similar type of order to Norwich Pharmacal orders: see **4.11** below.

4.3   THE DEFENDANT'S PRIVILEGE AGAINST SELF-INCRIMINATION

4.3.1   The defendant's privilege against self-incrimination may be relevant to the grant of an order to give discovery of assets, made in conjunction with a Mareva injunction, or the grant of an Anton Piller order. If giving the discovery or executing the Anton Piller order might expose the defendant to the risk of incrimination for a criminal offence in England and Wales, then such order should not be granted unless the case falls within one of the statutory exceptions to the privilege, or it is possible with the consent of the prosecuting authorities to ensure that the evidence disclosed will not be used against the defendant in a criminal trial.[1]

1   See *Rank Film Distributors Ltd v Video Information Centre* [1982] AC 380, CA and HL, and *Istel Ltd v Tully* [1992] 3 WLR 344, HL.

4.3.2   How much evidence of a danger of criminal prosecution does the defendant need to raise to show that the privilege applies? This was considered by Staughton LJ in *Sociedade Nacional de Combustiveis de Angola UEE v Lundqvist (Sonangol)*.[1] Having reviewed the authorities, he said:[2]

'The substance of the test is thus that there must be grounds to apprehend danger to the witness, and those grounds must be reasonable, rather than fanciful. Other points that emerge from the cases are these:

(i)   the affidavit claiming privilege is not conclusive (see *R v Boyes, ex p Reynolds* and *Khan v Khan*);

(ii)   the deponent is not bound to go into detail, if to do so would itself deprive him of protection (see *Short v Mercier* (1851) 3 Mac & G 205 at 217, 42 ER 239 at 244 and the *Rio Tinto Zinc* case [1978] AC 547, [1978] 1 All ER 434);

(iii)   ". . . if the fact of the witness being in danger be once made to appear, great latitude should be allowed to him in judging for himself of the effect of any particular question . . ." (see *R v Boyes* (1861) 1 B & S 311, [1861–73] All ER Rep 172 at 174, the *Rio Tinto Zinc* case and *Khan v Khan* [1982] 2 All ER 60, [1982] 1 WLR 513);

(iv) the privilege is not available where the witness is already at risk, and the risk would not be increased if he were required to answer (see *Brebner v Perry* [1961] SASR 177 and the *Rio Tinto Zinc* case); and

(v) "If it is one step, having a tendency to criminate him, he is not to be compelled to answer" (see *Paxton v Douglas* (1809) 16 Ves 239 at 242, 33 ER 975 at 976), ". . . as it is one link in a chain of proof" (see *Paxton v Douglas* (1812) 19 Ves 225 at 227, 34 ER 502 at 503).'

The effect of this is that, once the defendant has succeeded in showing that there are reasonable grounds to apprehend danger of prosecution of a defendant, he is to be allowed 'great latitude' in judging for himself the extent of the danger. Accordingly, the defendant who can show reasonable grounds for a fear of prosecution will be in a strong position to oppose discovery. In the *Sonangol* case, Staughton LJ held that it might incriminate the defendant to reveal the amount of his assets overseas, but that this did not apply to the nature and location of the assets. Accordingly, the defendant was ordered to disclose the nature and location but not the amount of the assets.

1   [1991] 2 QB 310, [1990] 3 All ER 283, CA.
2   [1990] 3 All ER at 292.

4.3.3   Extent of the privilege

In *Tate Access Floors Inc v Boswell*,[1] Sir Nicolas Browne-Wilkinson V-C considered the extent of the privilege. He analysed the *Rank Film Distributors* case.[2] He concluded that the privilege would not prevent the court from ordering the defendants to permit the plaintiffs to search the defendants' premises, under an Anton Piller order, and seize items which belonged to the plaintiffs themselves. It would, however, prevent the court from ordering that the defendants themselves should answer questions or provide any other evidence or documents, including documents relating to the plaintiffs' own items.

1   [1991] Ch 512 at 529–530.
2   Above.

4.3.4   Statutory exceptions

Parliament has enacted two statutory exceptions to the doctrine against self-incrimination which are relevant here.[1] First there is s 31(1) of the Theft Act 1968, which provides:

> 'A person shall not be excused, by reason that to do so may incriminate that person or the wife or husband of that person of an offence under this Act:
>
> (a) from answering any question put to that person in proceedings for the recovery or administration of any property, for the execution of any trust or for an account of any property or dealings with any property; or
>
> (b) from complying with any order made in such proceedings;
>
> but no statement or admission made by a person in answering a question put or complying with an order made as aforesaid shall, in proceedings for an offence under this Act, be admissible in evidence against that person or (unless they married after the making of the statement or admission) against the wife or husband of that person.'

The effect of this section is that a defendant in civil proceedings of the types set out in sub-s (a) may be required to answer questions or disclose documents which might tend to incriminate him in relation to offences under the Theft Act 1968. But the *Sonangol* case[2] is authority for the proposition that this section will not exclude the privilege against self-incrimination where there is a risk of a charge of conspiracy to defraud, either at common law or as a statutory conspiracy, because such a charge would not count as 'an offence under this Act' within the meaning of s 31.

---

1   Cf Companies Act 1985, s 434, Insolvency Act 1986, s 291 and Criminal Justice Act 1987, s 2, discussed by Lord Templeman in the *Istel* case, [1992] 3 WLR 344 at 351.
2   Above, [1990] 3 All ER 283 at 290H.

4.3.5   The second statutory exception is s 72 of the Supreme Court Act 1981.[1] That section applies to proceedings involving infringement of intellectual property rights or passing off. In *Universal City Studios Inc v Hubbard*,[2] the Court of Appeal held that s 72 should be given a broad interpretation. The effect of s 72 is essentially to abrogate the privilege against self-incrimination in relation to such civil proceedings, and enacts that answers given and evidence disclosed in such civil proceedings may not be used in criminal proceedings against the defendant or his spouse relating to the same matter.

1 See Appendix A.
2 [1984] Ch 225.

4.3.6 Protection by consent of the prosecuting authorities

If neither of the statutory exceptions applies, then the privilege may still not apply if the defendant can be given alternative protection from use of the evidence in a criminal prosecution. The civil court cannot, merely by its own order, prevent use of the documents in a criminal prosecution.[1] It can, however, make such an order on the basis that if the prosecuting authority consents not to use such evidence, then the privilege will not apply. For instance, in *Istel Ltd v Tully*,[2] Buckley J granted an ex parte injunction including the following clause:

> 'No disclosure made in compliance with paragraphs 18 to 32 inclusive of this order shall be used as evidence in the prosecution of the offence alleged to have been committed by the person required to make that disclosure or by any spouse of that person.'

The Crown Prosecution Service had, as a result of its own search and seizure in criminal proceedings, obtained evidence against the defendant before the grant of the civil court's order. In a letter, the Crown Prosecution Service gave an undertaking not to use the evidence which the plaintiffs might obtain in execution of their order. The reason was that the Service considered that it already had sufficient evidence and did not need to rely on evidence obtained by the plaintiffs. The House of Lords held that the Crown Prosecution Service was bound by its consent not to use the evidence in a criminal prosecution. It would be bound by such consent whether the consent was given after the Service had joined the civil proceedings as an intervenor,[3] or whether, as in the *Istel* case, consent had been given by letter without joining the proceedings. The result was that the defendant was no longer at risk of incrimination from the proposed order and so the privilege did not apply. It will be observed that, from the plaintiff's point of view, this means of obtaining discovery in spite of the privilege is rather haphazard: it all depends on the agreement of the prosecuting authorities. The House of Lords in the *Istel* case called for reform to reduce further the scope of the privilege against self-incrimination.

1 See the *Rank Film Distributors* case, above.
2 Above.
3 See *Re O* [1991] 2 QB 520.

4.3.7   Effect of the privilege on applications for Anton Piller orders

Where the privilege is raised as an objection to an order for discovery made with a Mareva injunction, the defendant should have time to argue the point on self-incrimination before he is obliged to give discovery. But in the case of an Anton Piller order, if the point is not taken at the ex parte hearing, the order is likely to have been executed and the damage done before the defendant has an opportunity to argue the point. For that reason, if there is a possibility that the privilege will arise, an ex parte Anton Piller order should not be granted.[1] This leads to a problem which requires the urgent attention of Parliament, as Sir Nicolas Browne-Wilkinson V-C has pointed out:[2]

> 'Anton Piller orders are only made when there is a strong prima facie case of dishonest conduct by the defendants which indicates that they are likely to destroy the evidence of their fraud. In such circumstances it is almost inevitable that the judge asked to make the order will consider that there is a real risk of prosecution for a criminal offence. If it is possible to say that the prosecution will be of a kind covered by section 31 of the Theft Act 1968 or section 72 of the Supreme Court Act 1981, that will cause no trouble. But if, as is likely too often to be the case, there is a real risk of a conspiracy charge, the judge will not be able to make an Anton Piller order at all and in consequence vital evidence will be destroyed. As it seems to me, apart from cases falling within section 72 (proceedings relating to intellectual property and passing off) in the future it will normally only be proper for the court to make an ex parte Anton Piller order for the recovery of property belonging to the plaintiffs without any related discovery as to documents. To a large extent, the Anton Piller jurisdiction will become incapable of being exercised. It is for this reason that, for myself, I would welcome the early consideration of the problem by Parliament.'

The effect of this decision is that, outside the area of intellectual property, in any case where there is a risk on reasonable grounds of criminal prosecution of the defendant for conspiracy to defraud, it is doubtful whether the court will or indeed should be asked to grant an ex parte Anton Piller order. The exception ought to be where the order relates only to items which the defendant does not dispute belong to the plaintiff, because the privilege does not extend to these (**4.3.3**). It is submitted that, even if it be thought that the application should nevertheless be made, the plaintiff's duty of full and frank disclosure will extend to require him to bring the attention of the court to the potential difficulty with self-incrimination, if there is a possibility it might apply.

1 *Tate Access Floors Inc v Boswell* [1991] Ch 512, per Sir Nicolas Browne-Wilkinson V-C at 530E.
2 Ibid at 532.

4.3.8 The Lord Chancellor's Department has published a consultation paper on Anton Piller orders.[1] The judges who wrote it agreed with Sir Nicolas Browne-Wilkinson's view of the problem raised by self-incrimination, and concluded that outside the area of intellectual property actions, which is governed by s 72 of the Supreme Court Act 1981:

> 'Privilege against self-incrimination remains a potential obstacle to execution of an Anton Piller order in all other types of proceedings.'[2]

They added that one of the commonest types of case in which Anton Piller orders had been granted was where an employer sued ex-employees who had entered into competition with him. In the committee's experience, dishonest conspiracy was almost invariably alleged. The result of the *Tate Access* case would be that the grant of Anton Piller orders in this type of case would generally be barred by the privilege against self-incrimination.[3]

1 'Anton Piller Orders – A Consultation Paper', published by the Lord Chancellor's Department, November 1992, and written by Staughton and Scott LJJ and Hollings, Hirst and Simon Brown JJ.
2 Ibid at para 2.16.
3 Ibid at para 2.18.

4.3.9 Risk of self-incrimination in foreign proceedings

The cases so far discussed concern privilege based on a danger of prosecution for offences in England and Wales. Can the defendant claim privilege on the basis that evidence might tend to incriminate him in foreign criminal proceedings? This was dealt with in *Arab Monetary Fund v Hashim (No 1)*.[1] Morritt J held that s 14 of the Civil Evidence Act 1968 intended that judges had no discretion to exclude evidence tending to incriminate defendants in relation to offences in foreign jurisdictions. But he added that when a judge was exercising his broad discretion to grant an order (such as an Anton Piller order or Mareva injunction) under s 37 of the Supreme Court Act 1981, the judge could take account of the danger of prosecution abroad and modify the terms of his order in light of such danger. In the *Hashim* case, it was said that the defendants were in danger of prosecution by the Iraqi regime. But they had been living openly in Canada or London for six years without any steps toward prosecution having been taken by the Iraqi authorities. Morritt J decided not to vary orders for discovery which he had earlier made.

1   [1989] 1 WLR 565.

4.3.10   Risk of incrimination of third parties in foreign proceedings

The *Hashim* litigation also raised the question of whether the court should order disclosure of documents which might endanger third parties living abroad. In *Arab Monetary Fund v Hashim (No 2)*,[1] Hoffmann J had to consider whether this should bar discovery by the defendants. They argued that to disclose the identities of certain parties from whom they had received moneys would place those persons in danger of prosecution by the Iraqi authorities, and that it was quite possible that the punishment for such offences under Iraqi law might be death. On the other hand, it appeared that the plaintiffs might have a tracing claim against the third parties and might be able to recover some funds from them. Hoffmann J started from the proposition that, at trial, the defendants would not be able to refuse to disclose identities of parties where such evidence was not part of a recognised privilege. If disclosure would have to be made at trial, he was inclined to order disclosure at the interlocutory stage unless the consequences of doing so for the third parties were likely to be very serious. He scrutinised the position of each of the third parties in turn. Many of them lived outside Iraq and were, he found, in no significant danger. Three were still in Iraq. Hoffmann J accepted that they might be in danger. On the other hand, their names would have to be disclosed at trial, unless there was no trial or the issues had changed by then to render them irrelevant. He ordered that their names be disclosed four weeks after the completion of discovery, unless the defendants on application could show that their identities were no longer relevant to the pleadings.

1   [1990] 1 All ER 673.

4.4 PASSAGE TO THIRD PARTIES OF DOCUMENTS AND OTHER INFORMATION OBTAINED IN EXECUTING THE ANTON PILLER ORDER

4.4.1   The Anton Piller order should contain a provision whereby the plaintiff and his solicitors undertake to keep in safe custody all documents and other articles which are obtained as a result of executing the order. A difficulty arises where the information or documents obtained suggest that the defendant has either committed a criminal offence, or infringed the civil law rights of a third party. Is it permissible for the plaintiff or his solicitors to pass on the information or documents obtained in executing the Anton Piller order, either to the police or to the third party? The courts have produced somewhat different answers, depending on whether the information is sought for the purpose of criminal or civil proceedings.

4.4.2   Criminal proceedings

In the case of possible criminal proceedings, it has been held that the plaintiff and his solicitors may disclose the documents to the prosecuting authorities only with the permission of the defendant or with the leave of the court. *EMI Records Ltd v Spillane*[1] concerned the provisions of the Value Added Tax Act 1983. Sir Nicolas Browne-Wilkinson V-C held that the plaintiffs' solicitors could not disclose to the Commissioners of Customs and Excise documents which they had obtained from the defendants pursuant to an Anton Piller order, without first obtaining the leave of the court or the defendants' permission. The Act negated any argument that the doctrine against self-incrimination might prevent disclosure. As to the obligations of the plaintiffs' solicitors, Sir Nicolas looked to the common law. The plaintiffs' undertaking to preserve the documents had been discharged by a consent order which settled the civil proceedings. But, in Sir Nicolas's view,[2]

> 'the documents were obtained by [the plaintiffs' solicitors] under procedures of the court providing for discovery of documents. Accordingly [the plaintiffs' solicitors] came under a further implied undertaking which in *Home Office v Harman* [1983] 1 AC 280 at 304 Lord Diplock defined in the following terms:
>> "the implied undertaking given by the solicitor personally to the court (of which he is an officer) that he himself will

not use or allow the documents or copies of them to be used for any collateral or ulterior purpose of his own, his client or anyone else; and any breach of that implied undertaking is a contempt of court by the solicitor himself." '

1   [1986] 1 WLR 967 (also reported sub nom *Customs and Excise Comrs v Hamlin Slowe* [1986] FSR 346).
2   [1986] 1 WLR at 972C–972D.

4.4.3   Sir Nicolas held that the plaintiffs' implied undertaking was an undertaking not to release the documents without the consent of the defendants or the leave of the court. As the defendants had not consented, the court had to exercise its discretion whether to order disclosure. Sir Nicolas exercised his discretion to order disclosure, on the basis that the civil action had already settled, and the consent order required the plaintiffs' solicitors to return the documents to the defendants in any event, so that the documents were held solely to the order of the defendants. But he emphasised that, had the civil proceedings not settled, he would not have given such leave:

'I wish to make it clear, however, that apart from the special circumstances flowing from [the consent order] whereby the documents are simply held to the order of *Spillane*, I would not have relaxed the undertakings so as to authorise production of the documents . . . So long as documents are held solely as the result of discovery, particularly discovery under compulsion under an Anton Piller order, it would be quite wrong to authorise their use in criminal proceedings brought under fiscal laws and having no connection with the original cause of action.'[1]

In this regard, he differed from Falconer J in the earlier case of *Customs and Excise Comrs v A E Hamlin & Co*,[2] who had been willing to exercise the discretion to give leave for documents to be disclosed to the Commissioners. Falconer J considered that the court would normally grant such leave.

1   [1986] 1 WLR at 977.
2   [1984] 1 WLR 509.

4.4.4   Further, in *General Nutrition Ltd v Pradip Pattni*,[1] Warner J declined to exercise his discretion to grant leave to disclose to the police documents obtained in executing an Anton Piller order. He held that the mere fact that such documents might show that a criminal offence had been committed did not, of itself, justify leave to disclose.

1   [1984] FSR 403.

4.4.5   It should be added that the implied undertaking not to use documents obtained on discovery for collateral or ulterior purposes does not apply once the document has been read to or by the court, or referred to in open court, unless the court makes an order that the document is to remain subject to the undertaking.[1]

1   RSC Ord 24, r 14A, Appendix E.

4.4.6   Civil proceedings

Having considered when the court will permit documents disclosed to be used for further criminal prosecution, one might conclude that similar principles would apply where application is made to use the documents for other civil actions. But this is not entirely so. There appear to be two streams of authority which are surprisingly inconsistent.

4.4.7   The first stream of authority culminates in *Crest Homes plc v Marks*.[1] Lord Oliver of Alylmerton delivered the leading judgment. He stated that discovery obtained in executing an Anton Piller order was discovery in advance of pleadings, and that:[2]

> '. . . a solicitor who, in the course of discovery in an action, obtains possession of copies of documents belonging to his client's adversary gives an implied undertaking to the court not to use that material nor to allow it to be used for any purpose other than the proper conduct of that action on behalf of his client: see *Home Office v Harman* [1983] AC 280.'

He went on to confirm that such document could not be used for any other purpose, for instance, as the foundation for a wholly different action.[3] Further,

> '. . . the implied undertaking applies not merely to the documents discovered themselves but also to information derived from those documents whether it be embodied in a copy or stored in the mind.[4] But the implied undertaking is one which is given to the court ordering discovery and it is clear and is not disputed by the appellants that it can, in appropriate circumstances, be released or modified by the court.'[5]

1   [1987] AC 829, [1987] 3 WLR 293, HL.
2   See [1987] 3 WLR at 297–298.
3   *Riddick v Thames Board Mills Ltd* [1977] QB 881.
4   See *Sybron Corpn v Barclays Bank plc* [1985] Ch 299.
5   See [1987] 3 WLR at 298.

4.4.8   Lord Oliver went on to consider when the court would release the undertaking. He accepted the importance of the integrity of the implied undertaking. There had to be strong reasons for the court to vary it. On the special circumstances of the *Crest* case, he was prepared to accept that the undertaking should be modified. The facts were that the plaintiffs had brought an action against the defendants for infringement of intellectual property rights in 1984. They had obtained an Anton Piller order and executed it. Then, again, in 1985, the plaintiffs had brought a similar action against the defendants. They had again obtained and executed an Anton Piller order. When executing the Anton Piller order in 1985, they had found documents which suggested that the defendants had acted in contempt of the 1984 proceedings. They sought leave to use the documents discovered in the 1985 proceedings to support a finding of contempt of the 1984 proceedings. The parties to the two sets of proceedings were not identical, but this was a technicality. The House of Lords granted the plaintiffs' application.

4.4.9   It therefore appears from the *Crest* case that the evidence obtained in executing an Anton Piller order may not be used to support further actions unless the court has given leave for the implied undertaking, referred to in *Home Office v Harman*,[1] to be released. This will be done only in special circumstances.[2] Unfortunately, that appears inconsistent with some other cases. The cases referred to above were not cited in this second stream of authority, and it may be that the second stream of authority requires reconsideration, or alternatively should be viewed as a set of exceptions to the general rule.

1   Above.
2   Cf *Prudential Assurance Co Ltd v Fountain Page Ltd* [1991] 1 WLR 756.

4.4.10   The second line of cases concern intellectual property. A number of parties may be involved in what is essentially one instance of infringement. For instance, the plaintiff may search the defendant's premises to find unlawful copies of his perfume, only to find that the defendant obtained them from someone else, or that the defendant is also selling other fake perfumes. It is necessary to distinguish two sets of circumstances. First, A may execute an Anton Piller order against B, and find at B's premises evidence that C, D and E have infringed A's copyright. Second, A may execute an Anton Piller order against B, and find evidence that B has infringed the copyright of C, D and E.

4.4.11 In the first example, there is authority that A may use the evidence to launch further actions against C, D and E. This applies both to documents obtained in executing the Anton Piller order, and to evidence of what A's solicitors see at B's premises when they execute the order. See *Sony Corpn v Anand*[1] and *Roberts v Jump Knitwear Ltd.*[2] But both those cases were decided before *Crest Homes plc v Marks*[3] or indeed *Home Office v Harman.*[4] It would appear that they cannot be good law in light of the House of Lords' decisions in those cases.[5] It is suggested that the prudent course in this type of case is to seek the leave of the court if disclosure is intended, and to bring to the attention of the court the *Crest* and *Harman* cases.

1 [1981] FSR 398.
2 [1981] FSR 527.
3 Above.
4 Above.
5 It would appear that the authors of note 29/2-3/8 in the *Supreme Court Practice 1993* have not considered this point.

4.4.12 As to the second example, one might think that this was little different from where A searches B's premises and finds evidence that B has broken the criminal law, so that similar principles would apply to the position discussed above regarding the criminal law: A would have to seek the leave of the court before disclosing the documents to C, D and E, and the court would rarely exercise its discretion in favour of this due to the rule that the documents were obtained as part of a process akin to discovery so that A would impliedly have undertaken not to use the documents for any purpose other than the proceedings in issue. But there is authority to the effect that the position is almost opposite to the cases concerning breaches of the criminal law. In *Piver SARL v S & J Perfume Co Ltd*,[1] Walton J said:

'. . . especially when a trained private investigator is going round a factory used by people who are counterfeiting perfumes, if he sees, as he is almost bound to see, other instances of counterfeiting, there can be absolutely nothing whatsoever to stop him reporting those instances to the people who are really concerned to stop it.'

The 'people who are really concerned to stop' such counterfeiting are the parties whose rights are being infringed by unlawful copying. It would therefore appear that A may pass on to C, D and E details of what his agent saw at B's premises, if that evidence suggests that B is infringing the rights of C, D and E. The report does not state whether *Crest Homes plc v Marks*[2] and *Home Office v Harman*[3] were cited in this case, and they were not mentioned in the judgment. As in paragraph **4.4.11**, it appears that the case cannot stand against those authorities.

1   [1987] FSR 159 at 162.
2   Above.
3   Above.

4.4.13   Further, in *Twentieth Century Fox Film Corpn v Tryrare Ltd*,[1] Harman J declined to vary a provision in an Anton Piller order which permitted A (the plaintiff)'s solicitors to disclose to C, D and E (third parties) what evidence of infringement of the rights of such third parties they had seen while executing an Anton Piller order over the premises of B (the defendant). What is somewhat surprising is the legal basis for this decision. The decision was based upon a quotation from the 1991 edition of the *Supreme Court Practice* to the effect that in relation to

> ' "information obtained pursuant to an Anton Piller order or Norwich Pharmacal order there is no implied undertaking that the information will be used solely for the purpose of the existing action." That is obviously a necessary consequence of the nature of Anton Piller orders.'[2]

This appears to be contradicted, however, by the *Crest*[3] and *Harman*[4] cases. Harman J did not have the benefit of considering either of those cases.

1   [1991] FSR 58.
2   Ibid at 60.
3   Above.
4   Above.

4.5   CROSS-EXAMINATION OF THE DEFENDANT

4.5.1   In granting a Mareva injunction or Anton Piller order, the court may also grant an order that the defendant swear an affidavit stating the whereabouts of his assets.[1] It is clear that, once such order has been served on the defendant, the court has power to grant a further order that the defendant be cross-examined on his evidence in reply.[2]

1   *A J Bekhor & Co Ltd v Bilton* [1981] QB 923.
2   *House of Spring Gardens Ltd v Waite* [1985] FSR 173, CA.

4.5.2   When will this power to order cross-examination be exercised? This is a question for the discretion of the judge. It was not raised in the *House of Spring Gardens*[1] case, as the defendants conceded it. There are two decisions at first instance which suggest that the power will be exercised in very limited circumstances. In *CBS (UK) Ltd v Perry*,[2] Falconer J approved the following passage from the judgment of Peter Gibson J in the unreported case of *RAC Ltd v Allsop*:[3]

> 'The object of the application must, I apprehend, truly be to obtain the further information which it is believed is in the possession of the person the subject of the order but which that person has failed to disclose notwithstanding the earlier order. The object of the application must not be to enable contempt proceedings to be brought so as to punish the person served with the order. Further, it must not be to obtain information which is to be used for the purpose of the action when that action comes to trial.'

1   Above.
2   [1985] FSR 421.
3   (1984) 3 October, unreported.

4.5.3   A similar approach was adopted by Scott J in *Bayer AG v Winter (No 2)*.[1] He refused an application by the plaintiffs for what their counsel openly admitted would be a 'free-ranging' cross-examination. Scott J considered that it was likely to cover 'almost the whole area on which [the defendant] would be cross-examined at trial'. This was before the plaintiffs had even served a statement of claim. Further, the answers given might be used to commit the defendant to prison for breach of the ex parte Anton Piller order. Scott J said:[2]

> 'For my part I find it very difficult to envisage any circumstances in which, as a matter of discretion, it would be right to make such an order as is sought in the present case and as was made by consent in the *House of Spring Gardens* case.'

This view is consistent with the general toughening of the court's approach toward these draconian orders, noted in Chapter 3.

1   [1986] 2 All ER 43, [1986] 1 WLR 540.
2   [1986] 2 All ER at 46H.

4.5.4   It therefore appears that the court will rarely exercise its discretion to order cross-examination on affidavits filed by the defendant. If cross-examination is ordered, it should generally be limited to the whereabouts of the defendant's assets. The purpose of the cross-examination would be to try to establish if there are assets which the defendant has dishonestly failed to mention in his affidavit. If the court does order cross-examination on an affidavit, made pursuant to an order contained in a Mareva order, as to the whereabouts of the defendant's assets, then the new RSC Ord 29, r 1A will apply to govern the procedure.[1] The court may order that the cross-examination take place before a master or indeed an examiner of the court. Some of the provisions of RSC Ord 68 will apply to the cross-examination. The cross-examination must take place in chambers; any record of it shall not be used other than for the purpose of the proceedings unless the court gives leave or the defendant consents.

1   See Appendix E.

4.6   DELIVERY UP OF THE PLAINTIFF OR DEFENDANT'S CHATTELS

4.6.1   Chattels which plaintiff alleges are his

A plaintiff applying for a Mareva injunction may at the same time apply for an order for interim delivery up of the chattels which are the subject matter of the action.[1] In this case, the plaintiff ought to give an undertaking to indemnify the defendant or any third party in respect of the costs, expenses, fees and liabilities reasonably incurred as a result of the making of the order.[2] These may be substantial.

1   RSC Ord 29, r 2A (Appendix E), and see Torts (Interference with Goods) Act 1977, s 4 (Appendix D).
2   See discussion of *Guiness Peat Aviation (Belgium) NV v Hispania Lineas Aereas SA* [1992] 1 Lloyd's Rep 190 in Chapter 2.

4.6.2   An Anton Piller order often contains a provision that the defendant deliver certain specified chattels, which belong to the plaintiff, into the custody of the plaintiff's solicitors.[1] This enables the plaintiff to remove infringing copies and any items relating to the making of infringing copies (eg invoices and video machines).

1 See Chapter 11.

4.6.3 Defendant's chattels

The court may also, as part of the Anton Piller procedure, order the removal not only of the evidence of infringement of the plaintiff's intellectual property rights but also of chattels which the defendant has bought with the proceeds of sale of articles in breach of such rights. Guidelines were laid down by the Court of Appeal in *CBS (UK) Ltd v Lambert*[1] in respect of such material: see Appendix H. There should be some evidence, or at least an inference, that the defendant acquired the chattels as a result of his wrongdoing. No order should normally be made for delivery up of the defendant's wearing apparel, bedding, furnishings, tools of his trade, farm implements, livestock or any machines (including motor vehicles) or other goods such as materials or stock-in-trade which it is likely he uses for the purposes of a lawful business.

1 [1983] Ch 37 at 44.

4.7 INJUNCTION TO RESTRAIN DISPOSAL OF ITEMS SUBJECT TO A TRACING CLAIM

4.7.1 If the plaintiff does not wish to go as far as seeking delivery to him of assets, he may instead apply for an order pursuant to RSC Ord 29, r 2 for the interim preservation of property which is the subject matter of the cause or action. The jurisdiction to grant this order is quite separate from the jurisdiction to grant a Mareva injunction or Anton Piller order, although the order may have a similar effect. The case of *Polly Peck International plc v Nadir (No 2)*[1] demonstrates the interrelationship between the two jurisdictions. The plaintiffs claimed a Mareva injunction against the central bank of the Republic of North Cyprus. In addition, in relation to £8.9m which the bank held, they launched a tracing claim on the basis that the £8.9m belonged to the plaintiffs and that the bank had constructive knowledge of this. The nature of tracing claims is discussed elsewhere.[2] In simple terms, they amount to a claim that an asset held by the defendant either belongs to the plaintiff or should be treated as so belonging. Accordingly, the basis of the interim injunction to preserve the asset is that the asset belongs to the plaintiff, the plaintiff is claiming its return, and therefore the defendant should not be permitted to dispose of it until the trial. This is different from the rationale of a Mareva injunction, which is that the defendant should not be permitted to dissipate assets which belong to him, the defendant, but which might enable him to meet a judgment in favour of the plaintiff.

1   [1992] 4 All ER 769, CA. Cf *A v C* [1981] QB 956.
2   See Goff & Jones *The Law of Restitution* (3rd edn, 1986) and the recent cases: *Agip (Africa) Ltd v Jackson* [1991] Ch 547, CA and *Eagle Trust plc v SBC Securities Ltd* [1993] 1 WLR 484.

4.7.2   As the injunction is based on the claim that the asset belongs to the plaintiff, if granted it will contain no proviso permitting the defendant to use the asset to meet his reasonable business or living expenses, as in the case of a Mareva injunction.[1] In deciding whether to grant the injunction, the court applies the principles of *American Cyanamid Co v Ethicon Ltd*.[2] This is different from the court's approach to an application for a Mareva injunction.[3]

1   *Polly Peck (No 2)* above, per Scott LJ at 785F.
2   [1975] AC 396, HL.
3   *Polly Peck (No 2)* above, per Scott LJ and Lord Donaldson of Lymington MR.

4.8   INJUNCTION TO RESTRAIN DEFENDANT FROM DAMAGING HIS OWN ASSETS

4.8.1   In *Standard Chartered Bank v Walker*,[1] Vinelott J held that the court had jurisdiction, on principles akin to the Mareva jurisdiction, to restrain the defendant from doing acts which would destroy or greatly injure his assets to the detriment of a creditor. The plaintiff banks were creditors of Brent Walker plc. Brent Walker owed them more than the value of its assets. They had proposed a reconstruction plan for Brent Walker. An extraordinary general meeting of Brent Walker had been arranged to consider the plan. In the bank's view, if the plan were rejected by the shareholders then Brent Walker would inevitably collapse. The defendants held shares which had voting rights of 5–10% of the meeting. Their votes might be crucial. They proposed to vote against the plan. Vinelott J granted an injunction to prevent them from doing so. In his view, for the defendants to vote against the plan would be[2]

'. . . so pointlessly harmful that, whatever motive inspired it, it would amount to the wilful dissipation of assets which the court has jurisdiction, consistently with the Mareva principles, to prevent.'

He added that such an order would be made only in extreme circumstances.

This approach might usefully be extended to matrimonial law.

1   [1992] 1 WLR 561.
2   At 566H.

4.9   INJUNCTION TO RESTRAIN THE DEFENDANT FROM LEAVING THE JURISDICTION

4.9.1   At the same time as making an Anton Piller order, the court has power to make an order that the defendant be restrained from leaving the jurisdiction and that he deliver up his passport to the plaintiff's solicitors. There are two separate streams of authority for this variety of order: a '*Bayer v Winter*' order[1] under s 37(1) of the Supreme Court Act 1981, and a prerogative *writ ne exeat regno*. It now appears that the plaintiff should apply for a *Bayer v Winter* order rather than a *writ ne exeat regno*.

1   From *Bayer AG v Winter (No 1)* [1986] 1 WLR 497, CA.

4.9.2   *Writ ne exeat regno*

The *writ ne exeat regno* originated in the thirteenth century as a prerogative writ. Gradually the scope of the writ was narrowed by the judges. The modern position was considered by Megarry J in *Felton v Callis*.[1] The writ would be granted only if, although the plaintiff's claim was not for a legal debt, the four conditions contained in s 6 of the Debtors Act 1869 were satisfied. Megarry J summarised those conditions as:

'(i)   The action is one in which the defendant would formerly have been liable to arrest at law.

(ii)   A good cause of action for at least £50 is established.

(iii)   There is "probable cause" for believing that the defendant is "about to quit England".

(iv) "The absence of the defendant from England will materially prejudice the plaintiff in the prosecution of his action".'

1   [1969] 1 QB 200 at 211.

4.9.3   The grant of a *writ ne exeat regno* in conjunction with Mareva injunctions was considered in *Al Nakhel for Contracting and Trading Ltd v Lowe*[1] and *Allied Arab Bank Ltd v Hajjar*.[2] The writ was issued together with a Mareva injunction in *Al Nakhel*. Tudor Price J relied upon an unreported note of a judgment of Anthony Evans J in *Yiu Wing Construction Co (Overseas) Ltd v Ghosh* ((1985) 21 February, unreported) for the proposition that:

'. . . such a writ could be issued to ensure that the defendant, by leaving the jurisdiction, did not defeat the very purpose for which a Mareva order had been granted.'[3]

But in *Hajjar*, Leggatt J declined to accept this proposition. He said:[4]

'. . . if it was intended to go further and to suggest that the writ may be ordered for the purpose of enforcing a Mareva injunction, I disagree: for that purpose the appropriate remedy is an injunction to restrain the defendant from leaving the jurisdiction.'

It appears that by 'an injunction to restrain the defendant from leaving the jurisdiction', Leggatt J meant a *Bayer v Winter* order (see below). Accordingly, the *Hajjar* case is authority for the proposition that a *writ ne exeat regno* will not be issued to support the enforcement of a Mareva injunction. Instead, the plaintiff should apply for a *Bayer v Winter* order. Further, in *Hajjar*, Leggatt J adopted a restrictive approach to some of the other conditions for the grant of a *writ ne exeat regno*: for instance, he held that Megarry J's condition (i) would be satisfied only if the plaintiff sued on a debt rather than for damages. The effect of the *Hajjar* case is that, while it may still technically be possible to obtain a *writ ne exeat regno* in a case where a Mareva injunction is granted, it will generally be far easier to apply for a *Bayer v Winter* order, because the *Bayer v Winter* order is not surrounded by technicalities from the past. As the *writ ne exeat regno* involves the arrest of the defendant, it is unlikely that the court will wish to develop it in preference to *Bayer v Winter* orders, which do not.

1   [1986] QB 235, [1986] 2 WLR 317.
2   [1987] 3 All ER 739.

3   See [1986] 2 WLR at 320C.
4   At 744A–B.

4.9.4   *Bayer v Winter* orders

As the basis for this order is s 37(1) of the Supreme Court Act 1981, it is not beset with the technicalities that surround the *writ ne exeat regno*. The basis for granting the order is that it is necessary in order to give effect to other parts of the order which the court is granting. In *Bayer v Winter (No 1)*,[1] the plaintiffs accepted that there was no jurisdiction to grant a *writ ne exeat regno*. The Court of Appeal held that the court had power, pursuant to s 37(1), to grant an order:

'1.   That the first defendant be restrained from leaving England and Wales until two days after the service of this order or further order in the meantime.

2.   That the first defendant do forthwith deliver up his passports to the person who shall serve this order upon him: provided that the plaintiffs' solicitors must return them to him upon the expiry of the time referred to in the preceding paragraph of the order.'

The facts were that the plaintiffs were manufacturers of an insecticide which was sold in many countries. They alleged that the defendants were involved in marketing a counterfeit product with a similar mark to the plaintiffs' product. At the ex parte hearing, Walton J ordered the defendants, inter alia, to disclose to the plaintiffs their knowledge of the whereabouts of documents relating to transactions in which the counterfeit product had been supplied or offered, and their assets inside and outside the jurisdiction. The plaintiffs claimed that without the bar on the first defendant leaving the jurisdiction, they might be denied the information required by the judge's order, because the first defendant had indicated that he would not answer the plaintiffs' questions, and the plaintiffs considered that the first defendant might leave the jurisdiction rather than answer their questions. The court emphasised that, if the first defendant was prejudiced, he could apply to discharge the order. Given that the order concerned the liberty of the subject, the court limited its operation to two days after service upon the defendant.

1   Above.

4.9.5   When the order was served, the plaintiffs executed the Anton Piller part of the order. Their solicitors questioned the first defendant.

They were not satisfied with some of his answers. They returned to court, four days after the grant of the original order, and asked Scott J to extend the restriction on leaving the jurisdiction, and grant an order that the first defendant be cross-examined further. The judge declined to grant the order.[1] He was very doubtful whether the court, on an ex parte application, should ever exercise its discretion to permit free-ranging cross-examination of parties as to all aspects of the proposed case against them, before the plaintiff had even served its statement of claim. As the application for further cross-examination failed, so did the application to extend the restriction on leaving the jurisdiction.

1   *Bayer AG v Winter (No 2)* [1986] 2 All ER 43.

4.9.6   The tendency of the courts to tighten the requirements for the grant of orders such as Anton Piller orders has already been noted.[1] This approach may in future extend to *Bayer v Winter* orders, and indeed the tenor of Scott J's judgment in *Bayer AG v Winter (No 2)* seems opposed to such orders. It is not clear from the report of *Bayer AG v Winter (No 1)*[2] whether there was strong evidence to show that the first defendant was about to leave the jurisdiction. The hearing was on 20 December, but this cannot have been enough to justify the order. It is suggested that there ought to be at least some evidence that the defendant, if unrestrained, is likely to leave the jurisdiction.[3]

1   See Chapter 3.
2   Above.
3   Cf the requirements for the *writ ne exeat regno*, above. Cf *Arab Monetary Fund v Hashim (No 1)* [1989] 1 WLR 565, for another case where a *Bayer v Winter* order was made.

4.10   ORDER 11

4.10.1   Order 11 provides for service of process out of the jurisdiction. Detailed consideration of its provisions is beyond the scope of this book, save to say that an affidavit is required for an application under Order 11. Sometimes it may be possible to rely upon only one affidavit for both an application for a Mareva injunction and an application under Order 11, although in more complex cases this may prove impossible.

4.11 DISCOVERY AGAINST THIRD PARTIES: NORWICH PHARMACAL ORDERS

4.11.1   In general, someone who is not a party to the plaintiff's action against the defendant has no obligation to give discovery of documents or evidence germane to that action. Norwich Pharmacal[1] orders are an exception to that principle. Where a third party has become mixed up in the wrongdoing of another (the intended or actual defendant), so as to facilitate its commission, the court has power under its inherent jurisdiction to order the third party to furnish the intended plaintiff with information in the third party's possession relating to the wrongdoing. The power exists regardless of whether the third party has itself done wrongful acts, or of whether the third party's involvement in the wrongdoing is voluntary or involuntary. For further discussion of this type of order see note 24/1/4 in the *Supreme Court Practice 1993*, and cases cited there.

1 See *Norwich Pharmacal Co v Customs and Excise Comrs* [1974] AC 133, HL.

4.11.2   As was noted in **4.2** above, it is conceivable that the doctrine against self-incrimination, discussed in **4.3**, might militate against this type of order. But as Norwich Pharmacal orders were established by the House of Lords, this seems highly unlikely.

4.12 OTHER ANCILLARY ORDERS

4.12.1   The court has wide powers under s 37(1) of the Supreme Court Act 1981[1] to grant an injunction or appoint a receiver where it appears to the court to be just and convenient. The powers may be used to ensure that the purposes of the Mareva or Anton Piller order are not frustrated. The appointment of a receiver may, however, prove very costly.

1   Appendix A.

4.12.2   The jurisdiction to prevent the defendant from leaving the country (**4.9**) is an example of the draconian powers which the court is prepared to employ in this regard. But, as has been mentioned in Chapter 3, especially as far as Anton Piller orders are concerned, the judicial tide is now running strongly against the making of intrusive and restrictive orders unless it is abundantly plain that they are absolutely necessary. Nevertheless, it appears that s 37 of the Supreme Court Act 1981 is sufficiently wide to permit the court to make numerous ancillary orders, depending on the circumstances of the case.[1] Orders which may be made ancillary to Anton Piller orders include injunctions against trading or dealing in infringing goods, to prevent identified confidential information being passed on by the defendant, and to prevent the defendant informing third parties, other than his lawyers, of the existence of the proceedings. The Anton Piller order will often include a term requiring the defendant to cause records, or documents stored in a computer's memory, to be printed out.[2] There may be an order that the defendant permits photographs to be taken.

1   Cf *House of Spring Gardens Ltd v Waite* [1985] FSR 173 per Cumming Bruce LJ at 183.
2   See Chapter 11.

4.12.3   In addition to the above powers, under RSC Order 29, r 3[1] the court has the power to order samples to be taken.

1   Appendix E.

PART II
The plaintiff's application

Obtaining the order

5.0 Chapters 5 and 6 consider how the order is obtained. The Mareva injunction and Anton Piller order should be regarded as drastic forms of relief. Before the orders are granted, the court requires certain pre-conditions to be satisfied and undertakings to be given by the plaintiff and, in the case of the execution of an Anton Piller order, the plaintiff's solicitor. Chapter 5 is divided into two parts: first, procedure, and second, the nature of the evidence which the plaintiff needs in order to persuade the court to grant the order. Chapter 6 deals with the obligations which the court imposes upon the plaintiff, if the order is granted, in order to safeguard the interests of the defendant. These chapters should be read in conjunction with Chapters 2 and 3 on the recent developments as to the form of the orders, Chapter 4 on self-incrimination, and Chapter 7 on execution of the orders, as the safeguards for the defendant include a number of important rules as to how the order should be executed.

5.1 PROCEDURE

5.1.1 Applications for either Mareva injunctions or Anton Piller orders are invariably made ex parte.[1] This is because it is implicit in either application that the defendant is essentially a rogue. If he is a rogue then he is likely to remove or dissipate assets or destroy evidence as soon as he knows of the proposed application. If the plaintiff were to make an inter partes application, giving the defendant at least two working days' notice of the proposed application, then, if he were a rogue, this would give him ample opportunity to remove assets or destroy evidence. The application should therefore be made ex parte and without notifying the defendant or his solicitors of the intended application.

---

1   Cf RSC Ord 29, r 1(2): ex parte applications to be made only in cases of urgency.

5.1.2   The need to keep the initial application secret from the defendant also means that consideration should be given to applying for a Mareva or Anton Piller order at a very early stage. The reason is the same as mentioned in paragraph **5.1.1**: the plaintiff is arguing that the defendant is the sort of person who will seek to dissipate or remove assets or destroy assets to frustrate the plaintiff's claim. If the defendant is indeed such a person, and if he does intend to take such steps, then it is likely that he will take them as soon as he knows of the plaintiff's claim, that is, as soon as he is served with the writ. If the action has begun and the defendant has not already removed or dissipated any assets or destroyed any evidence, then he can argue that he is not likely to do so in the future. Whether this is plausible will depend on the facts of the particular case. Further, the plaintiff may apply for a Mareva at any stage of the proceedings and indeed in aid of execution of judgment.[1] But it is generally better to consider whether to make the application at the earliest possible stage. That said, it is helpful to have formulated the statement of claim as this should clarify the nature of the plaintiff's case. The application could then be brought after the issue, but before the service, of the writ.

1   *Orwell Steel (Erection and Fabrication) Ltd v Asphalt and Tarmac (UK) Ltd* [1984] 1 WLR 1097.

5.1.3   In family cases the application is brought in the Family Division. Otherwise, the application must be made in either the Queen's Bench Division or the Chancery Division. If the action has already begun then the application is made in the division in which it is proceeding. If the application is made before issue of the writ then it should be made in the division in which it is intended to bring the action. To proceed in the Queen's Bench Division where the proposed cause of action involves matters assigned by statute to the Chancery Division, such as intellectual property,[1] invites criticism.[2]

1   See Schedule 1 to the Supreme Court Act 1981, at para 5347 of volume 2 of the *Supreme Court Practice 1993.*
2   See *McCain International Ltd v Country Fair Foods Ltd* [1981] RPC 69, CA and *Swedac Ltd v Magnet & Southerns plc* [1989] FSR 243.

5.2   PROCEDURE IN THE QUEEN'S BENCH DIVISION

5.2.1   The procedure in the Queen's Bench Division is as follows.[1] Unless there is extreme urgency, the applicant should prepare a writ, preferably endorsed with a statement of claim, an affidavit in support, and two copies of a draft of the order which it is proposed the court should make. The latter is known as a 'draft minute of order'. The form of the affidavit is crucial and is dealt with below. These papers should normally be lodged with the clerk to the Judge in Chambers at the Royal Courts of Justice by 3pm on the day before the application is to be made.

1   See the *Practice Direction (Judge in Chambers: Procedure)* [1983] 1 WLR 433 as amended, in Appendix G.

5.2.2   In *ALG Inc v Uganda Airlines Corpn*,[1] it was suggested that in all hearings concerning Marevas, whether ex parte or inter partes, the papers should be delivered to the court sufficiently long before the hearing to enable the judge to read and digest them all before the hearing. But this suggestion was made primarily in the context of applications for worldwide Marevas (see Chapter 2), and does not alter the *Practice Direction* (above).

1   (1992) Times, 31 July, per Mr Richard Southwell QC sitting as a deputy High Court Judge.

5.2.3   If the matter is too urgent to wait until the next day, then the applicant's counsel or solicitor should sign a certificate of extreme urgency. The applicant may then attend on the clerk to the judge in chambers, with the papers mentioned above, at 9.50am and be heard at 10am. Alternatively, the papers may be lodged with the clerk by 12.30pm and the application be heard at 2pm. If the matter is too urgent for either of those steps, then the applicant's advisers must give notice to the clerk to the judge in chambers who will if necessary interrupt what he is doing to hear the matter at once. The applicant's counsel must be able to explain to the judge why the matter is exceptionally urgent.

5.2.4   Exceptional circumstances may also prevent the applicant's advisers from preparing the papers in support of the application.[1] In this case, counsel or a solicitor may attend on the judge, explain the basis of the application and give various undertakings. The undertakings will be to issue the writ, have an affidavit sworn to confirm what the judge has been told, and draft and serve an order on the defendant. It is essential, in these circumstances, for a representative of the plaintiff other than the advocate to be present to note down precisely what the judge has been told. Indeed, this is a wise precaution in any ex parte application. An attendance note of the hearing may be crucial if the defendant challenges the order and alleges that the plaintiff has failed to draw the judge's attention to some material fact.

1 In *WEA Records Ltd v Visions Channel 4 Ltd* [1983] 1 WLR 721 counsel appeared armed only with a draft writ and instructions as to the nature and results of the plaintiff's enquiries. No affidavit evidence was produced nor did counsel have the advantage of being able to produce unsworn affidavits. Nevertheless the Court of Appeal confirmed that in such cases an order might be granted.

5.2.5 In even more extreme cases, if the court is not sitting, application for an ex parte injunction may be made to a judge at his or her home. The plaintiff's solicitors should telephone the Royal Courts of Justice, who will be able to put them in touch with the duty judge who is always available for the hearing of urgent applications. In *Refson & Co Ltd v Saggers*,[1] which concerned an application for Mareva relief, Nourse J stated, with the authorisation of Sir Robert Megarry V-C:[2]

> '. . . In cases where relief is sought over the telephone, the material part or parts of the draft indorsement should normally be read to the judge. Only in cases of very exceptional urgency should the court be asked to act without a sight or hearing of the material part or parts of a draft endorsement.'

1 [1984] 1 WLR 1025.
2 Ibid at 1030E–1030F.

5.2.6 The order will usually be expressed to last until trial or further order but will give the defendant liberty to apply to discharge or vary it on 24 or 48 hours' notice to the plaintiff's solicitors. In fact the defendant is entitled to apply for discharge of the order at any time, although if he gives the plaintiff's solicitors less than 48 hours' notice he may have to show why this was impracticable, and allow his application to be adjourned for a further period. Sometimes there is difficulty in obtaining a speedy listing in the Queen's Bench Division of the application to discharge. This occurred in *Re Capital Expansion & Development Corpn Ltd*.[1] The order gave the defendant leave to apply for discharge on 48 hours' notice. But when the defendant made the application, the Queen's Bench Division was unable to give a date for a further hearing within a month. The defendant applied instead to the Chancery Division, where the matter could be heard more quickly. In the Chancery Division, Millett J held that that Division had jurisdiction to discharge an order made in the Queen's Bench

Division 'until further order'. Further, it was right that if the court had granted a speedy hearing for the grant of the injunction, it should also grant a speedy hearing to consider its discharge. Millett J exercised his jurisdiction and discharged the order. This may be a useful procedure for those subject to Mareva injunctions.

1 (1992) Times, 30 November.

5.2.7 Practitioners who avail themselves of exceptional provisions for very speedy relief should, in spite of the need for urgency, continue to bear in mind the obligations on the plaintiff which are referred to in the rest of this chapter and in Chapter 6. In particular, it is essential to give full and frank disclosure of weaknesses in the plaintiff's case, of potential weakness in the plaintiff's finances which might cast doubt on the value of the undertaking in damages, and to give full details of what is known of the defendant's background, residence, place of work and family ties.[1] It is often better to delay the application by a few days in order to ensure that all of the numerous pitfalls have been carefully considered. Obtaining an injunction which is subsequently discharged may lose the plaintiff the initiative and damage his conduct of the whole action.

1 *O'Regan v Iambic Productions Ltd* [1989] NLJR 1378 per Sir Peter Pain.

5.3 PROCEDURE IN THE CHANCERY DIVISION

5.3.1 In the Chancery Division the applicant must lodge a Notice of Motion, the affidavit in support, and draft order. Three copies of each should be lodged. The papers should be lodged with the Clerk of the Lists in the Chancery Chambers at the Royal Courts of Justice by 12 noon on the day before the application is to be heard. The application will be heard before the Motions Judge the next day. If the matter is more urgent, the applicant's counsel or solicitor should telephone the clerk of the Motions Judge and explain how urgent it is. If there is time, arrangements will be made for the papers to be lodged and a time allocated for hearing before a judge. If the matter is very urgent then an immediate hearing will be arranged with an undertaking to lodge the papers thereafter. If it is urgent and requires to be heard out of business hours, then the applicant's counsel or solicitor should telephone the Royal Courts of Justice to arrange either to see or to speak by telephone to the duty judge who is always available to deal with very urgent ex parte applications.

5.3.2 If only a Mareva injunction is applied for, the hearing in the Chancery Division will normally be in open court. This is different to the Queen's Bench Division where the application is made in chambers. But if there is reason to believe that a hearing in open court may prejudice the plaintiff then the plaintiff's counsel may ask for the matter to be heard in camera. Where the application is made against a bank or other institution which depends on public confidence for the continuance of its business, the court should consider whether the hearing should be held and judgment given in camera.[1] Applications for Anton Piller orders will normally be heard in camera.

1   *Polly Peck International plc v Nadir (No 2)* [1992] 4 All ER 769, CA.

5.3.3 Unlike the usual practice in the Queen's Bench Division, the order will be made to last for at most a week. If the judge is in doubt as to whether to grant the order then he may require an inter partes hearing after only two or three days. At the further hearing the defendant should have been served by the plaintiff with all the papers in support of the application. The defendant may have prepared affidavits in response. The order will automatically expire after the period defined in the order; the defendant need not apply to discharge, he should merely appear to resist the reinstatement of the order. This differs from the Queen's Bench Division, where the defendant does have to apply to discharge the order.

5.4   PROCEDURE IN THE COMMERCIAL COURT

15.4.1 Many Mareva applications are made in the Commercial Court. RSC Ord 72, r 1 defines a commercial action.[1] The procedure is similar to that in the Queen's Bench Division. Reference should be made to the 'Guide to Commercial Court Practice'.[2]

1   Appendix E.
2   See note 72/A1 to the *Supreme Court Practice 1993*. See also A D Colman QC *The Practice and Procedure of the Commercial Court* (3rd edn).

5.5   PROCEDURE IN THE HIGH COURT DURING THE VACATION

5.5.1 During the High Court vacation, the procedure in either the Queen's Bench or Chancery Division is as described above except that counsel should provide a certificate to the effect that the application is of sufficient urgency to merit being heard during the vacation.[1]

1   RSC Ord 64, r 3 and *Practice Direction (Long Vacation Business)* [1983] 1 WLR 432, at note 64/3/1 in the *Supreme Court Practice 1993*.

5.6   PROCEDURE WHERE THE CLAIM IS WITHIN THE JURISDICTION OF THE COUNTY COURT

5.6.1   The law governing the county court's powers was changed by the County Courts Remedies Regulations 1991[1] which came into force on 1 July 1991. Apart from the Patents County Court,[2] the county court no longer has power to grant Anton Piller orders. It can grant Mareva injunctions only in three circumstances: in family proceedings; for preserving or ordering the detention of property the subject of actual or proposed proceedings; and in aid of execution of a judgment or order in proceedings in a county court to preserve assets until execution can be levied upon them.[3] As to the latter, money judgments of over £5,000 in the county court must be transferred to the High Court in any event.[4]

1   Appendix F.
2   Reg 3(2)(b).
3   Reg 3(3).
4   See art 8 of the High Court and County Courts Jurisdiction Order 1991. This does not apply where the judgment arises out of an agreement regulated by the Consumer Credit Act 1974.

5.6.2   Where the plaintiff wishes to apply for an Anton Piller order, or a Mareva injunction which the county court has no power to grant, but the size of the claim requires proceeding in the county court, the plaintiff should nevertheless apply to the High Court. The application for the order will be deemed to include an application for transfer.[1] Regulation 5 states that unless the High Court otherwise orders, the proceedings 'shall be transferred' to a county court after any application to vary or set aside has been heard, or, failing that, 28 days after the ex parte order. It is unclear whether this means that the plaintiff must transfer them or that they will automatically be transferred by the court. The former seems more likely.

1   County Courts Remedies Regulations 1991, reg 4.

5.6.3   It is inappropriate to invoke the Mareva jurisdiction where relatively small sums are in issue. See *Sions v Ruscoe-Price*.[1] In that case the Court of Appeal upheld the county court judge's refusal to grant a Mareva where the plaintiff's claim was for only £2,000. Woolf LJ stated:[2]

> '. . . having regard to the nature of the Mareva relief, basically it is inappropriate for use in relation to small sums of money. One can readily see that with people of modest means the costs involved in invoking the Mareva procedure, far from assisting the parties, may be prejudicial to their interests, because the amount of costs which could be incurred consequential to a Mareva order being made could be out of all proportion to the sum at stake.'

In practice, the courts have on occasion granted Mareva injunctions in support of relatively small sums. Further, before 1991, the county court had jurisdiction to grant Mareva injunctions even though it had jurisdiction only in cases worth less than £5,000. This suggests that Marevas may sometimes be granted where the sum in issue is under £5,000. But it is easy to incur costs which are very significant in relation to the value of the claim. The plaintiff must give full and frank disclosure of all points which could fairly be made against grant of the order (see Chapter 6). It is submitted that, where a small sum is in issue, the plaintiff is obliged to refer the judge to the *Sions* case and give some indication of what costs are likely to be incurred in prosecuting the application. Moreover, the client must be advised of the risk in costs.

1   (1988) Independent, 30 November, CA.
2   This passage is taken from the LEXIS transcript: the report in the Independent is only a summary.

5.7   PROCEDURE ON APPLICATION IN THE COURSE OF TRIAL

5.7.1   The court may grant a Mareva injunction during the course of a trial, but, in those circumstances, the application should be made inter partes. It is wholly wrong to make an application ex parte during the course of a trial, as this allows the applicant's counsel to make serious allegations against the respondent in the absence of the respondent's counsel.[1]

1   *Re All Starr Video Ltd* (1993) Times, 25 March, CA.

5.8 PROCEDURE AFTER GRANT OF THE INJUNCTION

5.8.1 Once the ex parte application has been made, the plaintiff's solicitor must not distribute copies of the affidavit to persons not party to the action.[1] Further, while the injunction remains on an ex parte basis, the plaintiff may become aware of new or altered facts of which he ought to have made disclosure had he known of them at the time of the original application. In that case, unless the court otherwise orders or the defendant consents, the plaintiff must return to court and apprise the court of the new facts.[2] See further **6.2**.

1 *Patel v Sharaby* (1992) Times, 29 October, per Millett J.
2 *Commercial Bank of the Near East plc v A, B, C and D* [1989] 2 Lloyd's Rep 319.

5.8.2 A plaintiff who obtains a Mareva injunction is under an obligation to proceed expeditiously with the action. If he does not do so, the court will regard this as a factor supporting discharge of the injunction.[1] If the plaintiff decides, after obtaining the Mareva, that he does not wish to proceed with his claim, even temporarily, then he ought of his own motion to seek discharge of the injunction. It is an abuse of the process of the court for the plaintiff to obtain a Mareva, not to proceed with prosecution of the action, but to retain the Mareva in force and then to recommence prosecuting the action in order to obtain security prior to third parties.[2] In these circumstances, if a plaintiff is in doubt as to whether to proceed he could seek directions, although of course this alerts the defendant to the argument that he has delayed for too long.

1 *Lloyds Bowmaker Ltd v Britannia Arrow Holdings plc* [1988] 1 WLR 1337, CA.
2 *Town and Country Building Society v Daisystar Ltd* [1989] NLJR 1563.

5.9 FORM OF THE AFFIDAVIT; SKELETON ARGUMENTS; PENAL NOTICE ON THE ORDER

5.9.1 The affidavit contains the basis of the plaintiff's application and its drafting is crucial. In particular, the affidavit should contain:

'. . . a clear and concise statement: (a) of the facts giving rise to the claim against the defendant in the proceedings; (b) of the facts giving rise to the claim for interlocutory relief; (c) of the facts relied on as justifying the application ex parte, including details of any notice given to the defendant or, if none has been given, the reasons for giving none; (d) of any answer asserted by the defendant (or which he is thought likely to assert) either to the claim in the action or to the claim for interlocutory relief; (e) of any facts known to the applicant which might lead the court not to grant relief ex parte; (f) of the precise relief sought, the nature of the plaintiff's cause of action, the nature of his claim for interlocutory relief, and why the application has been made ex parte.'[1]

The affidavit may contain hearsay evidence provided the deponent states the source of the information.[2] It must state what the plaintiff's evidence is to show that a Mareva or Anton Piller order is justified. As will be seen below, particularly in the case of an Anton Piller order, clear and strong evidence is required. As to Marevas, mere expressions of fear of dissipation are not enough to justify an order.[3]

1   *Practice Direction (Judge in Chambers: Procedure)* [1983] 1 WLR 433, part B, para 2 (Appendix G).
2   RSC Ord 41, r 5(2) (Appendix E).
3   *O'Regan v Iambic Productions Ltd* [1989] NLJR 1378 per Sir Peter Pain.

5.9.2   How much detail should the affidavit contain? In applying for either a Mareva or an Anton Piller order, it is imperative that the plaintiff should give full and frank disclosure of any points which it might be open to the defendant to take if he were present at the ex parte hearing.[1] This is dealt with further in Chapter 6. So far as this obligation is concerned, the plaintiff ought to go into considerable detail. That is particularly so where an Anton Piller order is sought. The affidavit

'. . . ought to err on the side of excessive disclosure. In the case of material falling into the grey area of possible relevance, the judge, not the plaintiffs' solicitors, should be the judge of relevance.'[2]

This means that the evidence on applications for Anton Piller orders is often inevitably voluminous.[3] When the plaintiff is setting out points which his opponent might take, he must not leave out anything, even if it is only of doubtful relevance. A useful rule is that if one has to ask oneself whether a point should be disclosed, then it should be disclosed. It is even arguable that a point raised by the defendant only in without prejudice correspondence should be brought to the attention of the court. These points as to the defendant's case should be raised in the text of the affidavit but, on the other hand, the plaintiff should not exhibit large numbers of documents to that affidavit. It is sufficient that the affidavit explains the point and exhibits a relatively small number of convenient documents.[4]

1 *Third Chandris Shipping Corpn v Unimarine SA* [1979] QB 645 at 669.
2 *Columbia Picture Industries Inc v Robinson* [1986] 3 WLR 542 at 571.
3 See 'Anton Piller Orders – A Consultation Paper' (Lord Chancellor's Department, November 1992) at para 3.5.
4 *National Bank of Sharjah v Delborg* (1992) Times, 24 December, CA.

5.9.3 When the plaintiff is setting out his own case, he must not 'flood the court with a large number of exhibits which are largely irrelevant and by their bulk conceal the real issue.'[1] Nor should the plaintiff, or indeed the defendant, provide several thousand pages of affidavits and exhibits: his evidence should be 'comparatively brief'.[2] In general, applications for Mareva injunctions should take hours and not days.[3] Having said that, the plaintiff must nevertheless attempt to ensure that all points which he can properly make are included in the affidavit.

1 *ALG Inc v Uganda Airlines Corpn* (1992) Times, 31 July, per Mr Richard Southwell QC sitting as a deputy High Court Judge.
2 *Derby & Co Ltd v Weldon (No 1)* [1990] Ch 48 per Parker LJ at 57.
3 Ibid, per Parker LJ at 58. Applied by Mervyn Davies J in *Ali & Fahd Shobokshi Group Ltd v Moneim* [1989] 1 WLR 710 at 714D–E.

5.9.4 Those applying for worldwide Mareva injunctions ought to send, with the other papers for the court, a skeleton argument for the precise grounds supporting the grant of a Mareva injunction, and explaining the special circumstances for granting a worldwide Mareva.[1] It has also been suggested that all applications for Marevas could be accompanied by a skeleton argument.[2] This would help ensure that the affidavit in support complied with the rule that it should not contain any arguments of law. The skeleton argument could identify briefly the key points in the case; highlight any special features of the case; highlight where in the evidence the key points appear; and even serve as a partial record of the submissions made at the ex parte hearing.

1 *ALG Inc v Uganda Airlines Corpn* (1992) Times, 31 July, per Mr Richard Southwell QC sitting as a deputy High Court Judge.
2 Ibid.

5.9.5 The order ought to contain a penal notice at the end.[1] The penal notice warns the defendant(s) of the consequences of disobeying the order, namely, committal to prison for contempt of court for individuals, and either committal to prison of directors or sequestration of assets for companies. If the order is not endorsed with such a notice then it is likely to prove impossible to bring an application for committal if the defendant(s) do not obey the order.[2]

1 See the precedent in **11.1A**.
2 RSC Ord 45, r 7(4) and note 45/7/6 at page 752 of volume 1 of the *Supreme Court Practice 1993*.

5.10   EVIDENCE: MAREVA INJUNCTIONS

5.10.0   The grant of Anton Piller orders and Marevas, being equitable relief, is discretionary.[1] But the principles on which the court's discretion will be exercised are now well established. The evidential requirements for Marevas and Anton Piller orders are different and will be treated separately.

1 *Ninemia Maritime Corpn v Trave Schiffahrtgesellschaft mbH Co KG, The Niedersachen* [1983] 1 WLR 1412 at 1426, per Kerr LJ.

5.10.1   In the case of Mareva injunctions, the plaintiff's evidence must demonstrate that

(i)   so far as the merits of his proposed action are concerned, he has a 'good arguable case';[1]

(ii)   the defendant has assets within the jurisdiction and that there is a real risk that, if not restrained, he will remove his assets from the jurisdiction or dissipate them within it.

In addition, the court will consider the broad justice of the case and, in particular, the prejudice which grant of the Mareva may cause to the defendant and third parties. These three factors will be considered in turn.

1 The *Ninemia* case, above, per Kerr LJ at 1422.

5.11   GOOD ARGUABLE CASE

5.11.1   If the plaintiff has already obtained judgment and now seeks a Mareva in aid of enforcement, then the requirement of a 'good arguable case' will of course not apply, as the plaintiff will already have proved his case. The requirement applies only to applications for Marevas before judgment.

5.11.2 The phrase 'good arguable case' is similar to the test of the merits of the plaintiff's case which the court applies in an application for an interlocutory injunction, and which is dealt with in the decision of the House of Lords in *American Cyanamid Co v Ethicon Ltd.*[1] But it is now clear that:

'The approach called for by the decision in *American Cyanamid Co v Ethicon Ltd* [1975] AC 396 has, as such, no application to the grant or refusal of Mareva injunctions which proceed on principles which are quite different from those applicable to other interlocutory injunctions.'[2]

1 [1975] AC 396.
2 Per Lord Donaldson of Lymington MR in *Polly Peck International plc v Nadir (No 2)* [1992] 4 All ER 769 at 786.

5.11.3 There is, however, one similarity between the two jurisdictions: in neither case will the court attempt to try the action at the interlocutory stage. In other words:

'It is no part of the court's function at this stage of the litigation to try to resolve conflicts of evidence on affidavit as to facts on which the claims of either party may ultimately depend nor to decide difficult questions of law which call for detailed argument and mature considerations. These are matters to be dealt with at trial.'

Lord Diplock said this in the *American Cyanamid* case,[1] but it was adopted as equally valid in the case of applications for Marevas by Parker LJ, with whom Nicholls LJ expressly agreed on this point, in *Derby v Weldon (No 1)*.[2] Echoing this, in *Polly Peck International plc v Nadir (No 2)*,[3] Scott LJ said:

'It must . . . be stressed that in this case, as in any other, the question whether an interlocutory injunction should be granted or continued is not the occasion for the trial of the action.'

1 [1975] AC 396 at 407–408.
2 [1990] 1 Ch 48 at 57–58 and 64.
3 [1992] 4 All ER 769 at 775F.

5.11.4   What is the difference between the 'serious arguable case' test for interlocutory injunctions and the 'good arguable case' test for Marevas? In *Derby v Weldon (No 1)*[1] Parker LJ stated:

> 'In my view the difference between an application for an ordinary injunction and a Mareva lies only in this, that in the former case the plaintiff need only establish that there is a serious question to be tried, whereas in the latter the test is said to be whether the plaintiff shows a good arguable case. This difference . . . is incapable of definition . . .'

There have, however, been attempts to give an alternative definition. In the *Ninemia* case,[2] Mustill J decided that the good arguable case test which the court would adopt was:

> 'a case which is more than barely capable of serious argument, and yet not necessarily one which the judge believes to have a better than 50% chance of success.'

More recently, in *Attock Cement Co Ltd v Romanian Bank for Foreign Trade*,[3] Staughton LJ had to decide what the burden of proof was on a party who had to establish a 'good arguable case', albeit for the purposes of RSC Ord 11, r 1(1). He said:

> '. . . I conclude that, where there is a disputed question of fact which is essential to the application of RSC Ord 11, r 1, the judge must reach a provisional or tentative conclusion that the plaintiff is probably right upon it before he allows service to stand. The nettle must be grasped, and that is what I take to be meant by a good arguable case.'

Although Staughton LJ was dealing with RSC Ord 11, the phrase 'good arguable case' is exactly the same as is used in the Mareva context. It is submitted that Staughton LJ's formulation of the test should be applied also in the context of Mareva injunctions.

1 Above.
2 [1984] 1 All ER 398.
3 [1989] 1 WLR 1147 at 1155G. Cf *Polly Peck International plc v Nadir (No 3)* (1993) Times, 22 March, CA.

5.11.5   There is some reason to believe that the courts are beginning to engage in a stricter degree of scrutiny of the merits of the plaintiff's case at the interlocutory stage. For instance, in *Polly Peck International plc v Nadir (No 2)*,[1] Scott LJ spent more than six pages of the report considering the strength of the plaintiff's case, before concluding that it was 'speculative'. In *Boobyer v Holman & Co Ltd*,[2] Saville J scrutinised and rejected the plaintiffs' claim to have a good arguable case. This case concerned an ordinary interlocutory injunction, rather than a Mareva, but the court's approach is similar with Marevas. Further, in the area of Anton Piller orders the case of *Lock International plc v Beswick*[3] suggests a stricter scrutiny of the plaintiff's case. It appears that there may be a general move to stricter scrutiny of the plaintiff's case at the interlocutory stage, although it is as yet too early to conclude that such a change has definitely occurred.[4]

1   [1992] 4 All ER 769; cf *Polly Peck International v Nadir (No 3)* (above) where a differently constituted Court of Appeal applied a similar degree of scrutiny and concluded, by a majority of two to one, that there was not a good arguable case and so there should be no leave to serve the Central Bank of the Republic of Northern Cyprus out of the jurisdiction.
2   [1993] 1 Lloyd's Rep 96. Cf *Aiglon Ltd v Gau Shan Co Ltd* [1993] 1 Lloyd's Rep 164.
3   [1989] 1 WLR 1268.
4   Zuckerman ('Mareva and Interlocutory Injunctions Disentangled' [1992] 108 LQR 559) believes there to have been a significant change of direction in the *Polly Peck* case.

5.12   SERIOUS RISK OF DISPOSAL OR DISSIPATION OF ASSETS

5.12.1   The plaintiff should give some grounds for believing that the defendant has assets within the jurisdiction[1] and that there is a risk of the assets being removed before the judgment or award is satisfied.[2] In *Ninemia Corpn v Trave Schiffahrtgesellschaft mbH & Co KG*[3] Kerr LJ stated:[4]

'. . . the test is whether, on the assumption that the plaintiffs have shown at least "a good arguable case", the court concludes, on the whole of the evidence then before it, that the refusal of a Mareva injunction would involve a real risk that a judgment or award in favour of the plaintiffs would remain unsatisfied.'

In addition, as Kerr LJ stated in *Z Ltd v A-Z*,[5] the assets should be identified as far as possible, even if their value is unknown. In the case of bank accounts or similar assets, the plaintiff should make every effort to determine the name of the bank, the name of the branch and the account number. This information will be set out in the order.

1   *Third Chandris Shipping Corpn v Unimarine SA* [1979] 3 WLR 122, CA per Lord Denning MR at 137. See also *Z Ltd v A-Z* [1982] 2 WLR 288, CA at 309 per Kerr LJ.
2   Ibid.
3   [1984] 1 All ER 398, [1983] 1 WLR 1412.

4   [1983] 1 WLR 1412 at 1422.
5   [1982] 2 WLR 288 at 309–310.

5.12.2   The court may grant an ancillary order of discovery requiring the party against whom the order is made to submit affidavit evidence of the precise extent and location of his assets (see Chapter 4).

5.12.3   An overdrawn bank account has been held to provide sufficient evidence of assets within the jurisdiction since it is presumed that a large overdraft by a commercial undertaking would be secured by a collateral security representing substantial assets.[1] What the plaintiff must prove to satisfy this requirement is incapable of precise definition. But a mere assertion by the plaintiff, unsupported by evidence, that the defendant will remove or dissipate the assets will not be enough.[2] When making its decision the court considers all the evidence. Evidence of the defendant's 'good character'[3] or 'bad character'[4] may influence the court's decision.

1   *Third Chandris Shipping Corpn v Unimarine* [1979] 3 WLR 122 at 138, CA.
2   The *Ninemia* case (above) – see [1984] 1 All ER 398 at 406 per Mustill J.
3   The injunction was not granted in a case where the defendant was shown to be an international bank closely connected with the government of a prosperous nation (*Etablissement Esefka International Anstalt v Central Bank of Nigeria* [1979] 1 Lloyd's Rep 445). In the *Ninemia* case (above), the injunction was discharged on the defendants' application. They had a policy of settling their debts, and evidence of their assets was put before the court.
4   The injunction was granted in a case where the defendants alleged that they had substantial assets within the jurisdiction but did not reveal their private addresses or otherwise indicate where the assets were (*Prince Abdul Rahman Bin Al Sudairy v Abu-Taha* [1980] 2 Lloyd's Rep 565).

5.12.4   In *O'Regan v Iambic Productions Ltd*,[1] Sir Peter Pain approved a checklist of relevant factors proposed by Steven Gee.[2] These include the ease with which the assets may be removed or dissipated; the nature and financial standing of the defendant's companies; the length of the defendant's establishment in business;[3] the defendant's past and present credit record; and the way in which the defendant has responded to the plaintiff's claims. In essence, factors which suggest the defendant is well established, honest and respectable, will mitigate against grant of the order, and vice versa.

1   [1989] NLJR 1378.
2   See now Gee *The Mareva Injunction and Anton Piller Order* (2nd edn, 1990) at pp 120–121 for the full list.
3   Cf **5.17** below.

5.13 OTHER FACTORS, INCLUDING PREJUDICE TO THE DEFENDANT AND THIRD PARTIES

5.13.0 In addition to the two factors mentioned above, the judge must consider, in exercising his discretion, possible prejudice to the defendant or third parties, and the conduct of the plaintiff.

5.13.1 Other factors where the plaintiff has not yet obtained judgment

Where the plaintiff has shown a good arguable case, but has not yet obtained judgment, then the court cannot be certain whether he will succeed. For that reason, in deciding whether to grant a 'pre-judgment' Mareva injunction, the court must take into account the prejudice which would be caused to the defendant by granting the injunction. In the *Ninemia* case,[1] Kerr LJ stated that a good arguable case was the 'minimum' which the plaintiff had to show in order 'to cross the threshold' for the exercise of the judge's discretion. He added:[2]

> 'The ultimate test for the exercise of the jurisdiction is whether, in all the circumstances, the case is one in which it appears to the court "to be just and convenient" to grant the injunction: see section 37 of the Supreme Court Act 1981 . . . Thus the conduct of the plaintiffs may be material, and the rights of any third parties who may be affected by the grant of an injunction may often also have to be borne in mind . . . Further, it must always be remembered that if, or to the extent that, the grant of the Mareva injunction inflicts hardship on the defendants, their legitimate interests must prevail over those of the plaintiffs, who seek to obtain security for a claim which may appear to be well founded but which still remains to be established at the trial . . .'

1 Above; see [1983] 1 WLR at 1417.
2 Ibid at 1426.

5.13.2 The principal means by which the interests of the defendant have been safeguarded have been the requirements of undertakings which the plaintiff must give (see Chapter 6), and the provisos which the order must contain (see Chapter 2). The provisos include the proviso that the Mareva will not prevent the defendant from making payments for the ordinary running of his business. As Lord Donaldson of Lymington MR has said,[1] it is not the purpose of the Mareva injunction 'to prevent a defendant carrying on business in the ordinary way'.

1   *Derby & Co Ltd v Weldon (Nos 3 and 4)* [1990] Ch 65 at 76E.

5.13.3   The recent case of *Polly Peck International plc v Nadir (No 2)*[1] develops this principle. The administrators of the plaintiff company claimed, inter alia, £45million from the fourth defendant. The fourth defendant was effectively the central bank of the Republic of North Cyprus, although this republic was not recognised by the United Kingdom. The claim against the fourth defendant was based on constructive trust or alternatively, as to £8.9million, in tracing. Millett J granted an ex parte Mareva injunction against the fourth defendant in respect of its assets in England and Wales, limited to £38.9million. The fourth defendant appealed to the Court of Appeal. The Court of Appeal discharged the Mareva injunction on the bases that the plaintiff's claim was speculative and that the Mareva injunction unduly interfered with the fourth defendant's business. It did grant an interlocutory injunction in respect of the tracing claim, but this was on a wholly different basis.[2]

1   [1992] 4 All ER 769, CA.
2   See Chapter 4.

5.13.4   The *Polly Peck (No 2)* case confirms that, in considering whether to grant a pre-judgment Mareva, the court must take into account prejudice which the injunction will cause to the defendant. Scott LJ stated that:[1]

'. . . the strength of the case sufficient to support the grant of a Mareva injunction is dependent to some extent on the consequences to the defendant of the injunction, as well, of course, as on the consequences to the plaintiff if an injunction is not granted.'

He went on to say:[2]

'It is, in my opinion, wrong in principle to grant a Mareva injunction so as, before any liability has been established, to interfere with the normal course of business of the defendant. To impose a Mareva injunction that will have that effect in order to protect a cause of action that is no more than speculative is not simply wrong in principle but positively unfair.'

1   Ibid, at 775H–775J.
2   Ibid, at 784E.

5.13.5   This echoes to some extent the same judge's criticism of Anton
Piller orders, namely that they tended to close down the defendant's
business, in *Columbia Picture Industries Inc v Robinson*.[1] That case
marked the beginning of a new trend where the court, in Anton Piller
cases, began to think more of the interests of the defendant. It could be
that the *Polly Peck (No 2)* case marks the start of a similar trend in the
Mareva jurisdiction. Zuckerman[2] has pointed out that allowing a
defendant to carry on trading means that he may well run out of assets
with which to meet the plaintiff's claim; nevertheless, *Polly Peck* shows
that the court will still permit expenses for the defendant's business
unless it can be shown that those expenses are in fact designed to
dissipate assets to avoid having to pay the plaintiff's claim. While this
case does emphasise that a Mareva injunction should not be allowed to
ruin the defendant's business, it remains to be seen whether it marks
the start of a thorough change in the courts' attitude toward Mareva
injunctions. After all, the business expenses proviso has been an
established feature of Mareva injunctions since 1981.[3] Further, the
result in *Polly Peck (No 2)* was based upon the nature of the defendant's business: it was a bank.

1   [1987] Ch 38. See Chapter 3.
2   'Mareva and Interlocutory Injunctions Disentangled' [1992] 108 LQR 559.
3   *Iraqi Ministry of Defence v Arcepey Shipping Co SA* [1981] QB 65.

5.13.6   As Lord Donaldson of Lymington MR explained, there were
two reasons why the court would be slow to grant a Mareva injunction
where the defendant was a bank. First, the normal way in which the
Mareva permitted the defendant to carry on its ordinary business
would not apply. If the defendant were a trading company, it would be
able to carry on its business, in spite of the Mareva, in the following
way:[1]

> '. . . there is no difficulty in leaving it free to trade on the
> footing that, in so far as it sells its stock, it will be required
> either to preserve the proceeds of sale or to use them to buy
> other stock to which the injunction will apply.'

But the stock in trade of a bank was money borrowed from depositors.
If the bank had to repay its debts, there were no 'proceeds of sale' to
which the Mareva could attach: the repayment simply reduced the
bank's debts. Hence, the Mareva could not switch to the 'proceeds of

sale' of the bank's goods. Second, the bank's business was based upon the trust of its customers. The grant of a Mareva might undermine that trust and so cause a 'run on the bank'. If this caused the bank to close down, it would not be in the interests of the plaintiff. Lord Donaldson concluded that it would be 'unusual' for a Mareva injunction to be granted against a bank.

1   *Polly Peck (No 2)* [1992] 4 All ER 769 at 786.

5.13.7   There may yet be scope for further development of the principle that the interests of the defendant should not be unduly prejudiced by the grant of a Mareva injunction, following upon the considerable changes to Anton Piller orders made on that basis.[1] For instance, what happens if the defendant is an individual whose employment depends largely upon his employer or customers trusting him? Is he in the same position as a bank, so that, on the basis of *Polly Peck (No 2)*,[2] no Mareva should be granted? As far as trading companies are concerned, however, Lord Donaldson of Lymington MR's explanation of the result in *Polly Peck (No 2)* would appear to preclude the use of that case to develop further protection for the defendant, beyond the safeguards which already exist.

1   The case of *Guiness Peat (Aviation) Belgium NV v Hispania Lineas Aereas SA* [1992] 1 Lloyd's Rep 190 shows an emphasis upon the rights to compensation of third parties – see Chapter 2. The court may consider possible prejudice to third parties in deciding whether to grant a Mareva injunction, and it is conceivable that this is also an area which case law could develop further.
2   [1992] 4 All ER 769.

5.13.8   Other factors where the plaintiff has already obtained judgment

If the plaintiff has already obtained judgment then, prima facie, he deserves to be able to enforce it. The court is likely to pay less attention to prejudice caused to the defendant by the Mareva, because the defendant has lost and ought to pay the plaintiff his damages.[1] This does not, however, mean that the plaintiff will be able to obtain a Mareva injunction to interfere with standard banking transactions between third parties.[2] Further, the purpose of obtaining a Mareva is different from a pre-judgment case. After judgment, the plaintiff is at liberty to use any method of enforcement. The purpose of the Mareva is to prevent dissipation or removal of assets before the plaintiff applies for one of the traditional forms of execution.[3] For this reason, the court may wish to limit the duration of the injunction:

'In passing, I would say that an injunction granted after judgment should normally, in my view, be of limited duration; the plaintiff should be encouraged to proceed with proper methods of execution; perpetual injunctions restraining a defendant from dealing with his assets until the crack of doom are undesirable.'[4]

1 Cf para **5.11.3** above.
2 *Lewis & Peat (Produce) Ltd v Almatu Properties Ltd* (1992) Times, 14 May. See Chapter 2.
3 See *Babanaft International Co SA v Bassatne* [1990] Ch 13 per Nicholls LJ at 43C.
4 Per Staughton LJ in *Republic of Haiti v Duvalier* [1990] 1 QB 202 at 214H.

5.14 EVIDENCE: ANTON PILLER ORDERS

5.14.1 In the case of Anton Piller orders, in addition to the 'ultimate test' of whether in all the circumstances the case appears to be one in which it appears to the court to be 'just and convenient' to grant the injunction,[1] the plaintiff must satisfy three essential pre-conditions laid down by Ormrod LJ in the *Anton Piller* case,[2] and which have been followed in subsequent cases:

'First, there must be an extremely strong prima facie case. Second, the damage, potential or actual, must be very serious for the applicant. Thirdly, there must be clear evidence that the defendants have in their possession incriminating documents or things, and that there is a real possibility that they may destroy such material before any application inter partes can be made.'

Ormrod LJ also expressed the view that Anton Piller orders are exceptional, and at the limit of the court's powers. That view has been repeated and wholly borne out in the excoriating judgments of Scott J in *Columbia Picture Industries Inc v Robinson*[3] and Hoffmann J in *Lock International plc v Beswick*.[4]

1 Section 37(1) of the Supreme Court Act 1981 (Appendix A).
2 *Anton Piller KG v Manufacturing Processes Ltd* [1976] Ch 55 at 62.
3 [1987] Ch 38.
4 [1989] 1 WLR 1268. See further Chapter 3.

5.14.2 It follows from these requirements that the court must be satisfied that the application is not a 'fishing expedition' by a plaintiff seeking evidence on which to base a subsequent action.

'Those who make the charges must state right at the beginning what they are, and what facts they are based on. They must not use the Anton Piller orders as a means of finding out what charges they can make.'[1]

1 *Hytrac Conveyors v Conveyors International Ltd* [1983] 1 WLR 44, per Lawton LJ at 47.

5.15 APPLICATION OF ORMROD LJ'S THREE CRITERIA

5.15.1 In *Lock International plc v Beswick*,[1] Hoffmann J dealt with the evidence that had been said to justify the grant of an Anton Piller order ex parte. The plaintiff company manufactured metal detectors. The defendants were a number of the plaintiff's employees who had left the plaintiff and set up a new company to design and then manufacture a new variety of metal detector. The plaintiff alleged that, in order to do so, the defendants must have committed various wrongs against the plaintiff including using the plaintiff's confidential information, breaching the plaintiff's copyright and passing off.

1 [1989] 1 WLR 1268.

5.15.2 Having considered the evidence adduced in support of the Anton Piller order, Hoffmann J stated:[1]

'The evidence came nowhere near disclosing "an extremely strong prima facie case" or "clear evidence that the defendants [had] in their possession incriminating documents or things" or that there was a "grave danger" or "real possibility" that the defendants might destroy evidence. The lack of specificity in the plaintiff's affidavit was such that I have some doubt whether it could be said to have raised a triable issue.'

1 [1989] 1 WLR 1268 at 1283.

5.15.3 Hoffmann J's approach was to examine each piece of alleged evidence provided by the plaintiff in its draft affidavit to see precisely what it showed. First, there was no evidence that the defendants had removed any of the plaintiff's commercial records. Second, there was almost no evidence that technical confidential information had been used, save that the defendants had found a supplier for their products and the plaintiff thought that they must have done so by use of confidential information of the plaintiff's which the defendants must have wrongfully divulged. This Hoffmann J described as 'conjecture'. It turned out to have been a mistaken conjecture. Third, it was said that the defendants could not have developed a metal detector as quickly as they had done, unless they had used the plaintiff's trade secrets and confidential information. But those secrets and that information were not particularised by the plaintiff. Hoffmann J stated:[1] 'In my view assertions like this are no substitute for evidence about what the plaintiff's secrets actually are.'

1   [1989] 1 WLR 1268 at 1275.

5.15.4   One problem for this interpretation of Ormrod LJ's three pre-conditions is the Court of Appeal's majority decision in *Yousif v Salama*.[1] The majority was prepared to infer the probability of disappearance or destruction of evidence where it was clearly established on the evidence before the court that the defendant was engaged in nefarious activity which rendered it likely that he was an untrustworthy person. The justification for the Court's decision was that direct evidence of a threat to destroy materials or documents is seldom available. The evidence relied upon was that the defendant had forged a cheque. So this decision would appear to show that mere evidence that a defendant has forged a cheque may be sufficient evidence from which the court may infer that there is a real possibility that the defendant will destroy evidence even if faced with a court order telling him not to do so. The weight of this authority is somewhat diminished by Donaldson LJ's strong dissent.

1   [1980] 1 WLR 1540.

5.15.5   One reading of *Yousif* suggests that it may not be particularly difficult to persuade the court to hold that Ormrod LJ's three pre-conditions have been satisfied. This argument was made by distinguished counsel in *Lock*. Hoffmann J dealt with it directly.[1] He rejected the argument on the basis of the *Anton Piller* case itself,[2] and *Booker McConnell plc v Plascow*.[3] One cannot be entirely sure of the status of the *Yousif* case until the Court of Appeal has again considered the matter. But the clear trend in the law is toward a rigorous application of Ormrod LJ's three pre-conditions, and careful attention to the plaintiff's evidence to see whether it satisfies them. The extent to which the court will in future be prepared to grant Anton Piller orders on the basis of broad inferences is doubtful. This trend forms part of the general move toward tighter control of Anton Piller orders.[4]

1   [1989] 1 WLR at 1280E–1280G.
2   Above.
3   [1985] RPC 425 esp per Dillon LJ at 441.
4   See generally the discussion of recent developments in Chapter 3.

5.16   LESSER ORDERS WHICH THE COURT MAY GRANT

5.16.1   Also in *Lock International plc v Beswick*,[1] Hoffmann J suggested orders less intrusive than a full Anton Piller order, which the court could make instead. In many cases it would be sufficient to order the defendant to deliver the plaintiff's documents to the plaintiff's solicitor. Alternatively, where the documents belonged to the defendant but might provide evidence against him, the court could order the defendant to preserve the documents pending further order, or to allow the plaintiff's solicitor to make copies.[2] The rationale of these lesser orders is this. If in fact the defendant is likely to obey such a lesser order, then there is no need to invoke the more intrusive powers of the Anton Piller order. The Anton Piller order is necessary only where the defendant would be likely to disobey such a lesser order. But the mere fact that a defendant has been dishonest in one respect does not show that he will flagrantly disregard a court order to preserve or deliver up documents.[3] It follows that lesser orders may well meet the need which is said to justify the grant of an Anton Piller order.

1   [1989] 1 WLR 1268.
2   Ibid, at 1281.
3   Ibid.

5.17   RESPECTABILITY OF THE DEFENDANT

5.17.1   It will be easier to obtain an Anton Piller order where the defendant is an apparently disreputable character with no community ties to prevent him from disappearing. On the other hand, it will be harder if the defendant is a large and well respected company of long-standing. In *Lock International plc v Beswick*,[1] Hoffmann J referred to the following as reasons militating against the grant of an Anton Piller order:

> '. . . these defendants were no fly-by-night video pirates. They were former long service employees with families and mortgages, who had openly said that they were entering into competition and whom the plaintiff knew to be financed by highly respectable institutions.'[2]

1 [1989] 1 WLR 1268 at 1283.
2 See also *Thermax Ltd v Schott Industrial Glass Ltd* [1981] FSR 289 at 297 per Browne-Wilkinson J. Cf **5.12.4**.

CHAPTER 6

Safeguards for the defendant before execution

6.0.1 Various provisos in the order for the protection of the defendant have already been considered in Chapter 2.[1] This chapter deals with the remaining safeguards for the defendant which the plaintiff must consider before making the application. These are the plaintiff's duty to give full and frank disclosure, and the plaintiff's undertakings. The next chapter deals with safeguards for the defendant in the execution of the order. There is inevitably an overlap and the two chapters should be read together.

1 See **2.3ff**.

6.0.2 The duty to give full and frank disclosure applies to applications for both Mareva injunctions and Anton Piller orders. There is no difference in the law between the two types of application. As to the undertakings, there are some which apply to both applications, some which apply only to Mareva cases, and some which apply only in Anton Piller cases. These three categories of undertaking are considered in turn. As to Anton Piller orders, the undertaking to use an independent solicitor to supervise execution is a major change from previous practice.

6.1   FULL AND FRANK DISCLOSURE

6.1.1   At the ex parte application for either a Mareva injunction or an Anton Piller order, the defendant will not be present or represented to make submissions. This is why the court imposes upon the plaintiff a duty to make full and frank disclosure to the court of any material facts or matters which, if the defendant were present, he might rely upon in opposing the grant of the order. If the plaintiff fails to do this at the ex parte application, then there is a serious danger that the injunction, if granted, will be discharged at the inter partes hearing and that the court will refuse to grant a further injunction. For this reason, it is essential for the plaintiff to give full consideration to what arguments could be raised and facts referred to on behalf of the defendant, and to ensure that his affidavit and his lawyer's submissions make proper reference to them. A good rule of practice is that if one has to consider whether a point should be disclosed, then it should be disclosed. Indeed, arguably the plaintiff's lawyers should scrutinise the plaintiff's case, investigate possible lines of argument which the defendant might take and disclose them to the court. The commonest way of trying to have a Mareva injunction set aside is for the defendant to allege that there has not been full and frank disclosure. As to Anton Piller orders, there is less danger of the order being set aside, but more danger of an award of damages against the plaintiff or his solicitors (see **7.7.3**). So the plaintiff's, lawyers must be alert to minimise the danger of such application succeeding.

6.1.2 This section will consider the steps the plaintiff must take in order to comply with this obligation. It should be read in conjunction with Chapter 8, which deals with how the court will react if it is shown later that the plaintiff has failed to give full and frank disclosure.

6.1.3 In *Siporex Trade SA v Comdel Commodities Ltd*,[1] discharging a Mareva injunction, inter alia for failure to make full and fair disclosure, Bingham J conveniently summarised the principles:

'. . . an applicant must show the utmost good faith and disclose his case fully and fairly. He must, for the protection and information of the defendant, summarise his case and the evidence in support of it by an affidavit or affidavits sworn before or immediately after the application. He must identify the crucial points for and against the application, and not rely on general statements and the mere exhibiting of numerous documents. He must investigate the nature of the cause of action asserted and the facts relied upon before applying and identify any likely defences. He must disclose all facts which reasonably could or would be taken into account by the judge in deciding whether to grant the application. It is no excuse for an applicant to say that he was not aware of the importance of matters he has omitted to state. If the duty of full and fair disclosure is not observed the court may discharge the injunction even if after full enquiry the view is taken that the order made was just and convenient and would probably have been made even if there had been full disclosure.'

1   [1986] 2 Lloyd's Rep 428 at 437. Cf the *Practice Direction (Judge in Chambers: Procedure)* [1983] 1 WLR 433, Appendix G.

6.1.4   The relevant principles were later set out by Ralph Gibson LJ in the later case of *Brink's-MAT Ltd v Elcombe*.[1] Both the other judges agreed with his reasoning, and the passage was cited by Woolf LJ in *Behbehani v Salem*.[2] Ralph Gibson LJ's first four principles concern the nature of the duty to give full and frank disclosure. It is worth quoting them in full:

'In considering whether there has been relevant non-disclosure and what consequence the court should attach to any failure to comply with the duty to make full and frank disclosure, the principles relevant to the issues in these appeals appear to me to include the following.

(1)   The duty of the applicant is to make a "full and fair disclosure of all the material facts": see *R v Kensington Income Tax Comrs, ex p Princess Edmond de Polignac* [1917] KB 486, 514, per Scrutton LJ.

(2)   The material facts are those which it is material for the judge to know in dealing with the application as made: materiality is to be decided by the court and not by the assessment of the applicant or his legal advisers: see *R v Kensington Income Tax Comrs*, per Lord Cozens-Hardy MR, at p 504, citing *Dalglish v Jarvie* (1850) 2 Mac & G 231, 238, and Browne-Wilkinson J in *Thermax Ltd v Schott Industrial Glass Ltd* [1981] FSR 289 at 295.

(3)   The applicant must make proper enquiries before making the application: see *Bank Mellat v Nikpour* [1985] FSR 87. The duty of disclosure therefore applies not only to material facts known to the applicant but also to any additional facts which he would have known if he had made such inquiries.

(4)   The extent of the inquiries which will be held to be proper, and therefore necessary, must depend on all the circumstances of the case including (a) the nature of the case which the applicant is making when he makes the application; and (b) the order for which the application is made and the probable effect of the order on the

defendant: see, for example, the examination by Scott J of the possible effect of an Anton Piller order in *Columbia Picture Industries Inc v Robinson* [1987] Ch 38; and (c) the degree of legitimate urgency and the time available for the making of inquiries: see per Slade LJ in *Bank Mellat v Nikpour* [1985] FSR 87 at 92–93.'

1   [1988] 1 WLR 1350, at 1356–1357, CA.
2   (Note) [1989] 1 WLR 723 at 726, CA.

6.1.5   Principle (2) makes plain that, if there is any doubt as to whether a fact is material, it ought to be disclosed so that the judge may consider for him or herself whether it is material. A party or his legal advisers should not decide whether a fact is material unless there can be no question that it is not material. What makes a fact material? In *Thermax Ltd v Schott Industrial Glass Ltd*,[1] an Anton Piller case, Browne-Wilkinson J stated:[2]

'It should be in the forefront of everybody's mind that the court must be fully informed of all facts that are relevant to the weighing operation which the court has to make in deciding whether or not to grant the order.'

In that case the plaintiff's evidence had implied that the defendant was a mere creature of three former directors of the plaintiff, but had failed to disclose that in fact it was a member of the Carl Zeiss group of companies. But the duty of full and frank disclosure does not require the plaintiff to disclose every relevant document, as it must on discovery. The plaintiff should make disclosure in the affidavit, exhibiting a few documents, but should not burden the judge with large quantities of documents if at all possible.[3]

1   [1981] FSR 289.
2   Ibid at 298.
3   *National Bank of Sharjah v Delborg* (1992) Times, 24 December, CA.

6.1.6   Ralph Gibson LJ's principles (3) and (4) relate to the extent to which a party should undertake enquiries before launching the application for the injunction. There is plainly a balance to be struck between, on the one hand, applying with such haste that one's application is defective in that it fails to disclose material facts which more enquiry would have revealed, and, on the other hand, taking too long to prepare the application so that the money or goods the subject of the injunction have been spirited away before it takes effect. Except where there is plainly a great need for urgency, it is usually better to spend more time on preparing the application so as to ensure that all possible lines of defence have been considered and disclosed. It is better for the applicant to have a well-prepared application which cannot be attacked and discharged on the ground of non-disclosure, than to prepare a hasty application which may succeed ex parte but then be discharged at the inter partes stage. The latter is not only a waste of substantial costs, but may also surrender the initiative in the action.

6.1.7   If, after the applicant has obtained an injunction ex parte, he discovers that he has mistakenly misled the court or given incomplete information on some material issue, he ought to return to the court and notify the judge of the point which he has discovered.[1] If the slip is minor and the applicant returns quickly to court, the court is unlikely to discharge the injunction. Similarly, if, before there has been an inter partes hearing, there is some change in circumstances which may be material, then, unless he receives the agreement of the party subject to the injunction or has the permission of the court, the applicant must return to court and apprise the judge of the new turn of events so that he may consider whether to continue the injunction.[2] The test of whether new events are material is the same as at the original ex parte application, so, applying Ralph Gibson LJ's definition, it must be: anything which, if it had occurred at the time of the ex parte application, would have been something that the judge ought to have known.

1   *Lloyds Bowmaker Ltd v Britannia Arrow Holdings* [1988] 1 WLR 1337 per Glidewell LJ at 1341E–1341F and 1343H.
2   *Commercial Bank of the Near East plc v A, B, C, and D* [1989] 2 Lloyd's Rep 319.

6.2   THE PLAINTIFF'S UNDERTAKINGS

6.2.1   The plaintiff must offer the court various undertakings, otherwise it will not exercise its discretion to grant the injunction. First considered are undertakings which must be given in both applications for Mareva injunctions and applications for Anton Piller orders; second, undertakings which must be given only if a Mareva injunction is sought; and third, undertakings which must be given only if an Anton Piller order is sought. It may assist to read this section in conjunction with the precedents contained in Chapter 11. The plaintiff should comply with these undertakings to the letter. Failure to do so may amount to a ground for discharge of the injunction.[1]

1   See Chapter 8.

6.3 UNDERTAKINGS COMMON TO APPLICATIONS FOR BOTH MAREVA INJUNCTIONS AND ANTON PILLER ORDERS

6.3.1 Undertaking to issue writ forthwith

Most applications for Mareva injunctions or Anton Piller orders will be made before the issue of proceedings. In such a case, the plaintiff must undertake to issue the writ or originating summons forthwith. See Ord 29, r 1(3),[1] which provides that a plaintiff may not apply ex parte for injunctive relief

'. . . before the issue of the writ or originating summons by which the cause or matter is to be begun except where the case is one of urgency and in that case the injunction applied for may be granted on terms providing for the issue of the writ or summons and such terms, if any, as the court thinks fit.'

The degree of urgency and appropriate procedure is dealt with in Chapter 5. The order should be headed 'In the matter of an intended action between A and B'.[2]

1 Appendix E.
2 *Re N (Infants)* [1967] Ch 512.

6.3.2 If the plaintiff does not comply with this undertaking it is likely that the order will be discharged. See **8.8** below.

6.3.3 Undertaking to make affidavit

Where the application is so urgent that there is no time for an affidavit to be sworn, the plaintiff must undertake to make and file an affidavit verifying what counsel told the judge. Alternatively, if the judge is presented with an unsworn affidavit, the plaintiff must undertake to make and file an affidavit in the terms of the unsworn draft.

6.3.4 Undertaking to serve papers on defendant

The plaintiff must also undertake to serve forthwith upon the defendant copies of the papers which were presented to the court in support of the order: the pleadings, affidavits, exhibits and order. It is essential that this undertaking is complied with, otherwise the defendant cannot know the case against him, or have a proper opportunity to apply to discharge the order or oppose its continuation.

6.4   UNDERTAKING IN DAMAGES

6.4.1   The plaintiff must undertake to compensate the defendant and third parties in damages for any loss which they may suffer by reason of the order having been made, if the court decides that he should pay them.[1] For discussion of when the court is likely to order such payment, see Chapter 8. For the moment, the plaintiff should note that it is certainly possible that a Mareva injunction or Anton Piller order may cause considerable damages to defendants or third parties, and he must be able to compensate such losses in the event that the court does decide to order him to do so. The undertaking will include compensation for the defendant in the event that the court holds that the injunction extended over more of the defendant's assets than was necessary, thus preventing the defendant from using some of those assets to make a profit.[2]

1   *Fenner v Wilson* [1893] 2 Ch 656.
2   See per Lord Donaldson of Lymington MR in *Jet West Ltd v Haddican* [1992] 1 WLR 487 at 491D–491E, CA. Cf *Guiness Peat Aviation (Belgium) Ltd v Hispania Lineas Aereas SA* [1992] Lloyd's Rep 190 – in Chapter 2.

6.5   SECURITY FOR THE UNDERTAKING

6.5.1   If the court suspects that the plaintiff may not have the funds to make good his undertaking in damages, it may order that he provide security for a certain sum, for example in the form of a bond or bank guarantee. In *The Mito*,[1] Hirst J said:

'May I make it plain at the start that there is no doubt in my judgment that the court has power at the time of either granting or extending a Mareva injunciton to order security in support of the usual cross-undertaking [in damages], in other words to fortify the injunction by security in the manner which was ordered, for example, by Roxburgh J in the case of *Baxter v Claydon* [1952] WN 376. In other words if the court considers that the cross-undertaker, usually the plaintiff, might not be worth powder and shot if it be held that he is obliged to fulfil his cross-undertaking, the court can strengthen the undertaking by requiring some sort of security.'

But Hirst J decided that, after the discharge of a Mareva injunction, the court had no power to order the plaintiff to give security for the undertaking. Why should the court have power to require security to be provided when it grants or continues a Mareva, but not after discharge? If the injunction is discharged this makes it likely that there will be something to pay on the undertaking. But it has often been said that the Mareva is not intended to give the plaintiff pre-judgment security. Hirst J said that the same applied to the undertaking in damages. It gave the defendant protection but not security.[2]

1   *Commodity Ocean Transport Corpn v Basford Unicorn Industries Ltd, The Mito* [1987] 2 Lloyd's Rep 197 at 198.
2   Ibid. Further, the court's power to require security was as a condition of granting the injunction. The court did not have independent power to require security: all it could do was tell the plaintiff that if he did not give security, the court would not exercise its discretion to grant the injunction.

6.5.2   If the defendant states that he is satisfied with the amount of security offered by the plaintiff, the judge should not refuse to grant the injunction on the basis that insufficient security has been provided.[1]

1   *Southway Group Ltd v Wolff* (1991) Times, 20 May, CA.

6.6   LEGALLY-AIDED PLAINTIFF

6.6.1   The court will not deny the plaintiff an interlocutory injunction to which he would otherwise be entitled simply on the grounds that he is legally aided and that his undertaking in damages is likely to be of limited value. See *Allen v Jambo Holdings Ltd.*[1]

1   [1980] 1 WLR 1252, CA.

6.7   FULL AND FRANK DISCLOSURE

6.7.1   If the plaintiff is not legally aided, part of his duty of full and frank disclosure is a duty to bring to the attention of the court any factors which might reasonably suggest that he might not be able to compensate the defendants if the order were found to have been wrongly made. See *Lock International plc v Beswick*.[1] At the ex parte hearing the plaintiff company had put before the court accounts showing no overdraft, assets of £800,000 and pre-tax profits of £1.76million over the previous 18 months. The affidavit had described the plaintiff as 'a substantial company' which was able to give an undertaking as to damages. The affidavit had not mentioned that, ten months before the ex parte hearing, the plaintiff had guaranteed a £94million overdraft facility of another company which had taken it over, or that the guarantee had been supported by a fixed and floating charge over all the plaintiff's assets. Hoffmann J held that this was a material non-disclosure. He discharged the Anton Piller order.

1   [1989] 1 WLR 1268 at 1278–1279. See also *Manor Electronics Ltd v Dickson* [1988] RPC 618 and *Swedac Ltd v Magnet & Southerns plc* [1989] FSR 243.

6.7.2   If the affidavit in support contains no reference to the financial position of the plaintiff then the judge is entitled to assume that the plaintiff's finances will be adequate to meet the possible liability on the undertaking.[1] Anything which might throw doubt on that should be disclosed. Indeed, even if it is believed that the plaintiff would have no difficulty in meeting the damages on the undertaking, the affidavit should state this and it is preferable to exhibit evidence such as company reports or an accountant's letter which backs this up. If there is doubt about whether factors suggesting financial weakness of the plaintiff should be disclosed, then they should be disclosed anyway.

1   *Manor Electronics Ltd v Dickson* [1988] RPC 618 per Scott J at 623.

6.8   LEVEL OF DAMAGES ON THE UNDERTAKING

6.8.1   Whether a plaintiff will be able to meet the potential liability on the undertaking in damages depends on how much that liability is likely to be. Because most Mareva and Anton Piller cases do not reach trial, there is little authority on this point. But the authority which does exist suggests that the damages may well be high, and practitioners should be aware of this in advising clients of the risk on the undertaking and in assessing the plaintiff's ability to meet the possible liability on the undertaking. This is particularly so in the case of Anton Piller orders. In *Columbia Picture Industries Inc v Robinson*[1] Scott J observed that it was common, possibly usual, for an Anton Piller order combined with a Mareva to have the effect of closing down the defendant's business. He held[2] that damages on the undertaking would have two functions: first, to compensate the defendant, including compensation for the loss of any legitimate business; second, there might be exemplary damages for the manner in which the plaintiff's solicitors executed the order, if they failed to comply with the terms of the order and acted in an oppressive or excessive way.

1   [1986] 3 WLR 542 at 567.
2   Ibid at 580–581.

6.8.2   If the order is unlawfully executed by the plaintiff's solicitors, who is liable for the exemplary damages to which this may give rise? Is it the plaintiff himself, or his solicitors? In the *Columbia Picture Industries* case, Scott J stated that:[1]

> '. . . the plaintiffs can, in my view, properly be held liable to the defendants in damages for this breach by [the plaintiffs' solicitors] of their undertaking. How the matter should be dealt with as between [the plaintiffs' solicitors] and the plaintiffs is not before me.'

In *Universal Thermosensors Ltd v Hibben*[2] the defendants alleged that there had been serious irregularities in the way in which the plaintiffs' solicitors had executed an Anton Piller order. They sued the plaintiffs' solicitors directly. The plaintiffs' solicitors settled by paying a total of £34,000 in damages plus costs on an indemnity basis. The basis of the settlement must have been that the solicitors accepted that they themselves were liable for errors in the execution of the order. It is very likely that solicitors will be liable in damages to the defendant for errors in the execution of the order.[3] It follows that the plaintiff need only demonstrate that he could meet, on the undertaking in damages, compensatory damages; the plaintiff need not show that he could pay exemplary damages for errors in execution of the order. Nevertheless, the compensatory damages may include damages for closing down the defendant's business.

1   [1986] 1 WLR 542 at 582.
2   [1992] 1 WLR 840.
3   See Chapter 7.

6.9   UNDERTAKINGS TO PROTECT THIRD PARTIES

6.9.1   In Chapter 2, three undertakings to protect third parties were considered.[1] Of these, the undertaking which is common to both Mareva and Anton Piller cases is the undertaking to pay the reasonable costs incurred by third parties by reason of the order.[2] The other two undertakings, namely to serve third parties and notify them of their right to apply for discharge of the order, are given only in Mareva cases. This is presumably because it is unlikely that third parties will be directly involved in Anton Piller cases.

1 **2.10** and **2.11**.
2 See Chapter 11 for the precise wording, which appears to be slightly different in the Chancery and Queen's Bench Divisions.

6.10 UNDERTAKINGS GIVEN ONLY IN APPLICATIONS FOR MAREVA INJUNCTIONS

6.10.1 There are three further undertakings which a plaintiff applying for a Mareva injunction must give. First, he must undertake to notify the defendant of the terms of the order forthwith. In order to assist an application by the defendant to seek to discharge the order, it is suggested that the undertaking should be in the following form:

> 'Forthwith to give notice of the terms of this order to the defendant by [means] and of the telephone number of a representative of the plaintiff's solicitors to whom any notice of an application to set aside or vary this order may be given out of office hours.'

6.10.2 Second, he must undertake to notify the defendant and any third party to whom he gives notice of the order of their right to apply to the court, on notice, to set aside the order. Third, he must undertake to serve a copy of the order on any third party whom he has notified of the existence of the order. For the position as to third parties, see Chapter 2. Put shortly, the applicant will wish to notify any third parties such as banks who hold assets of the respondent's. The effect of these undertakings is to give the third party (and the defendant) the ability to apply to set aside the order, if they wish to do so.

6.11 UNDERTAKINGS GIVEN ONLY IN APPLICATIONS FOR ANTON PILLER ORDERS

6.11.1 In this section are considered first the undertakings which the plaintiff himself must give, and second those which the plaintiff's solicitors must give.

6.12 UNDERTAKINGS BY THE PLAINTIFF: THE SUPERVISING SOLICITOR

6.12.1 In *Universal Thermosensors Ltd v Hibben*,[1] Sir Donald Nicholls V-C suggested that judges granting Anton Piller orders should seriously consider providing:

> '(a) that the order should be served, and its execution should be supervised, by a solicitor other than a member of the firm of solicitors acting for the plaintiff in the action; (b) that he or she should be an experienced solicitor having some familiarity with the workings of Anton Piller orders, and with judicial observations on this subject (eg as summarised in the notes in the *Supreme Court Practice 1991* [now 1993] to RSC, Ord 29, r 3); (c) that the solicitor should prepare a written report on what occurred when the order was executed; (d) that a copy of the report should be served on the defendants; and (e) that in any event and within the next few days the plaintiff must return to the court and present that report at an inter partes hearing, preferably to the judge who made the order. As to (b), I can see advantages in the plaintiff being required to include in his evidence, put to the judge in support of his application for an Anton Piller order, details of the name of the solicitor and of his experience.'

1   [1992] 1 WLR 840 at 861. See Appendix J.

6.12.2 The draft Anton Piller order now issued by the Chancery Division with judicial approval[1] contains the following undertakings:

> '(4) to serve on the Defendant(s) forthwith after the Plaintiff's solicitors receive the same a copy of a written report on the carrying out of this Order which shall be prepared by the supervising solicitor mentioned below;
>
> (5) to bring such motion before the court on the said date and on that occasion to place before the court the written report of the supervising solicitor . . .'

Further, paragraph 2 of the text of the draft order now contains the following provisos:

> '2. PROVIDED ALWAYS:
>
> (1) This order shall be served, and paragraph 1 hereof carried out, only by [name] of [firm] or failing [him] [her] by

[name] or some other solicitor approved for the purpose by the court (the solicitor serving the Order being referred to in this Order as "the supervising solicitor").

(2) Before any persons enter the premises pursuant to this Order the supervising solicitor shall offer to explain to the person served with the Order its meaning and effect in everyday language, and shall also advise such person of his/her right to obtain legal advice before permitting entry provided such advice is obtained at once.'

1   See **11.2**

6.12.3   In light of these changes, the safest course is plainly to prepare the application for an Anton Piller order on the basis that a supervising solicitor as described in the above provisions will be required. On the other hand, it appears that some judges of the Chancery Division may still grant Anton Piller orders without such provision. Further, it will save costs for the plaintiff if he does not need to pay for a supervising solicitor in addition, and it may be worth counsel's while trying to persuade the judge that it is unnecessary to make provision for a supervising solicitor.

6.12.4   If the court does require a supervising solicitor, then the effect of the passages quoted from the draft order is as follows. The supervising solicitor must be a solicitor from a firm different to the plaintiff's solicitors. He or she must be experienced in the law and practice of Anton Piller orders. The plaintiff ought, in his affidavit in support of the Anton Piller application, to have details of the name and experience of the solicitor whom it is proposed should fill this role. The supervising solicitor must serve the order on the defendant's premises. Before anyone may enter in pursuance of the order, the supervising solicitor must explain to the person served, in plain English,

(i)   the effect of the order;

(ii) the right of that person to seek legal advice before permitting entry, provided such advice is obtained at once.[1]

If and when the defendant or his responsible officer consents to entry, the order may be executed by the supervising solicitor and two (or however many the order authorises) other persons, not including anyone who might obtain commercial advantage over the defendant.[2] After execution of the order, the supervising solicitor must write a report on the execution. As soon as the report is prepared, a copy should be served on the defendant. A copy of the report should be placed before the court on the return date.

1 See Chapter 7.
2 See paragraph 1 of the draft Anton Piller order, 11.2.

6.12.5 The supervising solicitor will have every incentive to ensure that execution is done properly. If he fails to do so, he may be liable to the defendant in damages.[1] The supervising solicitor ought to be independent not only of the plaintiff's solicitors, but also of the plaintiff itself: it is undesirable that an Anton Piller order be executed by a solicitor closely related to the chief executive of the plaintiff company.[2]

1 See Chapter 7.
2 *Manor Electronics Ltd v Dickson* [1988] RPC 618.

6.12.6 If the court does not require a supervising solicitor, then the order should be executed by the plaintiff's own solicitors. See Chapter 7.

6.13 UNDERTAKINGS BY THE PLAINTIFF'S SOLICITORS: CUSTODY OF THE EVIDENCE SEIZED

6.13.1 Unlike in an application for a Mareva injunction, where an Anton Piller order is sought the plaintiff's solicitors must also give undertakings to the court. The draft order provides:[1]

'AND the solicitors for the Plaintiff(s) by counsel for the Plaintiff(s) (being their Counsel for this purpose) undertaking:

(1) to return the originals of all documents obtained as a result of this Order within two working days of their removal;

(2) where ownership of any article obtained as a result of this Order is disputed to deliver up any such article to the custody of solicitors acting on behalf of the Defendant(s) within two working days of receipt of a written undertaking by such solicitors to retain the same in safe custody and to produce the same if required by the Court;

(3) save as mentioned above to retain in their safe custody
until further Order all documents and articles obtained as
a result of this Order . . .'

1 **11.2.**

6.13.2   These undertakings are self-explanatory. Their rationale is to
ensure that the execution of the order causes the minimum necessary
disruption to the defendant.[1] Once documents have been copied, there
is no need for the plaintiff to retain the originals. If ownership of an
item is in dispute, then it is sufficient if the defendant's solicitors
undertake to keep the item in safe custody. Where the ownership of
items other than documents is disputed, it is only if the defendant's
solicitors give no such undertaking that the plaintiff may retain them,
and even then, it should be the plaintiff's solicitors rather than the
plaintiff him or herself who retains them. This minimises the danger of
the plaintiff taking unfair commercial advantage of the defendant. On
the other hand, if there is no dispute about ownership, so that the
defendant accepts that the plaintiff owns items, then these undertakings do not apply. The plaintiff may keep the items without
restraint. In any case, the plaintiff's solicitors should prepare a detailed
list of the items to be removed before removing them.[2]

1 See further Scott J's guidelines in *Columbia Picture Industries Inc v Robinson* [1987]
   Ch 38, Appendix I.
2 See **7.3** below.

Execution and the position of the defendant

CHAPTER 7

Execution of the order

7.0 Execution of the Mareva injunction is principally a question of informing banks and other third parties who hold assets of the defendant that they must not deal with them in breach of the injunction.[1] This is dealt with in the first part of this chapter. The second part of the chapter deals with execution of the Anton Piller order. This is a far more complicated matter. Due to the exceptionally intrusive nature of the order, detailed guidelines have been developed which must be observed with the utmost care.

1 See Chapter 2 for what the banks and third parties may and may not do, once informed of the terms of the order.

7.1 EXECUTION OF THE MAREVA INJUNCTION

7.1.1 From the moment it is granted, a Mareva injunction takes effect on every asset owned by the defendant. But third parties who hold such assets will not be liable for breach of the injunction until after they have been notified of the terms of the order. Accordingly, as soon as practicable after the grant of the order, the plaintiff's solicitors should notify all who hold assets of the defendant's to which the order applies. Once notified, all such third parties must do what they reasonably can to preserve the assets referred to in the order, otherwise they may be guilty of contempt of court.[1]

1 See Chapter 2.

7.1.2 The principles as to what the plaintiff's solicitors should do are dealt with in *Z v A-Z and AA-LL*.[1] They should tell the judge the names of the banks and other third parties to whom notice of the order is to be given, although they may inform others on further enquiry. They must notify the bank or other third party with as much precision as possible what such person is required to do or not to do. If possible, a bank should be told of the branch and account number which is to be frozen. The bank may insist that it search all its records to see whether it holds any other account of the defendant's, and may charge the cost to the plaintiff in accordance with his undertaking in damages.[2] If necessary the bank or other third party should be notified of the terms of the order by telephone or telex; it will often be quicker to notify the bank first by telephone and then to send a fax and indeed postal copy of the order afterwards.

1   [1982] QB 558.
2   See Chapter 6.

7.1.3   A bank or other third party which is served with a Mareva injunction may pass assets to the defendant unless it has 'notice of a probability that the asset will be dealt with or disposed of in breach of the order'.[1] What this means is discussed in Chapter 2.

1   See per Sir John Donaldson MR in *Law Society v Shanks* (1987) 131 Sol Jo 1626, 18 Fam Law 206, CA.

7.1.4   In *Columbia Picture Industries Inc v Robinson*,[1] in which an Anton Piller order and Mareva injunction were granted, bank managers at two of the bank's branches were telephoned and told of the Mareva injunction freezing the accounts of the defendant and his company. They were not told, during the telephone calls, of an 'ordinary living expenses' proviso which allowed the defendant to draw up to £200. The bank managers did not realise that this was allowed until they received a letter from the plaintiff's solicitors the following day. Scott J stated that this constituted a 'careless misinterpretation' of the effect of the order by the solicitors.

1   [1987] Ch 38.

7.2   EXECUTION OF THE ANTON PILLER ORDER

7.2.1   The general guidelines for the service and execution of Anton Piller orders are as follows. First, the order will generally provide that it must be served by a supervising solicitor who is well versed in the law of Anton Piller orders.[1] Alternatively, it may provide that it be served by the plaintiff's own solicitor alone. Second, the solicitor should serve copies of the affidavits and exhibits.[2] The solicitor should offer to explain to the defendant, in clear, everyday language, the terms of the order and should inform the defendant of his right to obtain legal advice, if he does so at once, before permitting entry of the premises. The plaintiff's solicitors should consider the likely bulk of material to be removed and provide appropriate transport.

1   See Chapter 6 and *Universal Thermosensors Ltd v Hibben* [1992] 1 WLR 840 at 861.
2   *International Electronics Ltd v Weight Data Ltd* [1980] FSR 423.

7.3   THE NEW GUIDELINES IN *UNIVERSAL THERMOSENSORS*

7.3.1   The guidelines have recently been thoroughly revised by Sir Donald Nicholls V-C in *Universal Thermosensors Ltd v Hibben*.[1] See appendix J for the full text of his judgment on this point. In addition, the approved form of Anton Piller order has been altered to take account of the new guidelines.[2] The requirement that the service and execution of the order be supervised by another solicitor has already been discussed.[3]

1   [1992] 1 WLR at 860–861.
2   See **11.2**.
3   See **6.12**.

7.3.2   The first point is that, in general, Anton Piller orders should be permitted to be executed only during working hours. This is so that the defendant has a proper opportunity to take legal advice before permitting the plaintiff's solicitors to enter his or her business or home.[1] The draft order suggests execution only between 9.30am and 5.30pm on weekdays. It appears that in cases of exceptional urgency this condition may not apply, but the plaintiff will have to show very strong evidence to the effect that if he or she waits until 9.30am on a weekday then the defendant is likely to destroy evidence or documents in the interim. The court is trying to discourage the knock on the door in the middle of the night.

1   See Chapter 8 for the position of the defendant.

7.3.3   Second, if the order is to be executed at a private house, and if it is at all likely that a woman may be in the house alone, then the solicitor serving the order must be, or must be accompanied by, a woman. In practice, there is a danger at most private houses that there might be a lone woman present, and so it would seem that the safer course would be always to have a woman present when the order is served unless it is plain that there will not be a lone woman at the house.

7.3.4   Third, in general the order should expressly provide that, unless seriously impracticable, a detailed list of the items being removed should be prepared at the premises before they are removed, and the defendant should be given an opportunity to check the list at the time.

7.3.5   Fourth, the order may restrain the defendant from informing others of the existence of the order, but this should be only for a very limited period, much less than a week.

7.3.6   Fifth, the order should provide that, except to the extent that it is impracticable, execution of the order on business premises may take place only in the presence of a responsible officer or representative of the company or trader in question.[1]

1   This deals with a question raised in *Bhimji v Chatwani* [1991] 1 WLR 989. An Anton Piller order provided that it could be served on 'a person appearing to be in control of the premises' of the defendant. It was served upon a book-keeper who had arrived early for work. At 997A, Scott J very much doubted whether he could be described as 'appearing to be in control of the premises.'

7.3.7   Sixth, the order will often be granted where the parties are commercial rivals. It must ensure that the representatives of the plaintiff company are not permitted carte blanche to search through the possessions of rival companies, thereby putting themselves in a position to obtain commercial advantage. The draft order states that those executing the order should not include anyone who might obtain commercial advantage over the defendants by carrying out the order. The same concern prompted Hoffmann J's dictum that the order should permit the passing of the documents or evidence only to the plaintiff's solicitors, not to the plaintiffs themselves; there should then be an inter partes application where the plaintiffs applied for inspection of the documents and evidence which had been taken.[1]

1   *Lock International plc v Beswick* [1989] 1 WLR 1268 at 1283. See Chapter 3.

7.4 AGREEMENTS TO EXTEND THE SCOPE OF THE ORDER

7.4.1 In *VDU Installations Ltd v Integrated Computer Systems and Cybernetics Ltd*,[1] Knox J made clear that agreements to extend the scope of the order which are made with the defendant at the time of the search are extremely suspect, because they are reached at a time when it is only natural that defendants are in a state of confusion and uncertainty. The wiser course is to eschew such agreements.

1 [1989] FSR 378.

7.5 ADDITIONAL GUIDELINES IN *COLUMBIA PICTURE INDUSTRIES INC V ROBINSON*

7.5.1 Prior to *Universal Thermosensors*, Scott J[1] had laid down guidelines for the removal and safeguarding of material taken during the execution of an Anton Piller order. These are reproduced at Appendix I.

1 [1987] Ch 38.

7.6 ATTENDANCE BY THE POLICE

7.6.1 In *ITC Film Distributors v Video Exchange Ltd*[1] the police had obtained a search warrant under the Obscene Publications Act 1959, s 3 on the same day that an Anton Piller order had been made. By previous arrangement the plaintiff's Anton Piller party and the police went to the defendant's premises together. The police produced the search warrant and eleven plain clothes police entered the defendant's premises together with the five representatives of the plaintiff permitted under the Anton Piller order.[2] The defendant was cautioned by the police and the Anton Piller order was then served inside the premises. After receiving advice from his solicitor, the defendant allowed entry and the Anton Piller search and seizure took place. Lawton LJ accepted that it might sometimes be necessary for the police to search premises at around the same time that an Anton Piller order was executed. But he stated that it was most undesirable that solicitors executing an Anton Piller order should appear to be hangers-on of a squad of police officers executing a search warrant. The order ought to ensure that the solicitors did not attend at the premises at the same time as the police.

1 (1982) Times, 17 June, CA. The case is reported elswhere but only at first instance.
2 The draft order now suggests two in addition to the supervising solicitor. See **11.2**.

7.6.2   Although it appears that it is not uncommon for the police to be present at the time when an Anton Piller order is executed,[1] this approach fits ill with the recent emphasis on the rights of defendants in Anton Piller cases.[2] The matter was considered recently by an eminent group of judges, who concluded:[3]

> 'We consider that in most cases there is no need for a police presence at the execution of the order. They need only be informed. The order should not be executed at the same time as a police search warrant. Criminal investigations should, so far as possible, be kept separate from Anton Piller proceedings.'

Although this is of course an *ex cathedra* statement which is in no sense legally binding, it shows the best practice in this area.

1 See per Scott J in *Columbia Picture Industries Inc v Robinson* [1986] 3 All ER 338 at 371.
2 See Chapter 3.
3 'Anton Piller Orders – A Consultation Paper' (Lord Chancellor's Department, November 1992) at para 4.12.

7.7   THE POSITION OF THE PLAINTIFF'S SOLICITORS

7.7.1   If the order is executed in a manner inconsistent with its terms, either the plaintiff will be liable on his undertaking in damages,[1] or his solicitors will be liable for contempt of court. In *Columbia Picture Industries Inc v Robinson*,[2] Scott J accepted an apology to the court for the breach of the plaintiff's undertaking to keep the material seized in safe custody. He awarded aggravated damages to be paid by the plaintiffs to the defendants pursuant to the plaintiffs' undertaking in damages. He left open the question of whether the plaintiffs' solicitors should compensate the plaintiffs.

1 See Chapter 8 for discussion of attempts to hold the plaintiff liable in damages for abuse of process or trespass.
2 Above. See discussion in Chapter 6.

7.7.2   In *VDU Installations Ltd v Integrated Computer Systems and Cybernetics Ltd*,[1] the plaintiff's solicitor told the defendant that the order permitted a wider search than it in fact did permit. He then carried out a search which was wider than the order permitted, and removed items which the order did not permit him to remove. Knox J held that the solicitor was liable for contempt. It was no defence that he had not deliberately breached the terms of the order; as long as he was merely negligent, he was in contempt.

1   [1989] FSR 378

7.7.3   As far as the defendant is concerned, a finding that the plaintiff's solicitors are in contempt may be of little value. The likely penalty is a fine rather than damages payable to the defendant. The defendant will probably prefer to be awarded the damages. In *Universal Thermosensors Ltd v Hibben*,[1] there had been serious irregularities in the execution of an Anton Piller order by the plaintiff's solicitors. After a number of days' hearing, the solicitors effectively conceded that they were liable to the defendants in damages for this. They paid £34,000 in damages, plus costs on the indemnity basis. In light of this, it is very likely that the court would hold that the plaintiffs' solicitors were liable in damages to the defendants in such circumstances. Trespass seems the most likely cause of action against the solicitors.

1   [1987] Ch 38.

CHAPTER 8

The position of the defendant: discharge and variation of the order; compensation; contempt; appeals by either party

8.0 DISCHARGE OR VARIATION OF THE ORDER

The defendant may make an application for the variation or discharge of either order. So far as a Mareva injunction is concerned, the defendant may wish to make the application quickly so as to reduce any damage to its business. The procedure is dealt with in the first part of this chapter. As to Anton Piller orders, the defendant is in contempt of court if he does not obey the terms of the order. There is, however, a risky alternative for the strong-minded but honest defendant. This is dealt with in **8.3**. The second part of the chapter deals with the grounds for discharge of the order. The third part of the chapter deals briefly with compensation for the defendant where the injunction is discharged, and the fourth part with the position of a defendant who breaches the order and is in contempt of court. Finally, the fifth part of the chapter considers appeals by either the plaintiff or the defendant.

8.1 PROCEDURE FOR DISCHARGE OR VARIATION OF MAREVA INJUNCTIONS

8.1.1 A short summary of what a defendant faced with a Mareva injunction should do is contained below at **9.2**.

8.1.2 Procedure governing Mareva injunctions has already been dealt with in Chapter 5. To recap, the procedure differs between the Queen's Bench Division and the Chancery Division. In the Queen's Bench Division, the order will normally last 'until further order', but will give the defendant liberty to apply on 24 or 48 hours' notice to discharge it. In the Chancery Division, the ex parte order will be expressed to last for at most a week. After that time, the plaintiff must return to court to ask the court to continue the injunction. Instead of applying for discharge of the order, the defendant resists its continuance. But the grounds on which the defendant may rely are the same in both divisions.

8.1.3 The defendant should prepare affidavit evidence in support of its challenge to the case set out in the plaintiff's evidence. The defendant's evidence will be based on the criteria set out in Chapter 5, but the defendant will of course seek to show that the criteria are not met or that the plaintiff's evidence is either a distortion of the picture or misses out evidence for the defendant. If there is evidence of prejudice to the defendant caused by the injunction this should also be included. For detailed discussion of the grounds on which the court may set aside the order, see **8.5**ff below, and for a short practical summary see **9.2**.

8.2 PROCEDURE GOVERNING THE DEFENDANT ON SERVICE OF AN ANTON PILLER ORDER

8.2.1 A person who is served with an Anton Piller order has to decide quickly whether to obey it. On service of the order, what should the defendant do?[1] It has been established since the *Anton Piller* case[2] that the defendant is likely to be held in contempt of court if he refuses to obey the order. Lord Denning MR stated:[3]

'It [the order] serves to tell the defendants that, on the evidence put before it, the court is of the opinion that they ought to permit inspection – nay it orders them to permit – and that they refuse at their peril. It puts them in peril not only of proceedings for contempt but also of adverse inferences being drawn against them; so much so that their own solicitor may often advise them to comply.'

The point was considered in *Columbia Picture Industries Inc v Robinson* by Scott J who stated:[4]

'. . . if respondents to Anton Piller orders were to be allowed to delay their execution while applications to apply to discharge were being made, the purpose of Anton Piller orders and procedure would be largely lost.'

---

1   See **10.2** for a quick practical summary of the defendant's position.

2   [1976] Ch 55.
3   Ibid at 61.
4   [1987] Ch 38 at 72.

8.3   *BHIMJI V CHATWANI*

8.3.1   The recent case of *Bhimji v Chatwani*[1] contains valuable and extensive guidance on the position of a defendant served with an Anton Piller order. The Anton Piller order was served on the defendants at 8am. The defendants did not grant permission to enter their premises at once: they wanted to take legal advice first. They contacted their solicitors. By 11am they had received the advice of the solicitors. Even at this stage, they did not permit entry. Instead, through their solicitors they offered a compromise. They suggested that there should be a joint search by both parties' solicitors and that the documents found by the plaintiffs' solicitors should be safeguarded by the defendants' solicitors for a short period to allow the defendants to make an application to the judge to have the order discharged or varied. The plaintiffs rejected this because they insisted that their solicitors be allowed to take photocopies of the documents to show to and consider with the plaintiffs.[2] The defendants applied to the judge to set aside his order. He heard the application at 5pm. He varied the order but declined to discharge it. As soon as the hearing had finished, at about 6pm, the defendants gave the plaintiffs permission to enter their premises in accordance with the terms of the amended order. The plaintiffs applied to commit the defendants to prison for contempt of court.

1   [1991] 1 WLR 989.
2   Since *Universal Thermosensors v Hibben* [1992] 1 WLR 840, it is likely that the order would prevent the plaintiffs themselves from seeing the documents, at least if there were any possibility of the plaintiffs gaining commercial advantage thereby. See Chapter 7.

8.3.2   The first question was what the order required the defendants to do. The undertaking in the order said that the defendants need not permit entry until they had taken legal advice, provided that they set about obtaining such advice 'forthwith'. Scott J construed the order as follows. The order required the defendants, if they intended to seek legal advice, to start trying to obtain it at once.[1] Once they had done so, their obligation to permit the plaintiffs' solicitors to enter did not arise until they had had a reasonable opportunity of obtaining such advice. How long they required for such 'reasonable opportunity' would depend on how sophisticated the defendants themselves were, and whether there were solicitors in their locality who understood Anton Piller orders.[2] On the facts of *Bhimji*, the defendants did obtain legal advice reasonably quickly. Their obligation to permit entry did not arise until they had obtained it. So they were not in contempt of court until after 11am, when they had received the legal advice.

1   The terms of the draft Anton Piller order now follow this judgment by stating that the defendant must start to seek legal advice 'at once', rather than 'forthwith'. See **11.2**. So the reasoning in *Bhimji* ought also to apply where the defendants are served with an order in the terms of the new draft order.

2   See *Bhimji* at 999–1000.

8.3.3   After they had obtained the legal advice, the order required the defendants to permit entry immediately. In *Bhimji*, they did not do so. Scott J applied the previous law that to refuse entry at this stage was in breach of the order. The defendants were therefore in contempt of court and liable to imprisonment as a punishment. But he then went on to consider what consequences flowed from the contempt on the particular facts of the *Bhimji* case. He concluded that the breach had not been contumacious; it was merely a technical breach of the obligation to allow entry forthwith on receipt of the legal advice, and so Scott J declined to make any order on the motion to commit. The motion was dismissed with costs.

8.3.4   Summary of when the defendant can refuse entry after service of the order

As a result, the position of the defendant who has received legal advice appears to be as follows. He must immediately permit the search, otherwise he will be in contempt of court and at risk of committal to prison. The safer course is therefore to permit entry immediately. What will happen if the defendant declines to do so? He is then at risk of imprisonment. If he refuses to permit entry and then interferes with documents or evidence in any way, he is liable to face consequences 'of the utmost gravity'.[1] Alternatively, he may do what the defendants did in *Bhimji*. He may offer a joint search by both parties' solicitors, with his solicitors undertaking to keep in safe custody any documents thought relevant pending an inter partes hearing, and he may make an immediate application to the court for discharge or variation of the order, with immediate obedience to whatever the court then orders, after the hearing. By 'immediate' is meant, within an hour or two. If, in the meantime, he ensures that no documents or evidence are tampered with in any way whatsoever, then, on the basis of *Bhimji*, he has a reasonable chance of defeating any application for committal. His defence will be that his breach is purely technical and not contumacious. It was the steps outlined above which caused Scott J to make such a finding in *Bhimji*.[2]

1   *WEA Records Ltd v Visions Channel 4 Ltd* [1983] 1 WLR 721, per Sir John Donaldson MR at 726.
2   Cf *HPSI Ltd v Thomas and Williams* [1983] NLJR 598.

8.3.5   What happens if the defendant attends court to seek a discharge of an order which has been granted ex parte, but in the absence of the plaintiff? There is authority that, in the case of an interlocutory injunction, the court has jurisdiction, on an ex parte application, to grant a stay of an order which was granted on an ex parte basis.[1] But it appears that where an Anton Piller order is granted ex parte, the court will refuse to vary it ex parte by imposing a stay until an inter partes hearing, unless there is very strong evidence in favour of so doing. Nevertheless, without the defendant's permission, the plaintiff will be unable to execute the order. The defendant will be in contempt of court, but it may be only a technical contempt if he succeeds in having the order discharged and does not destroy any evidence in the meantime.[2]

1   *London City Agency (JCD) v Lee* [1970] Ch 597.
2   *Hallmark Cards Inc v Image Arts Ltd* [1977] FSR 150, CA.

8.3.6   Risks for the defendant in not complying with the order on receipt of legal advice

It is important to emphasise that the defendant who declines to allow the search as soon as he has received legal advice is plainly at risk of committal. In *Bhimji*, a further factor mitigating the contempt was that the defendants claimed that their solicitor had told them that they need not obey the order until they had applied for its discharge. If that advice was given, it was wrong. So a defendant who is properly advised will not be able to rely upon this defence. As Scott J emphasised, the result in *Bhimji* turned on the particular facts of that case. A less careful defendant could easily be committed for contempt of court in refusing to obey the order at once.

8.3.7   The new safeguards introduced by Sir Donald Nicholls V-C in *Universal Thermosensors*[1] and the new draft form of order provide extra protection for the defendant. Their effect is that no plaintiff who might be a commercial rival of the defendants may see the evidence, and that all documents and any article whose ownership is disputed must be returned to the defendants' solicitors within two working days. This could mean that a refusal by the defendant to obey an order drafted in the new form might be thought less technical than it was in *Bhimji*, and thus lead to punishment. But a defendant may nevertheless be keen to seek to avoid the indignity of a thorough search of his premises, authorised by the court, if only because of the damage it might do to his reputation.

1   [1992] 3 WLR 840.

8.4   WILL THE COURT DISCHARGE AN ANTON PILLER ORDER AFTER IT HAS BEEN EXECUTED?

8.4.1   After an Anton Piller order has been executed, the court does have power to discharge it.[1] On the other hand, effluxion of time may weigh against discharge of the order: in *Columbia Picture Industries Inc v Robinson*[2] Scott J, refusing to discharge an Anton Piller order (executed some three years previously) on the ground of material non-disclosure by the plaintiff, stated:

'I am instinctively disinclined to make by judicial order what seems to me to be an empty gesture.'

But is it an empty gesture? The defendant may consider that it damages its reputation to have the public know that such order has been granted; the discharge of the order might undo or reduce this damage, and may well be desirable for the defendant.[3]

1   *Lock International plc v Beswick* [1989] 1 WLR 1268.
2   [1987] Ch 38 at 87.
3   Cf *Polly Peck International plc v Nadir (No 2)* [1992] 4 All ER 769, CA: the court took account of the damage to the defendant's business from public knowledge that there was a Mareva injunction in force against it.

8.5   GROUNDS FOR DISCHARGE OF THE ORDER

8.5.1   The grounds for discharge of Anton Piller orders and Mareva injunctions include the following.[1]

1   See *Siporex Trade SA v Comdel Commodities Ltd* [1986] 2 Lloyd's Rep 428.

8.6   FAILURE TO GIVE FULL AND FRANK DISCLOSURE

8.6.1   The commonest ground for an application for the discharge of a Mareva injunction is that the plaintiff failed to give full and frank disclosure of material facts at the ex parte hearing. The nature of the plaintiff's obligation to give such disclosure has already been discussed.[1] In short, at the ex parte hearing the plaintiff must draw the attention of the judge to all facts and arguments which, if the defendant were present, he might put forward in opposition to the grant of the order. The plaintiff has an obligation to make reasonable enquiries before he applies for the injunction, so that he is in a position to know what such arguments for the defendant might be.

1   See Chapter 5.

8.6.2   Principles in *Brink's-MAT Ltd v Elcombe*

If the court finds that there has been a material non-disclosure, it may discharge the injunction and decline to grant another. When will the court do this? The principles were set out by Ralph Gibson LJ in *Brink's-MAT Ltd v Elcombe*:[1]

'(5) If material non-disclosure is established the court will be "astute to ensure that a plaintiff who obtains [an ex parte injunction] without full disclosure . . . is deprived of any advantage he may have derived by that breach of duty:" see per Donaldson LJ in *Bank Mellat v Nikpour*,[2] at p 91, citing Warrington LJ in the *Kensington Income Tax Comrs'* case [1917] KB 486 at 509.

(6) Whether the fact not disclosed is of sufficient materiality to justify or require immediate discharge of the order without examination of the merits depends on the importance of the fact to the issues which were to be decided by the judge on the application. The answer to the question whether the non-disclosure was innocent, in the sense that the fact was not known to the applicant or that its relevance was not perceived, is an important consideration but not decisive by reason of the duty on the applicant to make all proper enquiries and to give careful consideration to the case being presented.

(7) Finally, it "is not for every omission that the injunction will be automatically discharged. A locus poenitentiae may sometimes be afforded": per Lord Denning MR in *Bank Mellat v Nikpour* [1985] FSR 87 at 90. The court has a discretion, notwithstanding proof of material non-disclosure which justifies or requires the immediate discharge of the ex parte order, nevertheless to continue the order, or to make a new order on terms.

> "when the whole of the facts, including that of the original non-disclosure, are before [the court, it] may well grant . . . a second injunction if the original non-disclosure was innocent and if an injunction could properly be granted even had the facts been disclosed": per Glidewell LJ in *Lloyds Bowmaker Ltd v Britannia Arrow Holdings plc* [[1988] 1 WLR 1337 at] 1343H–1344A.'

1 [1988] 1 WLR 1350, CA. And see **6.1.4**.
2 [1985] FSR 87, CA.

8.6.3 Ralph Gibson LJ's principle (7) shows that where it is shown that there has been a material non-disclosure, the most important factors in the exercise of the court's discretion are whether the non-disclosure was innocent and whether, if the matter had been disclosed, the injunction would nevertheless have been granted. In considering those factors, the court must take into account the practicalities of the case. Also in the *Brink's-MAT*[1] case, Slade LJ said:

> 'Nevertheless, the nature of the principle, as I see it, is essentially penal and in its application the practical realities of any case before the court cannot be overlooked. By their very nature, ex parte applications usually necessitate the giving and taking of instructions and the preparation of the requisite drafts in some haste. Particularly, in heavy commercial cases, the borderline between material facts and non-material facts may be a somewhat uncertain one. While in no way discounting the heavy duty of candour and care which falls on persons making ex parte applications, I do not think the application of the principle should be carried to extreme lengths. In one or two other recent cases coming before this court, I have suspected signs of a growing tendency on the part of some litigants against whom ex parte injunctions have been granted, or of their legal advisers, to rush to the *R v Kensington Income Tax Comrs* [1917] 1 KB 486 principle as a

tabula in naufragio,[2] alleging material non-disclosure on sometimes rather slender grounds, as representing substantially the only hope of obtaining the discharge of injunctions in cases where there is little hope of doing so on the substantial merits of the case or on the balance of convenience.'

In particular, if it transpires that the non-disclosure was entirely the fault of the plaintiff's solicitor rather than the plaintiff, the court is unlikely to discharge the injunction.[3]

1 *Brink's-MAT Ltd v Elcombe* [1988] 1 WLR 1350 at 1359C–1359E.
2 Ie a plank in a shipwreck.
3 *Eastglen International Corpn v Monpare SA* [1987] NLJR 56, CA.

8.6.4 The third judge in the *Brink's-MAT*[1] case, Balcome LJ, stated that the court's discretion to continue or grant a fresh injunction, after there had been a material non-disclosure, should be exercised sparingly.[2]

1 [1988] 1 WLR 1350.
2 Ibid at 1358F.

8.6.5 The Court of Appeal gave further consideration to discharge for non-disclosure in *Behbehani v Salem*.[1] The court confirmed that, in considering whether to discharge, the starting point would often be to consider whether the non-disclosure was innocent, and whether, if there had been full disclosure at the ex parte stage, the order would have been granted.[2] It was wrong for the judge, in deciding whether to discharge the injunction, to balance those factors against the strength of the merits of the plaintiff's case. If judges did this, it would water down the court's policy of treating material non-disclosures seriously. As to the innocence of the non-disclosure, this meant 'one where there was no intention to omit or withhold information which was thought to be material'.[3] In other words, the test is subjective and does not depend on matters which the plaintiff ought to have known or found out by the time of the ex parte application, but had not. Woolf LJ added that it would often be hard to determine at the interlocutory stage whether or not a non-disclosure had been innocent.[4]

1 (Note) [1989] 1 WLR 723.
2 See per Nourse LJ, [1989] 1 WLR 723 at 736E–F.
3 Ibid at 736F, citing the *Brink's-MAT* case [1988] 1 WLR 1350.
4 Ibid at 728G.

8.6.6 When will the court decide whether there has been a material non-disclosure?

There is a further point which has led to some confusion, although it is submitted that the authorities show a degree of agreement. The point is this. Allegations that there has been a material non-disclosure are often hotly contested. Both sides present prodigious quantities of affidavit evidence to support contentions that any non-disclosure was or was not material. How can the judge determine such an issue without trying the merits of the action, and without spending days considering the evidence and hearing argument? Should the judge attempt, at the interlocutory stage, to decide whether there has been a material non-disclosure, or should he adjourn this issue to be decided at the trial of the action? Both Mervyn Davies J[1] and Sir Nicolas Browne-Wilkinson V-C[2] have indicated that this question requires further consideration by the Court of Appeal, but that court has not yet had the opportunity to rule on the issue. One must therefore consider the authorities at first instance.

1   *Ali & Fahd Shobokshi Group v Moneim* [1989] 1 WLR 710 at 722F.
2   *Tate Access Floors Inc v Boswell* [1991] Ch 512 at 534A.

8.6.7   In *Dormeuil Frères SA v Nicolian International (Textiles) Ltd,*[1] Sir Nicolas Browne-Wilkinson V-C said:

'. . . save in exceptional circumstances, it is not the correct procedure to apply to discharge an ex parte injunction on the grounds of lack of full disclosure at the interlocutory stage of the proceedings.'

But this was before publication of the report of the Court of Appeal's decisions in *Behbehani v Salem.*[2] Sir Nicolas considered the matter further, and in light of the *Behbehani* case, in *Tate Access Floors Inc v Boswell.*[3] Referring to the *Dormeuil* case, he said:

'It is clear that I was in error in thinking that normally the question whether or not there has been a failure to disclose is not appropriate to be dealt with at the interlocutory stage. If, as seems probable, my decision in this case is appealed I, and I believe other first instance judges, would value guidance from the Court of Appeal as to how the test in *Behebhani v Salem* (Note) [1989] 1 WLR 723 should be applied having regard to the practical problems which I set out in full in the *Dormeuil* case [1988] 1 WLR 1362 . . . It may be that the reconciliation between the public interest in upholding the golden rule and the public interest in ensuring that the courts are not clogged with long interlocutory hearings is that the investigation of the circumstances in which the ex parte order was obtained should take place at an interlocutory stage only where it is clear that there has been a failure to make a material disclosure or where the nature of the alleged failure is so serious as to demand immediate investigation.'

1   [1988] 1 WLR 1362 at 1369.
2   [1989] 1 WLR 723.
3   [1991] Ch 512 at 533–534.

8.6.8 The basis of Sir Nicolas Browne-Wilkinson's dicta in *Dormeuil*[1] was that it took too long for the court to consider the question of non-disclosure at the interlocutory stage, and that, pending trial, if the injunction had been wrongly granted the defendant was nevertheless protected by the undertaking in damages. But in *Ali & Fahd Shobokshi Group Ltd v Moneim*,[2] Mervyn Davies J said that:

'Damages for non-disclosure awarded after trial may be an entirely inadequate remedy for a defendant who has to suffer the oppression of a Mareva order up to trial.'

An example of this is where the grant of the order of itself inhibits the defendant in performing its ordinary business: see *Polly Peck International plc v Nadir (No2)*.[3]

1   [1988] 1 WLR 1362.
2   [1989] 1 WLR 710 at 722D.
3   [1992] 4 All ER 769, discussed in Chapter 2.

8.6.9 In the *Ali & Fahd*[1] case, at the inter partes hearing Mervyn Davies J considered *Behbehani v Salem*[2] and said:

'. . . I come to the conclusion that I must consider (a) whether the non-disclosure complained of was innocent and (b) whether an injunction could properly have been granted if full disclosure had been made to Peter Gibson J [at the ex parte hearing]. If (a) and (b) are answered in the affirmative then the court has a discretion [to grant a new injunction].'

Mervyn Davies J accepted that in many cases it would be sufficient to leave examination of non-disclosure until trial, as suggested in the *Dormeuil* case.[3] But he also stated that:

'. . . a defendant should be at liberty to require the discharge of an ex parte Mareva injunction (without its immediate reimposition) as soon as he can show non-disclosure of a substantial kind.'[4]

This would appear to accord with the dicta of Sir Nicolas Browne-Wilkinson V-C in *Tate Access Floors Inc v Boswell*.[5] It therefore appears that, in the absence of further elucidation from the Court of Appeal, the court will consider whether to discharge an injunction for material non-disclosure if either there has clearly been material non-disclosure, as was the case in *Behbehani v Salem*,[6] or if it appears that there has been serious non-disclosure which warrants examination. It might be argued, on the basis of the *Ali and Fahd* case, that prejudice to the defendant from the injunction continuing in force is a relevant factor. Compare also the Court of Appeal's approach to the separate question of whether the undertaking in damages should be discharged (**8.12.2**).

1 [1989] 1 WLR 710.
2 Above.
3 [1988] 1 WLR 1362.
4 [1989] 1 WLR 710 at 722C.
5 [1991] Ch 512.
6 Above.

8.6.10 Further, in *Arab Monetary Fund v Hashim (No 1)*,[1] Morritt J distinguished Sir Nicolas Browne-Wilkinson V-C's dicta in the *Dormeuil*[2] case on the basis that the return date for the ex parte injunction had not yet arrived, and the ex parte order for disclosure had not been complied with. As has been indicated above, it would now appear that those dicta carry less weight in any event.

1 [1989] 1 WLR 565 at 569H.
2 [1988] 1 WLR 1362.

8.6.11   Full and frank disclosure of plaintiff's finances

The plaintiff's duty to give full and frank disclosure extends to his ability to compensate the defendant in damages if the order is subsequently discharged. Accordingly, if the plaintiff fails to disclose any inability to do this, or gives a misleading picture of his financial position, that in itself may amount to grounds for the discharge of the order. See **6.7**.

8.7   BREACH OF THE BASIC REQUIREMENTS OF THE GRANT

8.7.1   The defendant may apply for discharge of the order on the grounds that its grant does not satisfy the 'ultimate test' of being just and reasonable in all the circumstances or that the evidence adduced in support of its grant falls below the requisite standard of proof (see Chapter 5). Save in exceptional circumstances, the order may be discharged if the plaintiff has no cause of action to maintain the injunction. This is discussed in Chapter 2.

8.8   BREACH OF AN UNDERTAKING

8.8.1   The plaintiff must carry out undertakings which he gave to the court as a condition of the grant of the injunction to the letter. If he does not, this may amount to grounds for discharge of the order. But it may not lead to discharge, as it may be treated as less serious than material non-disclosure, especially if the undertaking was honestly and genuinely given, and no prejudice followed from the failure to observe it.[1]

1   *Sabani v Economakis* (1988) Times, 17 June.

8.8.2   In *Siporex Trade SA v Comdel Commodities Ltd*[1] a Mareva injunction had been issued without an undertaking to issue an originating summons forthwith. At the application to discharge the injunction, some two months after it had been issued, no originating summons (and no writ) had been issued. The papers bore no serial number, the order had never been formally drawn up and, in the absence of originating process, could not be drawn up. Bingham J discharged the injunction. He said:

'This history highlights in a vivid way the laxity of practice which the Mareva injunction has indirectly caused. It is not so very long ago since ex parte applications for injunctive relief were infrequently made and even more exceptionally granted. The conditions were strict and (at least in my experience) scrupulously observed. If the urgency of the case was demonstrably such as to preclude issue of proceedings, an undertaking to issue forthwith was given and performed. The advent of the Mareva injunction has, as is notorious, led to such applications becoming commonplace, hundreds being made each year and relatively few refused. As often as not the proceedings have not been issued and supporting affidavit is in draft. Appropriate undertakings are then given but cases occur in which an impermissibly generous construction is given to the important word "forthwith".

Even by these relaxed standards, the present case must be regarded as an extreme example of procedural irregularity. [The plaintiffs] urge that the absence of originating process is no more than an irregularity, which I should cure by a suitable order under Order 2, rule 1. They urge that [the defendants] were fully aware of the injunction and that neither they nor the bank have suffered from this procedural oversight which (I assume) was not the fault of [the plaintiffs] themselves. There is undoubted force in these considerations. It is none the less unacceptable, in my judgment, that an undertaking should remain in force for over two months after its grant without any originating process to sustain it, and that the court should appear to countenance that neglect of its procedure by maintaining an injunction in force in those circumstances. I feel the only appropriate course is to discharge the injunction.'

1   [1986] 2 Lloyd's Rep 428 at 436.

8.9   THE PLAINTIFF'S NON-COMPLIANCE WITH THE TERMS OF THE ORDER

8.9.1   The plaintiff's failure to comply with the terms of the order may also be a ground for, or factor supporting, the discharge of the order.[1]

1   *Columbia Picture Industries Inc v Robinson* [1987] Ch 38.

8.10   THE PLAINTIFF'S FAILURE TO PROSECUTE THE ACTION QUICKLY

8.10.1   The plaintiff who obtains a Mareva injunction has a duty to prosecute the action as rapidly as he can. If he fails to do so, this is a factor which may weigh heavily with the court in favour of discharging the order. See further Chapter 5.

8.11   ORDERS INVOLVING A BREACH OF THE PRIVILEGE AGAINST SELF-INCRIMINATION

8.11.1   It might be thought that if the grant and execution of an Anton Piller had breached the defendant's privilege against self-incrimination (see Chapter 4), the court would discharge the order. But in *Universal City Studios Inc v Hubbard*[1] the Court of Appeal observed that there were serious doubts as to whether the judge's finding was correct that documents seized under Anton Piller order should be returned if the defendant's claim to privilege had been made good. It now appears from *Tate Access Floors Inc v Boswell*,[2] however, that an Anton Piller order should not be granted if there is any danger that the defendant's privilege against self-incrimination will be breached, and so the question ought not to arise.

1   [1984] Ch 225 at 236.
2   [1991] Ch 512 and see **4.3.7**.

8.12   COMPENSATION OF DEFENDANT ON DISCHARGE

8.12.1   If the order is discharged, the defendant's principal means of obtaining compensation is to seek an enquiry as to damages payable pursuant to the undertaking in damages. The general nature of this undertaking has already been discussed (**6.4**ff). The defendant may not plead a claim based upon the undertaking in damages until after the injunction has been discharged. If he does, it may be struck out.[1]

1   *Fletcher Sutcliffe Wild Ltd v Burch* [1982] FSR 64.

8.12.2   Procedure on seeking an enquiry as to damages

Should the discharge of the injunction lead automatically to an order that there be an enquiry as to the damages which the defendant has been caused, as soon as possible? The case of *Cheltenham & Gloucester Building Society v Ricketts*[1] shows that the position is complex. Sir

Peter Pain sitting as a High Court Judge discharged two injunctions, one a Mareva, and ordered that there be an enquiry as to what damages two of the defendants had suffered. The Court of Appeal overturned his decision. The Court of Appeal's decision shows that one has to distinguish two separate questions. These will be referred to as 'stage (a)' and 'stage (b)'.

Stage (a)   Should the application to enforce the undertaking be granted? This depends on 'liability' on the undertaking: in other words, to what extent is it just that the plaintiff should compensate the defendant for the losses which the defendant has suffered by reason of the order? In deciding this question, the first issue is whether the injunction was wrongly granted, which the court considers on the basis of the facts available at the time the order was made. But the court must also consider all the circumstances in exercising its discretion as to whether to order enforcement of the undertaking as to damages. Peter Gibson LJ said that it was inappropriate to exercise the discretion if there were material matters as to which the parties were in dispute, until the court had resolved such disputes. Such matters could not normally be resolved until trial, and so the court would not usually exercise its discretion on the application until trial if such disputes were material.

Stage (b)   The enquiry as to damages. Unless otherwise ordered (see option (iv) below), this is purely a question of the quantum of damages which the injunction has caused the defendant. Accordingly, once the court has ordered that there be an enquiry as to damages, there is no scope for reducing the sums payable by the plaintiff on the basis that in all the circumstances it is not fair the plaintiff should pay so much. That is why the court has to exercise its discretion on the application (stage (a)) so carefully.

1   (1993) Times, 9 April, CA.

8.12.3   Peter Gibson LJ distinguished five separate courses which the court could follow where it discharged the injunction at an interlocutory stage and the question of damages on the undertaking arose:

Option (i)   The court grants the application (stage (a)) and proceeds to assess the damages caused (stage (b)) there and then.

This course would be appropriate only in the most straightforward of cases where all the facts were already known at the interlocutory stage. It was unlikely that the court would choose this option.

Option (ii)   The court could grant the application (stage (a)) and order that the enquiry (stage (b)) should follow at a specified time, rather than at trial. This was the course which Sir Peter Pain had adopted.

Option (iii)   The court could stand over the application (stage (a)) to a specified time. If there was a question as to whether the injunction had rightly been granted, the court would normally stand the application over until trial, to be determined by the trial judge at the conclusion of the trial when all the facts were known.

Option (iv)   The court could order an enquiry (stage (b)) but direct that the question of liability of the plaintiff on the undertaking (most of stage (a)) be determined at the enquiry.

Option (v)   The court could refuse the application (stage (a)). This would be done only in the clearest cases where it was plain that the defendant had suffered no loss by reason of the injunction.

8.12.4   The effect of the *Ricketts* case may be summarised as follows. Where it is clear at the inter partes hearing either precisely what loss the defendant has suffered by reason of the order, or alternatively that the defendant has suffered no loss at all, then the court will deal with both the application for an enquiry as to damages (stage (a)) and the enquiry itself (stage (b)) there and then. Where it is clear what the defendant has suffered (option (i)), the court will assess damages in that sum, and where it is clear the defendant has suffered no loss (option (v)), the court will reject the application. But these two courses of action will rarely be followed because the facts will rarely be sufficiently clear for all to be decided at the interlocutory stage.

8.12.5   The more usual case will be as follows. Before the court can assess whether it is fair that the plaintiff pay on the undertaking, it will have to consider all the circumstances including disputed matters of fact between the parties which will be determined at trial. For instance, in the *Ricketts* case the plaintiff building society alleged that the defendants, its employees, had defrauded it of mortgage moneys by overvaluation of properties. The truth of this allegation was material to whether the plaintiff should pay on the undertaking in damages. But the allegation was disputed and the court could not determine the dispute until trial. So it was inappropriate to order the plaintiffs to pay on the undertaking until trial, when the court would be able to determine the truth of the allegation. Accordingly, in the normal case, where disputes of fact which cannot be determined until trial are relevant, the court will not grant the application for an enquiry (stage (a)) until trial. In other words, in the normal case the court will follow option (iii). Peter Gibson LJ said that in these circumstances the court might, as an alternative, adopt option (iv), that is, ordering that both liability (stage (a)) and damages (stage (b)) be determined at the enquiry as to damages. This appears to be a novel solution and it is not as yet clear precisely when or why the court might choose it instead of option (iii). But it does have a clear advantage: most cases settle before trial. The problem with option (iii) is that if the case does settle, the defendant may never obtain his damages on the undertaking. At least with option (iv) it is possible that he might obtain some damages, even if the main case ultimately settled.

8.12.6 Alternative causes of action for the defendant?

In the case of an Anton Piller order, if the defendant alleges that more persons entered his property than were authorised by the order, then that gives him a cause of action in trespass which may be pleaded separately. But if the claim is proceeding in the Chancery Division, the defendant ought to plead this in a separate action in the Queen's Bench Division rather than by way of counterclaim in the Chancery Division.[1] Apart from those circumstances, any claim for loss suffered due to the existence of the injunction ought to be brought on the basis of the undertaking in damages, rather than based on a separate cause of action. In particular, the defendant should not sue in negligence or for abuse of the process of the court.[2]

1   *Fletcher Sutcliffe Wild Ltd v Burch* [1982] FSR 64.
2   *Digital Equipment Corpn v Darkcrest Ltd* [1984] Ch 512.

8.12.7 Burden of proof at the enquiry

At the enquiry as to damages (stage (b) above), the burden of proof that the defendant has suffered loss due to the imposition of the injunction lies upon him. But once he has established a prima facie case that damage which he has suffered was caused exclusively by the injunction, then, in the absence of further evidence, the court will generally infer that it has been so caused.[1]

1   *Financiera Avenida SA v Shiblaq* (1988) Times, 21 November.

8.13   COSTS ON DISCHARGE

8.13.1   If it is shown that a Mareva injunction has been obtained on the basis of fabricated evidence, the plaintiff will be ordered to pay the costs of the application and the discharge forthwith, to be taxed on the indemnity basis. It does not matter that the plaintiff was not himself aware of the fabrication, or that it was done by someone else who did not tell him of it.[1]

1   *Bir v Sharma* (1988) Times, 7 December.

8.14   CONTEMPT

8.14.1   It has already been stated that the defendant who refuses to obey an Anton Piller order or Mareva injunction is in contempt of court.[1] It is open to the plaintiff to apply for his committal for contempt. If the contempt is proved beyond reasonable doubt, then the court may fine or imprison the defendant. An example is *Wardle Fabrics v Myristis*.[2] The plaintiff had obtained an Anton Piller order. The defendant by its managing director refused consent to the entry to its premises that the order required and applied for the order to be discharged on the ground that all material facts had not been disclosed to the court by the plaintiffs when applying for the order. The plaintiffs applied to punish the defendant and its managing director for contempt in failing to obey the Anton Piller. Goulding J found the contempt proved and, after contemplating fining the defendant, dealt with the contempt by requiring the defendant to pay the plaintiff's costs of the contempt application on an indemnity basis. But see **8.3** for discussion of when the court may regard a party's contempt of court as purely technical.

1   **8.3.3**.
2   [1984] FSR 263.

8.14.2 In *Canadian Imperial Bank of Commerce v Bhattessa*,[1] Harman J found the defendant guilty of contempt and fined him £10,000. The facts are stated in **2.1.5** above.

1 (1991) Times, 10 September.

8.14.3 The law of contempt, and the procedural rules which must be followed by the plaintiff seeking to commit, are detailed and are beyond the scope of this book.[1]

1 See RSC Ord 52, CCR Ord 29, and Miller *Contempt of Court* (2nd edn, 1989).

8.15 APPEAL

8.15.1 '... appeals should be rare and [the Court of Appeal] should be slow to interfere.' So stated Parker LJ in an appeal to the Court of Appeal in a Mareva case, *Derby & Co Ltd v Weldon (No 1)*.[1] The decision to grant or refuse a Mareva or Anton Piller order is essentially discretionary. As long as the judge at first instance has complied with the rules that do exist, it is unlikely that the Court of Appeal will interfere with the exercise of his discretion. Accordingly, it is worth considering carefully whether an appeal is justified.

1 [1990] 1 Ch 48.

8.16 APPEAL BY THE DEFENDANT

8.16.1 The defendant against whom a Mareva injunction or Anton Piller order has been granted ex parte, and who wishes to challenge the order, should not appeal to the Court of Appeal. He should first return to the judge who granted the order, or, if he is not available, to another High Court judge, and apply at an inter partes hearing for the discharge of the order. Only if the defendant is dissatisfied with the decision of the High Court judge at the inter partes hearing should he consider appeal to the Court of Appeal.[1] A party who wishes to appeal from the decision of a High Court judge granting or refusing a variation in an injunction does not require leave to appeal.[2]

1   *WEA Records v Visions Channel 4 Ltd* [1983] 1 WLR 721, CA. (Contra, *Bestworth Ltd v Wearwell Ltd* [1979] FSR 320, but this is only a decision at first instance and so overridden by *WEA*.)
2   *Atlas Maritime Co SA v Avalon Maritime Ltd (No 2)* [1991] 1 WLR 633, CA.

8.16.2   A similar rule applies where the defendant is found to have breached a Mareva injunction and is committed for contempt of court as a result. If he wishes to put forward new evidence to explain the contempt, or to apologise in the hope of reducing the punishment, he should apply to the first instance judge who originally made the committal order, rather than to the Court of Appeal. An appeal should be launched only if he alleges that the judge at first instance made a mistake.[1]

1   *Irtelli v Squatriti* [1992] 3 WLR 218 at 226C–226F, CA.

8.16.3   The Court of Appeal may itself grant a Mareva injunction or Anton Piller order. To which court should further applications in respect of such order be made? This depends on the nature of the application. If a party seeks the 'amendment, execution and enforcement' of the order then, by virtue of s 15(3) of the Supreme Court Act 1981, the application must be made to the Court of Appeal itself. But if the application is for anything else, for instance for discharge of the order, it must be made to the High Court as the Court of Appeal will have no jurisdiction.[1]

1   *Ocean Software Ltd v Kay* (1992) Times, 29 January, CA.

8.17   APPEAL BY THE PLAINTIFF

8.17.1   The plaintiff may appeal to the Court of Appeal if the ex parte order applied for is refused. The appeal is by way of a further ex parte application to the Court of Appeal which must be made within seven days of the date of the refusal.[1] The seven days do not include weekends or bank holidays.[2] The application will be heard in open court unless there is some special factor which requires a hearing in camera.[3] If counsel decides that the appeal ought to be held in camera, he should contact the Registrar of Civil Appeals, indicating his view; his written reasons, signed by him, should be sent to the Registrar. The court may then make a preliminary decision whether the application should be made in camera or in open court. It is likely that appeals concerning banks, building societies and other institutions which depend entirely upon confidence for their financial stability will be heard in camera.[4]

1   RSC Ord 59, r 14(3).
2   RSC Ord 3, r 2(5).
3   *Practice Note* [1982] 1 WLR 1420.
4   *Polly Peck International plc v Nadir (No 1)* (1991) Times, 11 November, CA.

8.17.2   *Bayer AG v Winter*[1] is a case where the plaintiff successfully appealed to the Court of Appeal. The judge at first instance granted ex parte relief in Anton Piller and Mareva form but refused to grant orders that the first defendant be restrained from leaving England and Wales, and that he deliver up his passports forthwith. The judge considered that, as the law then stood, if such novel relief were to be granted ex parte it should be done by the Court of Appeal. The plaintiffs appealed to the Court of Appeal which granted the plaintiffs the relief sought.

1   [1986] 1 WLR 497. See further Chapter 4.

Quick summaries, synopses and precedents

CHAPTER 9

Quick summaries and synopsis: Mareva injunctions

9.0 QUICK SUMMARIES

This chapter contains two short summaries, and a longer synopsis. The summaries are designed to state in very short form the points that should be considered by a plaintiff intending to apply for a Mareva injunction, and a defendant who finds him or herself subject to one. The synopsis, which is in longer form, is based on the form of the order. It should be read in conjunction with the precedents and the passages in the main text to which reference is made.

9.1 PLAINTIFF CONSIDERING APPLYING FOR A MAREVA INJUNCTION: MAIN POINTS

1   Effect of order: freezes defendant's assets, up to value of plaintiff's proposed claim, within the jurisdiction as soon as order made. In practice banks etc must be notified of the existence of the order, eg by telephone, before they will give it effect. Assets outside the jurisdiction may be covered, by a 'worldwide Mareva', but usually the court grants this only for very large claims.

2   Rationale: stop defendant frustrating plaintiff's proposed claim by removing his assets from the jurisdiction, or spending or hiding them within it.

3   Procedure: application ex parte in Queen's Bench Division or Chancery Division, depending on type of cause of action. County court cases: save in limited circumstances (**5.6**), automatically transferred up to the High Court for application to be made. Plaintiff requires: draft statement of claim and endorsement for writ, affidavits (sworn or draft), exhibits (if relevant), draft order to be made by court. In very urgent cases counsel may attend before judge and indicate orally what his evidence is, but generally far

better to prepare papers properly: less danger of order being overturned later.

4   Plaintiff's evidence (or proposed evidence) must show:
   (i)   plaintiff has a good arguable case on his proposed cause of action against defendant, and what the claim is likely to be worth;
   (ii) some grounds for believing defendant has assets within the jurisdiction, and, if at all possible, should identify where and what they are;
   (iii) objective factors (not just expressions of fear) which tend to show that if no injunction is granted defendant is likely to remove his assets from the jurisdiction or dissipate them within it;
   (iv) plaintiff has sufficient assets to compensate any loss which defendant or third parties may suffer by reason of the order being made. This requirement does not apply to legally-aided plaintiffs.

5   Plaintiff's evidence (and his counsel's submissions) should also give full and frank disclosure, ie should set out in full detail any points which defendant might make if he were present. Plaintiff's affidavit should state or exhibit any evidence plaintiff possesses which might assist defendant. If in doubt, disclose it. It is plaintiff's lawyers' responsibility to ensure this is done and it is imperative they consider it with the utmost care if they wish to avoid having the order set aside later.

6   Plaintiff must give various undertakings to the court: to issue the writ, serve it, have the affidavit(s) sworn and served on defendant, all as soon as practicable; to notify defendant of terms of the order forthwith; to serve any third parties who may be affected and notify them, and the defendant, of their right to apply to have the order set aside; to pay the costs or losses incurred by defendant or third parties if the court decides it is just to make the plaintiff pay them.

7   Plaintiffs should consider what their undertaking as to the defendant or third party's losses might cost them if the order is set aside, before applying for the order.

8   Third parties will not be bound by the order until the plaintiff has notified them of its terms.

9   Once order is granted, plaintiff should proceed speedily with the action, and notify court if he subsequently discovers information material to the application for the injunction which might assist the defendant.

9.2 WHAT SHOULD A DEFENDANT FACED WITH A MAREVA INJUNCTION DO? MAIN POINTS

1 The injunction takes immediate effect to prevent defendant dealing with his or her assets within the jurisdiction of England and Wales except
   (i) for a weekly or monthly sum or sums stated in the order. These should be for reasonable living, legal and business expenses;
   (ii) in so far as defendant's assets in the jurisdiction exceed the amount of plaintiff's claim.

2 Defendant will wish to take immediate steps to have order discharged or alternatively varied, eg to allow larger sums for living or business expenses. In addition, order may provide for such sums to be increased by agreement: defendant should try this, without prejudice to application to discharge.

3 Procedure for discharge: depends on which division of High Court granted the order. In the Chancery Division, order should recite a date for a renewed hearing. In the Queen's Bench Division, it is up to defendant to apply to set the order aside. Either way, defendant needs to prepare affidavit evidence challenging plaintiff's case and serve it on plaintiff and court. If possible, serve it a few days before renewed hearing.

4 First step: consider what plaintiff's evidence says. Plaintiff ought to serve his evidence on defendant very quickly after grant of injunction. Second step: prepare evidence for defendant raising as many of following points as possible.

5 Defendant may seek discharge of order on a number of bases.
   (i) Failure of plaintiff to give full and frank disclosure, at ex parte hearing, of all points or evidence which could properly be made or referred to for defendant. This is the commonest way of obtaining discharge. But sometimes court will not consider this point at the interlocutory hearing: see Chapter 8. Defendant's evidence should (if possible) show that defendant will suffer great prejudice if injunction is allowed to continue, and that the non-disclosure was plainly serious. Also include material changes in evidence of which plaintiff has learnt since ex parte application: he should have gone back and told the court of the change. Also consider plaintiff's financial standing: failure to disclose difficulty in meeting the undertaking in damages may lead to discharge of the order: *Lock International plc v Beswick* [1989] 1 WLR 1268.

(ii) Plaintiff does not have a good arguable case, or has no cause of action against defendant (but sometimes the cause of action can be against a related company: see Chapter 2).

(iii) There are no objective factors to show that defendant intends to remove his assets from the jurisdiction or dissipate them within it, and defendant has no such intention. Plaintiff's case is based on unsupported expressions of fear: see **5.12**.

(iv) Defendant will suffer significant prejudice from the injunction, eg if operation of his business will be harmed by restrictions on payments. See **5.13**. This factor may alternatively lead to variation of order to allow defendant to run business more easily.

(v) Breach of plaintiff's various undertakings, eg, not serving papers swiftly or failing to notify defendant of existence of order or his right to apply to vary it.

(vi) Delay by plaintiff in prosecuting the action, after grant of injunction.

9.3   SYNOPSIS

A Mareva injunction restrains a defendant from removing from the jurisdiction, or disposing or dealing with his assets within the jurisdiction, in order to defeat a plaintiff's claim or potential claim for a certain or approximate sum. It has been said that the order will not be needed in relation to the majority of defendants, as they are either honest or unable to dissipate their assets within the jurisdiction.[1]

1   See per Kerr LJ in *Z Ltd v A-Z* [1982] 2 WLR 288 at 307, CA.

9.4   The power to grant a Mareva injunction is now statutory, under s 37(3) of the Supreme Court Act 1981,[1] although the jurisdiction was developed principally by the Court of Appeal.[2]

1   Appendix A.
2   *Mareva Compania Naviera SA v International Bulkcarriers SA* [1980] 1 All ER 213 and *Nippon Yusen Kaisha v Karageorgis* [1975] 1 WLR 1093, CA.

9.5   The Mareva injunction takes effect from the moment it is pronounced on every asset of the defendant which it covers. It operates in rem, in other words it binds third parties, such as banks, who hold assets frozen by the injunction. Third parties risk committal for contempt of court if they assist the defendant in breaching the injunction. But:

'. . . mere notice of a Mareva injunction cannot render it a contempt of court for a third party to make over an asset to the defendant direct . . . A distinction must be drawn between notice of the injunction on the one hand and notice of a probability that the asset will be disposed of or dealt with in breach of it on the other. It is only in the latter case that the third party can be guilty of contempt of court.'[1]

1 *Bank Mellat v Kazmi* [1989] 1 QB 541 per Nourse LJ at 547, CA. See **2.9.4**.

9.6 The court has jurisdiction to order a defendant who is properly joined to an action in England or Wales not to dissipate assets anywhere in the world (a 'worldwide Mareva injunction'). See **2.20**. But the practical use of such an order may depend on whether the countries in which the defendant has assets are willing to give effect to it, after an application in those countries. This order is probably appropriate only in cases involving millions of pounds.

9.7 All divisions of the High Court have jurisdiction to grant Mareva injunctions. County courts, apart from the Patents County Court, may not grant them (except in very limited circumstances), but cases may be transferred from the county court to the High Court purely for the purpose of applying for a Mareva injunction.[1] In the Queen's Bench Division the application is made, ex parte, to the judge in chambers.[2] In the Chancery Division it is made to the motions judge; it will be heard in open court unless the plaintiff's counsel requests a hearing in camera and provides a good reason.[3] The applicant should prepare an affidavit or affidavits, draft statement of claim, and a draft order. In the Queen's Bench Division the applicant should provide two copies of the draft order; in the Chancery Division he should provide three copies of all documents. Skeleton arguments are helpful in complex cases. The papers should be lodged with the court the day before unless the matter is of great urgency, in which case the plaintiff's counsel and solicitor may be able to see a judge more quickly, or even instantly in very urgent cases. There is always a duty judge available to hear urgent applications. See generally Chapter 5.

1 See **5.6**.
2 For procedure in the Queen's Bench Divison see **5.2**.
3 For procedure in the Chancery Division see **5.3**.

9.8 The plaintiff's evidence must persuade the judge as to four matters.

(i) On the merits of the plaintiff's proposed action against the defendant, he has a 'good arguable case', as to a specified or approximate sum (see **5.11**).

(ii) There are some grounds for believing the defendant has assets within the jurisdiction.[1]

(iii) There is a real risk that the defendant, if not restrained, will remove his assets from the jurisdiction or dissipate them within it (see **5.12**).

(iv) It is just to grant the injunction in all the circumstances, and, in particular, bearing in mind any prejudice which granting it might cause to the defendant, his business, or third parties (see **5.13**).

The information in (ii) is essential because the plaintiff is under a duty if an injunction is granted to inform an innocent third party what he is to do or not to do and identify for the third party with as much certainty as possible the assets which are affected by the injunction. A mere assertion by the plaintiff, unsupported by evidence, that the defendant will remove or dissipate assets will not be sufficient to satisfy ground (iii).[2]

1   *Z Ltd v A-Z* [1982] 2 WLR 288 per Kerr LJ at 309–310, CA (see also **2.20**, as to worldwide Mareva injunctions).
2   *O'Regan v Iambic Productions Ltd* [1989] 139 NLJ 1378 per Sir Peter Pain.

9.9   Before applying for a Mareva injunction, the plaintiff should make reasonable enquiries as to what defences the defendant might raise if he or it were present at the ex parte application. The plaintiff should then make full and frank disclosure to the court, in his affidavit, of any fact or argument which the defendant might use, if he were present, to oppose the grant of the order. It is for the court and not the plaintiff to decide whether potential arguments for the defendant are relevant. If the plaintiff failed to disclose matters which were material, the order may be discharged on the application of the defendant.[1]

1   See **6.1** and **8.6**.

9.10   The court will require the plaintiff to give the following undertakings.

1   To issue a writ of summons if an application is made before the action has been commenced, and serve it on the defendant as soon as reasonably practicable (see **6.3.1**, and the first undertaking in

precedent 11.1A). It should be remembered that the jurisdiction may be exercised at any time during the course of an action, even in aid of execution.[1]

2 To swear and file affidavits verifying what the judge was told at the application, or in the form of draft affidavits presented to the judge (see **6.3.3** and second undertaking in the precedent).

3 To give notice of the terms of the order to the defendants forthwith and give a telephone number they may use to give notice of an application to discharge the order (see **6.3** and **6.10** and the third undertaking in the precedent). In the Queen's Bench Division, the injunction is likely to last 'until further order', and so it is up to the defendant to apply to set it aside.

4 To serve copies of the affidavit and exhibits on the defendant and third parties as soon as reasonably practicable (see **6.3.4**, **6.10** and the fourth and seventh undertakings in the precedent). This enables the defendant to know the case made against him, and to decide whether he can challenge it.

5 The undertaking in damages (the fifth undertaking in the precedent, and see **6.4**ff). If it suspects that the plaintiff could not satisfy the undertaking, the court may require security, for example in the form of a bond or bank guarantee (**6.5**).

6 To pay the expenses of a bank or any other innocent third party which are incurred in complying with the injunction and to indemnify such party in respect of any liability to which it is exposed by complying with the injunction (see the sixth undertaking in the precedent, and **2.10**).

7 To notify the defendants and third parties of their rights to apply to set aside the order (the eighth undertaking in the precedent and see **2.11**).

1 *Orwell Steel (Erection and Fabrication) Ltd v Asphalt and Tarmac (UK) Ltd* [1984] 1 WLR 1097.

9.11 THE INJUNCTION

9.11.1 The body of the injunction

'. . . removing from the jurisdiction, . . . otherwise dealing with any of their assets within the jurisdiction . . .'

9.11.2   This can be divided into two parts:

(a) the general restraint; and

(b) the specific restraint.

(a) The general restraint

'. . . removing from the jurisdiction, disposing of, mortgaging, assigning, charging or otherwise dealing with any of their assets within the jurisdiction . . .'

This provides a general or blanket restraint over all assets belonging to the defendant preventing any form of dissipation of such assets (see **2.1**).

(b) The specific restraint

'. . . including and in particular (i) the freehold property known as . . . or (if the same has been sold) the net proceeds of sale thereof after discharge of any subsisting mortgage or charge (ii) the property and assets of the business known as . . . carried on by the Defendant(s) from premises at . . . or (if and in so far as the same have been sold) the proceeds of sale thereof (iii) any moneys in (any) account(s) (numbered . . .) at . . . at . . .'

This identifies certain specific assets of the defendant which he is restrained from dissipating. The order may identify only one specific asset (eg a bank account) or a number of assets (eg bank account, house and aeroplane). Any assets may be restrained (for example, ships, aeroplanes, and cars – see **2.1**). The court may in some circumstances restrain dealings with a joint account of the defendant (effectively freezing the account). See **2.1.4**.

9.12   THE PROVISOS TO THE INJUNCTION

9.12.1   The provisos limit the effect of the injunction. They are as follows.

(a) The maximum sum

'Save in so far as the unencumbered value of those assets exceeds £....'

The courts prefer to grant an injunction which freezes the defendant's assets only up to the level of the plaintiff's claim, leaving the defendant free to deal with the balance. There are two reasons for this approach: it represents no more than a plaintiff can obtain from a defendant and an order which freezes all the assets of a defendant will have to be adjusted, especially if the defendant is resident or carries on a business within the jurisdiction (see **2.7**).

(b) Ordinary living expenses

> '. . . the Defendants shall be entitled to draw and expend from a bank account or other source the identity of which shall first be notified by them to the Plaintiffs' solicitors:
>
> (a) A sum not exceeding £.... per week for ordinary living expenses; . . .'

The defendant should not be left without funds for ordinary living expenses (see *PCW (Underwriting Agencies) Ltd v Dixon*[1]). This proviso can be particularly important if the defendant's assets are less than the estimate of them given by the plaintiff on an ex parte application as it permits the defendant to use his assets below the maximum sum restrained by the injunction for his ordinary living expenses (see **2.4**).

(c) Other expenses

> '(b) A sum not exceeeding £.... per week for ordinary business expenses
>
> (c) A sum not exceeding £.... per week for ordinary legal expenses . . .'

These provisions relate to ordinary business and legal expenses. As with ordinary living expenses, a defendant must not be left without the sums to pay ordinary business expenses. It is also to the plaintiff's advantage that the defendant continues his business, as the business represents an asset which could go towards satisfying any judgment given to the plaintiff. Further, the court permits the defendant reasonable sums for legal representation. (See **2.5** and **2.6**.)

(d) Set-off

> '(3) Nothing in this order shall prevent any bank from exercising any rights of set-off it may have in respect of

facilities afforded by any such bank prior to the date of this order . . .'

This proviso protects any right of set-off a bank may have in respect of facilities and the accounts of a defendant. (See *Oceanica Castelana Armadora SA v Mineralimportexport, The Theotokos*[2] per Lloyd J and **2.12**.)

1   [1983] 2 All ER 158; on appeal [1983] 2 All ER 697, CA.
2   [1983] 1 WLR 1294.

9.13   DISCOVERY OF THE DEFENDANT'S ASSETS

9.13.1   The court may order the defendant to disclose the full value of his assets and make and file an affidavit verifying the same.[1]

1   *A v C* [1981] 2 WLR 629; *AJ Bekhor & Co Ltd v Bilton* [1981] 2 WLR 601; and *Z Ltd v A-Z* [1982] 2 WLR 288, and see **4.1**.

9.14   DELIVERY UP OF THE DEFENDANT'S CHATTELS

9.14.1   The court may also order the defendant to deliver up all or certain of his chattels into the custody of the plaintiff's soliticitors, or possibly a receiver appointed by the court, although the latter may be expensive for the plaintiff. See **4.6**.

9.14.2   On ex parte Mareva injunctions the defendant will always be given liberty to apply to discharge the injunction after giving notice to the plaintiff or the plaintiff's solicitors (see Chapter 5).

9.15   Many Anton Piller orders also include Mareva injunctive relief as well (see precedent 11.3).

CHAPTER 10

Quick summaries and synopsis: Anton Piller orders

10.0 QUICK SUMMARIES

As with Chapter 9, this chapter contains two short summaries, and a longer synopsis. The summaries are designed to summarise in very short form the points which should be considered by a plaintiff intending to apply for an Anton Piller order, and a defendant who finds him or herself subject to one. The synopsis, which is in longer form, should be read in conjunction with the precedents and the passages in the main text to which reference is made.

10.1 Plaintiff considering applying for an Anton Piller order: main points

1 Effect of order: permits plaintiff's solicitor to enter defendant's premises (with consent of defendant) to search for evidence in plaintiff's proposed action against defendant. The order should specify the type of evidence or documents to be taken. Where appropriate, also includes orders for immediate delivery up of items which belong to plaintiff; for defendant to disclose to plaintiff's solicitor names of persons to whom he has supplied items which breach plaintiff's intellectual property rights; and restraining defendant from telling others of existence of the order for a few days.

2 Rationale: stop defendant frustrating a fair trial by destroying evidence and documents before trial, and not giving proper discovery. (See **1.8** for a good example of the successful use of the order.)

3 Procedure: application ex parte in Queen's Bench Division or Chancery Division, depending on type of cause of action. County court cases: automatically transferred up to the High Court for

application to be made. Plaintiff requires: draft statement of claim and endorsement for writ, affidavits (sworn or draft), draft order to be made by court. In very urgent cases counsel may attend before judge and indicate orally what his evidence is, without any documents, but generally far better to prepare papers properly.

4   Plaintiff's evidence (or proposed evidence) must show:
    (i)   plaintiff has extremely strong prima facie case, on the merits, against defendant;
    (ii) very serious potential damage to plaintiff from defendant's activity;
    (iii) clear evidence defendant has incriminating evidence and a real possibility he will destroy it before an inter partes application for discovery by plaintiff.

5   Plaintiff's evidence (and his counsel's submissions) should also give full and frank disclosure, ie should set out in full detail any points which defendant might make if he were present. Plaintiff's affidavit should state or exhibit any evidence plaintiff possesses which might assist defendant. If in doubt, disclose it. It is plaintiff's lawyers' responsibility to ensure this is done and it is imperative they consider it with the utmost care if they wish to avoid having to pay substantial damages later.

6   In general, the order will not be granted, outside the area of intellectual property law, if there is a danger that the evidence would breach defendant's privilege against self-incrimination on a possible charge of conspiracy to defraud: this will rule out most cases outside intellectual property law. There may be an exception to this if the articles in relation to which the order is sought all belong to the plaintiff. See **4.3.7**.

7   Plaintiff must give various undertakings to the court: to issue the writ, serve it, have the affidavit(s) sworn and served on defendant, all as soon as practicable; and to pay the costs incurred by defendant or third parties if the court decides it is just that the plaintiff should pay them.

8   Plaintiff's solicitors must undertake: to return originals of all documents seized within two working days of removal; to return articles whose ownership is disputed, within two working days; to retain all other articles obtained as a result of the search.

9   Execution: generally, the order will provide that the plaintiff must have an independent solicitor who explains the effect of the order to the defendant in plain English and supervises execution, by the plaintiff's own solicitors. The order will provide that execution

should be between hours of 9.30am to 5.30pm on a week day. (Alternatively, it may provide for this to be done by the plaintiff's own solicitors, unsupervised.)

10 Execution cannot occur until defendant consents. Defendant need not consent until he has obtained legal advice. Defendant is then in contempt if he refuses entry (see **10.2** below).

11 Execution should be by the supervising solicitors with plaintiff's solicitor, generally not plaintiff. If execution at a private house and any danger a woman will be there alone, party executing should include a woman. Solicitor should make detailed list of items removed. See **7.3ff** for full list of points on manner of execution. It is vital to comply with these: £34,000 damages in *Universal Thermosensors Ltd v Hibben* [1992] 1 WLR 840, just for the manner of execution by plaintiff's solicitors.

10.2 Defendant subject to an Anton Piller order: summary of what to do

1 Plaintiff's solicitors cannot enter without the consent of defendant. Before consenting, defendant has a right to receive legal advice, as long as he starts obtaining the legal advice at once. So defendant should decline to let plaintiff in until he has received legal advice, and should start seeking it at once.

2 DEFENDANT MUST NOT REMOVE, DESTROY OR HIDE ANY EVIDENCE OR DOCUMENTS WHICH MIGHT BE SUBJECT OF THE ORDER, AT ANY STAGE BEFORE LETTING PLAINTIFF'S SOLICITORS IN. If he does he is in contempt of court and faces very serious penalties, ie prison or heavy fines.

3 Defendant has a reasonable period to get the legal advice. The order should have been served between 9.30am and 5.30pm on a working day unless exceptional circumstances. If it is served in those hours, a defendant in a city should be able to get competent legal advice within two hours or so. In country areas it will take longer and defendant need not open his doors until he has had a reasonable time to get it. See Chapter 7.

4 Once solicitor arrives, he will advise defendant that he has essentially two options (see **8.3**).

   (a) Allow plaintiff in to carry out search. If this is chosen, see further below.

(b) Make immediate application to court (eg that day if at all possible) to set aside or vary the order by challenging the plaintiff's evidence in his affidavit. The defendant can offer plaintiff's solicitors a visit to the premises (with both sets of solicitors) in the meantime, and defendant must undertake not to damage remove etc any of the matters covered by the order. Defendant could offer to give it into custody of his solicitor in the meantime, pending inter partes hearing where plaintiff seeks order for discovery of the material, a few days later.

If defendant takes option (b), then

(i) his solicitor should immediately instruct counsel who has experience of Anton Piller orders;

(ii) DEFENDANT IS TECHNICALLY IN CONTEMPT OF COURT, although there is a reasonable chance that as long as the defendant does not damage, remove, etc any evidence while he makes his application to the court, no order will be made on the contempt. See **8.3** and exercise great care.

5   Grounds which might support an immediate application to set aside or vary the order:

(i) plaintiff has not made full and frank disclosure of arguments which could properly be made for defendant (see summary re Marevas: paragraph 5 of **9.2**);

(ii) plaintiff has failed to show an extremely strong prima facie case, or that there is very serious potential damage to plaintiff if injunction not granted, or clear evidence that defendant has incriminating evidence or documents, or a real possibility that without injunction defendant will destroy them;

(iii) defendant very respectable and will not destroy evidence; if defendant is a well-established company then Anton Piller may well be inappropriate (see **5.17**);

(iv) privilege against self-incrimination applies. If the cause of action does not concern intellectual property, and there is any chance plaintiff's case suggests a criminal charge of conspiracy to defraud (ie if more than one person is involved), then there is a good argument the order should never have been granted, unless it relates only to the plaintiff's own property. See **4.3**.

6   If defendant chooses option (a), his solicitor should still read through the order carefully to make sure that the plaintiff is proposing to execute it properly. Defendant's solicitor should consider the following.

(i) Does the order provide for a supervising solicitor? If so, check there is one.

(ii) If it is to be executed at a private house, is there a woman present?

(iii) Does it provide for a detailed list of items to be removed to be made? If so, make sure the list is made.

(iv) If it prevents defendants telling others of the existence of the order, this should be for a period of much less than a week.

(v) If it relates to business premises, it should provide that execution may take place only in the presence of a responsible officer of the company or trader. Is one present?

(vi) It should provide that those who execute the order should not include anyone who might gain commercial advantage over defendant. Does it? Have plaintiff's solicitors complied with this?

(vii) Order will limit the number of people who can execute it. Check this is complied with.

(viii)
Defendant should not agree to extend the scope of the order.

(ix) Make sure plaintiff's solicitors take only items which are actually covered by the terms of the order.

See **7.3**ff.

10.3 SYNOPSIS

This synopsis should be read in conjunction with the draft Anton Piller order in precedent 11.2A. It may assist where an emergency application has to be made. But it must be emphasised that Anton Piller orders should not be applied for or executed without the most careful preparation and consideration of obligations on the plaintiff, otherwise the plaintiff or his solicitors may find themselves paying tens of thousands of pounds in compensation: see *Universal Thermosensors Ltd v Hibben.*[1]

1 [1992] 1 WLR 840; **1.9** and **7.3**.

10.4 The Anton Piller order allows search of the defendant's premises and seizure of items or documents found there which might form evidence in the plaintiff's action or proposed action against the defendant. The search is made by solicitors. Generally the court will order that it be served and executed by a supervising solicitor, from a firm other than the plaintiff's solicitors' firm. The supervising solicitor should have experience of the workings of Anton Piller orders.[1] If evidence of a type specified in the order is found, then the plaintiff's solicitors may remove it for limited periods for copying or photographing. The rationale of the order is that, if it is not granted, the defendant may destroy the evidence or documents before the trial, and thus evade justice. In the case which gave its name to Anton Piller orders, Lord Denning MR said:[2]

> 'It seems to me that such an order can be made by a judge ex parte but it should only be made where it is essential that the plaintiff should have inspection so that justice can be done between the parties; and when, if the defendant were forewarned, there is a grave danger that vital evidence will be destroyed, that papers will be burnt or lost or hidden or taken beyond the jurisdiction and so the ends of justice be defeated; and when inspection would do no real harm to the defendant or his case.'

1   *Universal Thermosensors Ltd v Hibben* [1992] 1 WLR 840.
2   *Anton Piller KG v Manufacturing Processes Ltd* [1976] Ch 55 at 60, CA.

10.5   It is said that an Anton Piller order differs from a search warrant, in that the plaintiff may enter only with the permission of the defendant.[1] But in reality this may make little difference, as the defendant risks committal to prison for contempt of court if he refuses entry.[2] At best, he is permitted to postpone entry while he seeks legal advice, as long as he begins to seek it at once. But the legal advice is likely to be that he must permit entry. The alternative is to apply immediately to the court to discharge the order, and, meanwhile, to ensure that no evidence is destroyed. This alternative is risky. If evidence is destroyed in the meantime then the defendant faces very severe penalties.[3]

1   See per Waller LJ in *Ex p Island Records Ltd* [1978] Ch 122 at 145, and per Lord Denning MR in the *Anton Piller KG* case [1976] Ch 55 at 60.
2   See *Bhimji v Chatwani* [1991] 1 WLR 989; **8.3**.
3   See **8.3**; *Bhimji* (above), and *WEA Records Ltd v Visions Channel 4 Ltd* [1983] 1 WLR 721 at 726.

10.6   There are three principal areas of law in which the order is used:

> 'They are, first, the infringement of rights in intellectual property, such as trade marks, copyright and trade secrets;

secondly, anti-competition cases brought by ex-employers against ex-employees; and thirdly, matrimonial proceedings where it is thought that a spouse has failed to make truthful disclosure of his or her assets. There is a notable difference between the practice in the first two classes and the third. In the first two there is likely to be a pre-emptive strike, the application being made upon the issue of the writ and before it is served. In the third class [an Anton Piller] order is likely to be made as a last resort, when other measures are thought not to have resulted in truthful disclosure.'[1]

Anton Piller orders may, however, be made in other classes of case where the evidential requirements (see **10.8**) are satisfied. They may be granted in the High Court. County courts, apart from the Patents County Court, may not grant them, but cases may be transferred from the county court to the High Court purely for the purpose of applying for an Anton Piller order.[2]

1 See 'Anton Piller Orders – A Consultation Paper' (the Lord Chancellor's Department, November 1992) at para 1.9.
2 **5.6**.

10.7 The application is made, ex parte, to the judge in chambers in the Queen's Bench Division and in camera in the Chancery Division. In the Queen's Bench Division, the applicant should prepare an affidavit or affidavits, draft statement of claim, writ and two copies of a draft order; in the Chancery Division he should prepare three copies of all these documents.[1] Skeleton arguments are helpful in complex cases. The papers should be lodged with the court the day before unless the matter is of great urgency, in which case the plaintiff's counsel and solicitor may be able to see a judge more quickly, or even instantly in very urgent cases. There is always a duty judge available to hear urgent applications. See generally Chapter 5.

1 See Chapter 5.

10.8 The plaintiff's evidence must persuade the court that three essential pre-conditions for the grant of the order are satisfied:

'First, there must be an extremely strong prima facie case. Secondly, the damage, potential or actual, must be very serious for the applicant. Thirdly, there must be clear evidence that the defendants have in their possession incriminating documents or things, and that there is a real possibility that they may destroy such material before any application inter partes can be made."[1]

The court is likely to scrutinise the plaintiff's evidence carefully to see precisely what, if true, it shows. The order will not be granted purely on the basis of suspicion unsupported by hard evidence.[2]

1　*Anton Piller KG v Manufacturing Processes Ltd* [1976] Ch 55 per Ormrod LJ at 62.
2　See **5.15** and *Lock International plc v Beswick* [1989] 1 WLR 1268.

10.9　Although Anton Piller orders are plainly appropriate in cases of blatant fraud, the clear trend in the law is to emphasise that exceptional circumstances are required to justify making them.[1] The reason is that they are exceptionally intrusive on the privacy of the defendant, and may easily ruin his or its business, at a stage when the plaintiff's case has in no sense been proved.

1　See the judgments of Scott J in *Columbia Picture Industries Inc v Robinson* [1987] Ch 38; Hoffmann J in *Lock International plc v Beswick* [1989] 1 WLR 1268 and Sir Donald Nicholls V-C in *Universal Thermosensors Ltd v Hibben* [1992] 1 WLR 840. See also **1.9**, **3.2**, and **3.8**.

10.10　The court will not grant Anton Piller orders where, outside the area of intellectual property law, the evidence to be used against the potential defendant might also give rise to a criminal charge of conspiracy against him, unless it relates only to the plaintiff's own property: *Tate Access Floors Inc v Boswell*.[1] This is due to the development of the doctrine against self-incrimination. Although judges of the highest eminence have criticised this application of the doctrine,[2] it can be changed only by Parliament, which so far has not acted.

1　[1991] Ch 512, per Sir Nicolas Browne-Wilkinson V-C at 529–530, and **4.3**.
2　See eg the judgment of Lord Templeman in *Istel Ltd v Tully* [1992] 3 WLR 344 at 351.

10.11　Before applying for an Anton Piller order, the plaintiff should make reasonable enquiries as to what defences the defendant might raise if he or it were present at the ex parte application. The plaintiff should then make full and frank disclosure to the court of any fact or argument which the defendant might use, if he were present, to oppose the grant of the order. It is for the court and not the plaintiff to decide whether potential arguments for the defendant are relevant, and the plaintiff's affidavit should err on the side of excessive disclosure.[1] If the plaintiff does not give full and frank disclosure, the order may be discharged. This in itself may not cause the plaintiff much damage, as the order is likely to have been executed already. What may be more serious is the possibility of the plaintiff or his solicitors having to pay large sums in compensation, including possibly exemplary damages.[2]

1   *Columbia Picture Industries Inc v Robinson* [1987] Ch 38.
2   Ibid, and see the *Universal Thermosensors case* [1992] 1 WLR 840; **7.3**.

10.12   Many Anton Piller orders also include Mareva injunctive relief.[1]

1   *Johnson v L & A Philatelics Ltd* [1981] FSR 286 and *AJ Bekhor & Co Ltd v Bilton* [1981] QB 923 at 955 where Stephenson LJ commented that such a course was 'to pile Piller on Mareva'.

10.13   The plaintiff will be required to give a number of undertakings before an Anton Piller order is granted.

1   Where, as is normal, the application is made before the action has been commenced: to issue a writ of summons (see the first undertaking in precedent 11.2A and **6.3**).

2   To make and file any draft affidavits read to the court or an affidavit verifying what has been alleged by counsel for the plaintiff (see the second undertaking in the precedent and **6.3**).

3   To serve upon the defendant copies of (a) any affidavits, and (b) draft affidavits when sworn read to the court together with (in the Chancery Division) notice of motion for the judge. (See the third undertaking in the precedent and **6.3**.) In the Chancery Division the injunction will be granted until the return day, which may be no more than a week later. Unless the defendant makes an immediate application to discharge the order on receipt of it, the order will have been executed by the time of the return day.

4   To serve on the defendant a copy of the report of the supervising solicitor (see **6.12**) as soon as the plaintiff receives it (the fourth undertaking in the precedent).

5   (In the Chancery Division) to bring the motion before the court on the return day and, on that occasion, to place the supervising solicitor's report before the court (see the fifth undertaking in the precedent, and **6.12**).

6   The undertakings in damages in respect of the defendant and third parties (the sixth and seventh undertakings in the precedent, and

see **6.4**ff). If it suspects that the plaintiff could not satisfy the undertaking, the court may require security, for example in the form of a bond or bank guarantee (**6.5**).

10.14   The solicitors for the plaintiff will be required to give the following undertakings (**6.13**).

1   To return the originals of all documents obtained as a result of the order within two working days (first solicitor's undertaking in the precedent). This should give time to copy the documents, but avoids excessive damage to the defendant's business through loss of all his working papers for an excessive period. See the *Universal Thermosensors case.*[1]

2   Where ownership of any article obtained as a result of the order is disputed, to deliver the article to solicitors for the defendant within two working days of receipt of a written undertaking, from such solicitors, to retain the article in safe custody (second solicitor's undertaking).

3   To retain in their safe custody all other items recovered as a result of the order, until further order. It is more appropriate for solicitors to preserve evidence recovered; being officers of the court, they are directly answerable to the court. In *Columbia Picture Industries Inc v Robinson*[2] Scott J laid down guidelines to be followed with regard to material seized. (These are set out in Appendix I, and see **7.5**.)

1   [1992] 1 WLR 840.
2   [1987] Ch 38.

10.15   The order

(a) The injunction (paragraph 1 after 'it is ordered' in the precedent)

10.15.1   This orders the defendant or a person 'appearing to be in control of the premises' to permit the plaintiff's solicitors entry. For who counts as a person 'appearing to be in control of the premises' see *Bhimji v Chatwani.*[1] The plaintiffs may not enter if permission is refused: instead, they must seek to commit the defendant for contempt of court. Service of the order should take place between 9.30am and 5.30pm on a weekday unless is there is exceptional urgency. Persons who may gain commercial advantage over the defendant should not enter the premises: for instance the plaintiff himself or any of his employees.

1   [1991] 1 WLR 989; and **7.3.6** note 1.

(b) The proviso (paragraph 2 of the order)

10.15.2   The proviso regulates the manner of execution. Generally, the order will provide that it must be served by the supervising solicitor (above). The supervising solicitor, when serving the order, must explain its meaning to the defendant or his agent in plain English. The supervising solicitor must compile a report on the execution, to be sent to the defendant and presented to the court on the return day.

(c) Disclosure (paragraph 3 of the order)

10.15.3   It is now standard to include a provision requiring defendants to give details of their suppliers in Anton Piller orders, at least where the case relates to infringement of intellectual property rights and the defendant has received infringing merchandise from a third party supplier.[1]

1   See the Chancery Division's precedent issued with judicial approval, 'The Supreme Court Practice News', April 1992.

(d) Order for delivery up (paragraph 4 of the order)

10.15.4   In a case involving infringement of intellectual property rights such as trademarks, this enables the plaintiff to take all infringing copies and any items relating to the making of infringing copies (eg invoices, video machines, etc) (see **4.6**).

(e) Order relating to material stored on computers (paragraph 5 of the order)

10.15.5   This provision is self-explanatory.

(f) Order preventing defendant communicating with third parties (paragraph 6(1) of the order)

10.15.6   In cases involving intellectual property or unlawful competition with an ex-employer, the plaintiff may wish to pursue third parties in addition, and possibly to apply for Anton Piller orders against them too. This provision prevents the defendant warning such third parties before the plaintiff has had time to act. But the period for which this part of the order lasts should never be for as long as a whole week: see per Sir Donald Nicholls V-C in the *Universal Thermosensors case*.[1]

1   [1992] 1 WLR 840 at 860G.

(g) Further injunction (paragraph 6(2) of the order)

10.15.7   Here may be inserted further injunctions upon the defendant, for instance, a Mareva injunction (but see precedent 11.3 for this) or an interlocutory injunction to prevent unlawful competition.

10.16   The defendant will be given liberty to apply to discharge the order after giving notice to the plaintiff or the plaintiff's solicitors. Once the order has been executed, the court may take the view that it will be an empty gesture to discharge the order, and so refuse to do so.[1] On the other hand, it is arguable that the mere existence of an undischarged Anton Piller order may be a blot on the reputation of the defendant. On that basis, if the order was wrongly obtained it should be discharged even after execution.

1   See per Scott J in the *Columbia Picture Industries* case [1987] Ch 38 at 87; and **8.4**.

CHAPTER 11

Precedents

11.0 The precedents are cross-referenced to the synopsis. The drafting of Mareva injunctions and Anton Piller orders is a technical task of considerable importance. For that reason, the courts have taken the unusual step of issuing draft orders, with judicial approval. The precedents which follow are adapted from the drafts issued by the Commercial Court[1] and the Chancery Division.[2]

1 'Guide to Commercial Court Practice', published at note 72/A1 in the *Supreme Court Practice 1993*.
2 In 'The Supreme Court Practice Practice News,' April 1992.

11.1A PRECEDENT OF A MAREVA INJUNCTION (QUEEN'S BENCH DIVISION)

IN THE QUEEN'S BENCH DIVISION 199 No
THE HON MR(S) JUSTICE
IN CHAMBERS

IN THE MATTER OF AN INTENDED ACTION

BETWEEN:

Intended Plaintiffs

and

Intended Defendants

UPON hearing Counsel for the Intended Plaintiffs ('the Plaintiffs') and upon reading the [draft] Affidavit(s) of
sworn [to be sworn] herein on

AND upon the Plaintiffs by their Counsel undertaking:

[9.10.1]   (1) Forthwith to issue a Writ of Summons in the form of the draft produced to the Court and initialled by the Judge and to serve the same on the Intended Defendants ('the Defendants') as soon as is reasonably practicable thereafter.

[9.10.2]   (2) Forthwith to swear and file an Affidavit(s) [in the form of the draft initialled by the Judge] [covering the additional information given to the Court].

[9.10.3]   (3) Forthwith to give notice of the terms of this Order to the Defendants by [means] and of the telephone number of a representative of the Plaintiff's solicitors to whom any notice of an application to set aside or vary this Order may be given out of office hours.

[9.10.4]   (4) [Forthwith] to serve copies of this Order and the said affidavit(s) and the copiable exhibits thereto on the Defendants [as soon as is reasonably practicable].

[9.10.5]   (5) To abide by any order which the Court may make as to damages in case this Court is hereafter of the opinion that the Defendants or any other person served with notice of this Order have suffered any by reason of this Order which the Plaintiffs ought to pay.

[9.10.6]   (6) (a) To indemnify any third party in respect of any costs, expenses, fees or liabilities reasonably incurred, from the time when this Order first adversely affected such third party, as a result of the making of this Order;

   (b) to pay the reasonable costs and expenses incurred by any third party to whom notice of the terms of this Order has been given, in ascertaining whether any assets to which this Order applies are within their control and in complying with this Order and to indemnify any such person against all liabilities which may flow from such compliance.

   (7) To serve a copy of this Order upon any third party to whom the Plaintiffs have given notice of this Order.

[9.10.7]   (8) To notify the Defendants and any third party to whom notice of this Order is given by the Plaintiffs or their solicitors of their right to apply to the Court on notice to carry or set aside this Order in so far as it may affect them.

IT IS ORDERED THAT:

1   The Defendants be restrained and an injunction be [9.11.2(a)] granted restraining them until trial or further order in the case of the [   ] Defendant whether by its directors or by its servants or agents or any of them or otherwise howsoever and as regards the [   ] Defendant whether by himself, his servants or agents or otherwise howsoever, from removing from the jurisdiction, disposing of, mortgaging, assigning, charging or otherwise dealing with any of its/their [respective or joint] assets within the jurisdiction, including, but not limited to:
[here set out any particular accounts or other assets which it is intended should be specifically covered by the injunction, eg:]

    (i)   the freehold property known as [name] or (if the [9.11.2(b)] same has been sold) the net proceeds of sale thereof after discharge of any subsisting mortgage or charge

    (ii) the property and assets of the business known as [name] carried on by the Defendant(s) from premises at [address] or (if and in so far as the same have been sold) the proceeds of sale thereof

    (iii) any moneys in [any] account(s) [numbered] at [bank's name] at [bank's address] and without prejudice to the foregoing pledging charging or otherwise parting with title to or possession of such assets

    save in so far as the unencumbered value of those [9.12.1(a)] assets exceeds £....

2   Notwithstanding paragraph 1 hereof, the Defendants shall be entitled to draw and expend from a bank account or other source the identity of which shall first be notified by them to the Plaintiffs' solicitors:

    (a) A sum not exceeding £.... per week for ordinary [9.12.1(b)] living expenses;

    [(b) A sum not exceeding £.... per week for ordinary [9.12.1(c)] business expenses]

    [(c) A sum not exceeding £.... per week for reasonable legal expenses]

(d) Such further sum or sums, if any, as the Plaintiffs' solicitors may from time to time agree in writing.

Provided, however, that nothing in sub-paragraph (a), (b), (c) or (d) of this paragraph shall impose any obligation on any third party to enquire into the purpose or purposes for which any sum or sums drawn by the Defendants thereunder are in fact required or used.

[9.12.1(d)] 3 Nothing in this Order shall prevent any bank from exercising any rights of set-off it may have in respect of facilities afforded by such bank prior to the date of this Order.

[9.13.1] 4 The Defendant(s) [and each of them] do forthwith disclose the full value of his/her/its/their [respective and joint] assets within the jurisdiction of this Court identifying with full particularity the nature of all such assets and their whereabouts and whether the same be held of his/her/its/their own names or by nominees or otherwise on his/her/its/their behalf and the sums standing in such accounts such disclosures to be verified by affidavit(s) to be made by the Defendant(s) [and in the case of the [   ] Defendants by its/their proper officer] and served on the Plaintiffs' solicitors within [insert] days of service of this Order or notice thereof being given.

[9.14.1] 5 The Defendant(s) [and each of them] do forthwith upon the service of this Order deliver up or cause to be delivered up into the custody of the Plaintiffs' solicitors the items specified in the Schedule hereto.

[6 The Plaintiffs have leave to issue and serve the Writ on the Defendants at [address] or elsewhere in [country]. The time for acknowledgment of service shall be .... days.]

7 Liberty to the Defendants or any other person affected by this Order to apply, on [48 hours'] notice to the Plaintiffs' solicitors, to set aside or vary this Order.

8 Costs reserved.

DATED the   day of   199

If you, the within-named [name(s)] disobey paragraph 1 of this order, or if you neglect to obey paragraphs 4 and 5 of this order by the time stated, you may be held to be in contempt of Court and liable to imprisonment.

[*OR, in the case of a body corporate:*
If you, the within-named X Ltd, disobey paragraph 1 of this order, or if you neglect to obey paragraphs 4 and 5 of this order by the time stated, you may be held in contempt of court and liable to sequestration of your assets.

OR, in the case of a body corporate where the plaintiff may wish to take enforcement proceedings against a director or other officer of the company:

If X Ltd disobey paragraph 1 of this order, or if X Ltd neglects to obey paragraphs 4 and 5 of this order by the time stated, you, Uriah Heep (a director or officer of the said X Ltd) may be held in contempt of Court and liable to imprisonment.][1]

THE SCHEDULE

The Specified Items

1 See RSC Ord 45, r 7(4) and note 45/7/6 at page 752 of volume 1 of the *Supreme Court Practice 1993*.

11.1B   PRECEDENT OF A MAREVA INJUNCTION GRANTED
IN A CASE CONCERNING A DISPUTE OVER
DISSOLUTION OF A PARTNERSHIP
(CHANCERY DIVISION)

IN THE HIGH COURT OF JUSTICE   199   Ch No
CHANCERY DIVISION
MR JUSTICE

the   day of   199

IN THE MATTER OF AN INTENDED ACTION

BETWEEN:

Intended Plaintiff

and

(1)
(2)
(3)   Intended Defendants

UPON MOTION made by the Counsel for the Intended Plaintiff
('the Plaintiff')

AND UPON READING the draft Affidavits of
and

AND the Plaintiff by his Counsel undertaking

[9.10.1]   (1) Forthwith to issue a Writ of Summons in the form of
the draft produced to the Court and initialled by the
Judge and to serve the same on the Intended
Defendants ('the Defendants') as soon as is reasonably practicable thereafter.

[9.10.2]   (2) Forthwith to swear and file an Affidavit(s) [in the form
of the draft initialled by the Judge] [covering the
additional information given to the Court].

[9.10.3]   (3) Forthwith to give notice of the terms of this Order to
the Defendants by [means] and of the telephone
number of a representative of the Plaintiff's solicitors
to whom any notice of an application to set aside or
vary this Order may be given out of office hours.

(4) [Forthwith] to serve copies of this Order and the said affidavit(s) and the copiable exhibits thereto on the Defendants [as soon as is reasonably practicable].

(5) To abide by any order which the Court may make as to [9.10.5] damages in case this Court is hereafter of the opinion that the Defendants or any other person served with notice of this Order have suffered any by reason of this Order which the Plaintiffs ought to pay.

(6) (a) To indemnify any third party in respect of any [9.10.6] costs, expenses, fees or liabilities reasonably incurred, from the time when this Order first adversely affected such third party, as a result of the making of this Order;

    (b) to pay the reasonable costs and expenses incurred by any third party to whom notice of the terms of this Order has been given, in ascertaining whether any assets to which this Order applies are within their control and in complying with this Order and to indemnify any such person against all liabilities which may flow from such compliance.

(7) To serve a copy of this Order upon any third party to whom the Plaintiffs have given notice of this Order.

(8) To notify the Defendants and any third party to whom [9.10.7] notice of this Order is given by the Plaintiffs or their solicitors of their right to apply to the Court on notice to carry or set aside this Order in so far as it may affect them.

IT IS ORDERED THAT:

1   The first and second Defendants and each of them be restrained until after [date] or until further Order in the meantime from doing (whether by themselves or by their servants or agents or any of them or otherwise howsoever) the following acts or any of them that is to say disposing or dealing with any assets within the possession or control of the first or second Defendants which are either former assets of the partnership ('the partnership') formerly subsisting between the Plaintiff and the first and second Defendants or consist of proceeds of sale of any such assets of the partnership or consist of proceeds or sums thereby realised by any

charge on or other dealing with any assets of the partnership or which represent any such proceeds of sale of those assets.

2 Notwithstanding paragraph 1 hereof, the Defendants shall be entitled to draw and expend from a bank account or other source the identity of which shall first be notified by them to the Plaintiffs' solicitors:

[9.12.1(b)]   (a) A sum not exceeding £.... per week for ordinary living expenses;

[9.12.1(c)]   [(b) A sum not exceeding £.... per week for ordinary business expenses]

[(c) A sum not exceeding £.... per week for reasonable legal expenses]

(d) Such further sum or sums, if any, as the Plaintiffs' solicitors may from time to time agree in writing.

Provided, however, that nothing in sub-paragraph (a), (b), (c) or (d) of this paragraph shall impose any obligation on any third party to enquire into the purpose or purposes for which any sum or sums drawn by the Defendants thereunder are in fact required or used.

[9.12.1(d)] 3 Nothing in this Order shall prevent any Bank from exercising any rights of set-off it may have in respect of facilities afforded by such Bank prior to the date of this Order.

[9.13.1]   4 The Defendant(s) [and each of them] do forthwith disclose the full value of his/her/its/their [respective and joint] assets within the jurisdiction of this Court identifying with full particularity the nature of all such assets and their whereabouts and whether the same be held of his/her/its/their own names or by nominees or otherwise on his/her/its/their behalf and the sums standing in such accounts such disclosures to be verified by affidavit(s) to be made by the Defendant(s) [and in the case of the [   ] Defendants by its/their proper officer] and served on the Plaintiffs' solicitors within [insert] days of service of this Order or notice thereof being given.

[9.14.1]   5 The Defendant(s) [and each of them] do forthwith upon the service of this Order deliver up or cause to be delivered up into the custody of the Plaintiffs' solicitors the items specified in the Schedule hereto.

[6   The Plaintiffs have leave to issue and serve the Writ on the Defendants at [address] or elsewhere in [country]. The time for acknowledgment of service shall be .... days.]

7   The Plaintiff is at liberty to serve Short Notice for [date].

8   The Defendant(s) is/are to be at liberty to apply to discharge this Order upon giving to the Plaintiff's solicitors [24/48] hours' notice of their intention to do so.

If you, the within-named [name(s)] disobey paragraph 1 of this order, or if you neglect to obey paragraphs 4 and 5 of this order by the time stated, you may be held to be in contempt of Court and liable to imprisonment.

THE SCHEDULE

The Specified Items

11.2A   PRECEDENT OF AN ANTON PILLER ORDER
(CHANCERY DIVISION)

IN THE HIGH COURT OF JUSTICE   199   Ch No
CHANCERY DIVISION
MR JUSTICE

IN THE MATTER OF AN INTENDED ACTION

BETWEEN:

                                          Intended Plaintiffs
                       and
                                          Intended Defendants

UPON MOTION made by Counsel for the Intended Plaintiff(s)
('the Plaintiff(s)')

AND UPON READING the documents recorded on the Court file as
having been read

AND the Plaintiff(s) by Counsel undertaking

[10.13.1]   (1) forthwith to issue a writ of summons claiming relief
                 similar to or connected with that hereafter granted

[10.13.2]   (2) to make and file an affidavit (verifying what was
                 alleged by Counsel) [OR] (in the terms of the draft
                 Affidavit of [name])

[10.13.4]   (3) as soon as practicable to serve upon the Intended
                 Defendant(s) ('the Defendant(s)') a copy of such
                 affidavit and the exhibits capable of being copied and a
                 Notice of Motion for [Date] 199

            (4) to serve on the Defendant(s) forthwith after the
                 Plaintiff's solicitors receive the same a copy of a
                 written report on the carrying out of this Order which
                 shall be prepared by the supervising solicitor
                 mentioned below

[10.13.5]   (5) to bring such motion before the Court on the said date
                 and on that occasion to place before the Court the
                 written report of the supervising solicitor

(6) to obey any Order this Court may make as to damages   [10.13.6]
     if it shall consider that the Defendant(s) has/have
     sustained any damages because of this Order which the
     Plaintiff(s) ought to pay

(7) to obey any Order this Court may make as to damages
     if it shall consider that any innocent parties other than
     the Defendant(s) shall have sustained any damages by
     result of this Order which the Plaintiff(s) ought to pay.

AND the solicitors for the Plaintiff(s) by counsel for the
Plaintiff(s) (being their Counsel for this purpose) undertaking:

(1) to return the originals of all documents obtained as a   [10.14.1]
     result of this Order within two working days of their
     removal

(2) where ownership of any article obtained as a result of   [10.14.2]
     this Order is disputed to deliver up any such article to
     the custody of solicitors acting on behalf of the
     Defendant(s) within two working days of receipt of a
     written undertaking by such solicitors to retain the
     same in safe custody and to produce the same if
     required by the Court

(3) save as mentioned above to retain in their safe custody   [10.14.3]
     until further Order all documents and articles obtained
     as a result of this Order

IT IS ORDERED

1   THAT the Defendant(s) (and each of them), either   [10.15.1]
     himself/herself/itself/themselves or by a responsible
     officer or person appearing to be in control of the
     premises in question, do permit the person serving this
     Order upon him/her/it/them and such other persons
     duly authorised by the plaintiff (such other persons not
     to exceed [two] in number) [and not to include any
     person who might obtain commercial advantage over
     the Defendant(s) by carrying out this Order] to enter
     forthwith on any weekday between 9.30am and 5.30pm
     the premises mentioned in the schedule to this Order
     (herein referred to as 'the premises') and any vehicles
     on the premises, to the extent that such premises or

vehicles are in the occupation, possession or control of the Defendant(s), for the purpose of looking for, inspecting, photographing and delivering into the custody of the Plaintiff's solicitors all documents and articles which are specified in the schedule to this Order (referred to herein as the 'specified items') or which appear to the supervising solicitor to be specified items.

2　PROVIDED ALWAYS:

[10.15.2]　(1)　This order shall be served, and paragraph 1 hereof carried out, only by [name] of [firm] or failing [him] [her] by [name] or some other solicitor approved for the purpose by the court (the solicitor serving the Order being referred to in this Order as 'the supervising solicitor').

(2)　Before any persons enter the premises pursuant to this Order the supervising solicitor shall offer to explain to the person served with the Order its meaning and effect in everyday language, and shall also advise such person of his/her right to obtain legal advice before permitting entry provided such advice is obtained at once.

(3)　Save to the extent that it is impracticable, no documents or articles shall be removed from the premises until after a list thereof has been prepared and a copy of the list has been supplied to the person served with this Order, and he or she has been given a reasonable opportunity to check the same.

(4)　Save to the extent that this is impracticable, the premises shall not be searched, or any document or articles removed, except in the presence of an officer of the Defendant(s), or a person being, or appearing to be, a suitably responsible employee of the Defendant(s).

3　THAT the Defendant(s) do disclose forthwith to the Plaintiff's solicitor:

[10.15.3]　(1)　the whereabouts of all specified items which are in his/her/its/their possession custody or power; and

(2)　to the best of the Defendant(s)'(s) knowledge and belief

(a) the names and addresses of all persons to whom he/she/it/they has/have supplied or offered to supply any specified items; and

(b) the names and addresses of all persons to whom he/she/it they has/have supplied or offered to supply any specified items; and

(c) full details of the dates and quantities of each offer to supply and supply referred to in (a) and (b) above.

4   THAT the Defendant(s) do forthwith deliver to the Plaintiff(s)'(s) solicitor all specified items in his/her/its/ their possession custody or power.   [10.15.4]

5   THAT if any such item exists in computer readable form only the Defendant(s) shall cause it forthwith to be printed out and shall deliver the print out to the Plaintiff's Solicitors or (failing a printer) shall cause it forthwith to be displayed to the Plaintiff's solicitors in a readable form.   [10.15.5]

6   IT IS FURTHER ORDERED:

(1) That the Defendant(s) (and each of them) be restrained until after [date] 199   or further Order in the meantime from (in the case of the (first) Defendant whether itself or by its officers or employees or agents or otherwise howsoever and as regards the (second) Defendant whether himself/herself or by his/her employees or agents or otherwise howsoever) directly or indirectly informing any person company or firm of the existence of these proceedings or of the provisions of this Order or otherwise warning any person company or firm that proceedings may be brought against him/her/it/them by the Plaintiff(s) otherwise than for the purpose of such Defendant obtaining legal advice from his/her/its/their lawyers.   [10.15.6]

(2) That the Defendant(s) (and each of them) be likewise restrained until after [DATE] 199   or further Order in the meantime from doing the following acts or any of them: [10.15.7]

(a)

(b)

[10.16]   7   THE Defendant(s) is/are to be at liberty to apply to discharge or vary this Order upon giving to the solicitors for the Plaintiff [   ] hours' notice of his/her/its/their intention to do so.

THE SCHEDULE

The Premises

The Specified Items

DATED THIS   day of [month] 199

If you, the within-named [name(s)] neglect to obey this order, you may be held to be in contempt of Court and liable to imprisonment.

[OR, in the case of a body corporate:
If you, the within-named X Ltd, neglgect to obey this order, you may be held in contempt of court and liable to sequestration of your assets.

OR, in the case of a body corporate where the plaintiff may wish to take enforcement proceedings against a director or other officer of the company:

If X Ltd neglects to obey this order, you, Uriah Heep (a director or officer of the said X Ltd) may be held in contempt of Court and liable to imprisonment.]

11.2B PRECEDENT OF AN ANTON PILLER ORDER
(QUEEN'S BENCH DIVISION)

IN THE QUEEN'S BENCH DIVISION   199   No
THE HON MR(S) JUSTICE IN CHAMBERS

IN THE MATTER OF AN INTENDED ACTION

BETWEEN:

Intended Plaintiffs

and

Intended Defendants

UPON hearing Counsel for the Intended Plaintiffs ('the Plaintiffs') and upon reading the [draft] Affidavit(s) of [name(s)] sworn [to be sworn] herein on [date]

AND upon the Plaintiffs by their Counsel undertaking

(1) forthwith to issue a writ of summons claiming relief similar to or connected with that hereafter granted   [10.13.1]

(2) to make and file an affidavit (verifying what was alleged by Counsel) [OR] (in the terms of the draft Affidavit of [name])   [10.13.2]

(3) as soon as practicable to serve upon the Intended Defendant(s) ('the Defendants') a copy of such affidavit and the exhibits capable of being copied

(4) to serve on the Defendant(s) forthwith after the Plaintiff's solicitors receive the same a copy of a written report on the carrying out of this Order which shall be prepared by the supervising solicitor mentioned below   [10.13.4]

(5) to place before the Court the written report of the supervising solicitor at any application by the Defendants to discharge this order   [10.13.5]

(6) to obey any Order this Court may make as to damages if it shall consider that the Defendant(s) has/have sustained any damages because of this Order which the Plaintiff(s) ought to pay   [10.13.6]

AND the solicitors for the Plaintiff(s) by counsel for the Plaintiff(s) (being their counsel for this purpose) undertaking:

[10.14.1]   (1)   to return the originals of all documents obtained as a result of this Order within two working days of their removal

[10.14.2]   (2)   where ownership of any article obtained as a result of this Order is disputed to deliver up any such article to the custody of solicitors acting on behalf of the Defendant(s) within two working days of receipt of a written undertaking by such solicitors to retain the same in safe custody and to produce the same if required by the Court

[10.14.3]   (3)   save as mentioned above to retain in their safe custody until further Order all documents and articles obtained as a result of this Order

IT IS ORDERED:

[10.15.1]   1   THAT the Defendant(s) (and each of them), either himself/herself/itself/themselves or by a responsible officer or person appearing to be in control of the premises in question, do permit the person serving this Order upon him/her/it/them and such other persons duly authorised by the plaintiff (such other persons not to exceed [two] in number) [and not to include any person who might obtain commercial advantage over the Defendant(s) by carrying out this Order] to enter forthwith on any weekday between 9.30am and 5.30pm the premises mentioned in the schedule to this Order (herein referred to as 'the premises') and any vehicles on the premises, to the extent that such premises or vehicles are in the occupation, possession or control of the Defendant(s), for the purpose of looking for, inspecting, photographing and delivering into the custody of the Plaintiff's solicitors all documents and articles which are specified in the schedule to this Order (referred to herein as the 'specified items') or which appear to the supervising solicitor to be specified items.

2 PROVIDED ALWAYS:

(1) This order shall be served, and paragraph 1 hereof [10.15.2] carried out, only by [name] of [firm] or failing [him] [her] by [name] or some other solicitor approved for the purpose by the court (the solicitor serving the Order being referred to in this Order as 'the supervising solicitor').

(2) Before any persons enter the premises pursuant to this Order the supervising solicitor shall offer to explain to the person served with the Order its meaning and effect in everyday language, and shall also advise such person of his/her right to obtain legal advice before permitting entry provided such advice is obtained at once.

(3) Save to the extent that it is impracticable, no documents or articles shall be removed from the premises until after a list thereof has been prepared and a copy of the list has been supplied to the person served with this Order, and he or she has been given a reasonable opportunity to check the same.

(4) Save to the extent that this is impracticable, the premises shall not be searched, or any document or articles removed, except in the presence of an officer of the Defendant(s), or a person being, or appearing to be, a suitably responsible employee of the Defendant(s).

3 THAT the Defendant(s) do disclose forthwith to the Plaintiff's solicitor:

(1) the whereabouts of all specified items which are in [10.15.3] his/her/its/their possession custody or power; and

(2) to the best of the Defendant(s)'(s) knowledge and belief
   (a) the names and addresses of all persons to whom he/she/it/they has/have supplied or offered to supply any specified items; and
   (b) the names and addresses of all persons to whom he/she/it they has/have supplied or offered to supply and specified items; and
   (c) full details of the dates and quantities of each offer to supply and supply referred to in (a) and (b) above.

[10.15.4]   4   THAT the Defendant(s) do forthwith deliver to the Plaintiff(s)'(s) solicitor all specified items in his/her/its/ their possession custody or power.

[10.15.5]   5   THAT if any such item exists in computer readable form only the Defendant(s) shall cause it forthwith to be printed out and shall deliver the print out to the Plaintiff's Solicitors or (failing a printer) shall cause it forthwith to be displayed to the Plaintiff's solicitors in a readable form.

6   IT IS FURTHER ORDERED:

[10.15.6]   (1) That the Defendant(s) (and each of them) be restrained until [after the hearing of a summons returnable at ... on [date] or] further Order from (in the case of the (first) Defendant whether itself or by its officers or employees or agents or otherwise howsoever and as regards the (second) Defendant whether himself/herself or by his/her employees or agents or otherwise howsoever) doing any of the following acts or any of them, that is to say:

(a) directly or indirectly informing any person company or firm of the existence of these proceedings or of the provisions of this Order or otherwise warning any person company or firm that proceedings may be brought against him/her/it/them by the Plaintiff(s) otherwise than for the purpose of such Defendant obtaining legal advice from his/her/its/their lawyers.

(b) [Insert any particular further relief sought]

[10.16]   7   THE Defendant(s) is/are to be at liberty to apply to discharge or vary this Order upon giving to the solicitors for the Plaintiff [   ] hours' notice of his/her/ its/their intention to do so.

THE SCHEDULE

The Premises

The Specified Items

DATED THIS   day of [month] 199

If you, the within-named [name(s)] neglect to obey this order, you may be held to be in contempt of Court and liable to imprisonment.

[*OR, in the case of a body corporate:*
If you, the within-named X Ltd, neglgect to obey this order, you may be held in contempt of court and liable to sequestration of your assets.

OR, in the case of a body corporate where the plaintiff may wish to take enforcement proceedings against a director or other officer of the company:

If X Ltd neglects to obey this order, you, Uriah Heep (a director or officer of the said X Ltd) may be held in contempt of Court and liable to imprisonment.]

11.3   PRECEDENT OF A COMBINED MAREVA/ANTON
         PILLER ORDER (CHANCERY DIVISION)

IN THE HIGH COURT OF JUSTICE   199 Ch No
CHANCERY DIVISION
MR(S) JUSTICE

IN THE MATTER OF AN INTENDED ACTION

BETWEEN:

                                            Intended Plaintiff
                        and
                                            Intended Defendant

UPON MOTION made by Counsel for the Intended Plaintiff(s) ('the
Plaintiff(s)')

AND UPON READING the documents recorded on the Court file as
having been read

AND the Plaintiff(s) by Counsel undertaking

[10.13.1]   (1) forthwith to issue a writ of summons claiming relief
                  similar to or connected with that hereafter granted

[10.13.2]   (2) to make and file an affidavit (verifying what was
                  alleged by Counsel) [OR] (in the terms of the draft
                  Affidavit of [name])

[10.13.4]   (3) as soon as practicable to serve upon the Intended
                  Defendant(s) ('the Defendant(s)') a copy of such
                  affidavit and the exhibits capable of being copied and a
                  Notice of Motion for [Date] 199

             (4) to serve on the Defendant(s) forthwith after the
                  Plaintiff's solicitors receive the same a copy of a
                  written report on the carrying out of this Order which
                  shall be prepared by the supervising solicitor
                  mentioned below

[10.13.5]   (5) to bring such motion before the Court on the said date
                  and on that occasion to place before the Court the
                  written report of the supervising solicitor

(6) to obey any Order this Court may make as to damages if it shall consider that the Defendant(s) has/have sustained any damages because of this Order which the Plaintiff(s) ought to pay   [10.13.6]

(7) to obey any Order this Court may make as to damages if it shall consider that any innocent parties other than the Defendant(s) shall have sustained any damages by result of this Order which the Plaintiff(s) ought to pay.   [9.10.6]

(8) To serve a copy of this Order upon any third party to whom the Plaintiffs have given notice of this Order.

(9) To notify the Defendants and any third party to whom notice of this Order is given by the Plaintiffs or their solicitors of their right to apply to the Court on notice to carry or set aside this Order in so far as it may affect them.   [9.10.7]

(10) To notify any third party to whom notice of this Order is given by the Plaintiffs or their solicitors of their right to apply to the Court on notice to carry or set aside this order in so far as it may affect them.

AND the solicitors for the Plaintiff(s) by counsel for the Plaintiff(s) (being their counsel for this purpose) undertaking:

(1) to return the originals of all documents obtained as a result of this Order within two working days of their removal   [10.14.1]

(2) where ownership of any article obtained as a result of this Order is disputed to deliver up any such article to the custody of solicitors acting on behalf of the Defendant(s) within two working days of receipt of a written undertaking by such solicitors to retain the same in safe custody and to produce the same if required by the Court   [10.14.2]

(3) save as mentioned above to retain in their safe custody until further Order all documents and articles obtained as a result of this Order   [10.14.3]

IT IS ORDERED:

Anton Piller Order

[10.15.1]   1   THAT the Defendant(s) (and each of them), either himself/herself/itself/themselves or by a responsible officer or person appearing to be in control of the premises in question, do permit the person serving this Order upon him/her/it/them and such other persons duly authorised by the Plaintiff (such other persons not to exceed [two] in number) [and not to include any person who might obtain commercial advantage over the Defendant(s) by carrying out this Order] to enter forthwith on any weekday between 9.30am and 5.30pm the premises mentioned in the schedule to this Order (herein referred to as 'the premises') and any vehicles on the premises, to the extent that such premises or vehicles are in the occupation, possession or control of the Defendant(s), for the purpose of looking for, inspecting, photographing and delivering into the custody of the Plaintiff's solicitors all documents and articles which are specified in the schedule to this Order (referred to herein as the 'specified items') or which appear to the supervising solicitor to be specified items.

2   PROVIDED ALWAYS:

[10.15.2]   (1)   This order shall be served, and paragraph 1 hereof carried out, only by [name] of [firm] or failing [him] [her] by [name] or some other solicitor approved for the purpose by the court (the solicitor serving the Order being referred to in this Order as 'the supervising solicitor').

(2)   Before any persons enter the premises pursuant to this Order the supervising solicitor shall offer to explain to the person served with the Order its meaning and effect in everyday language, and shall also advise such person of his/her right to obtain legal advice before permitting entry provided such advice is obtained at once.

(3)   Save to the extent that it is impracticable, no documents or articles shall be removed from the premises until after a list thereof has been prepared and a copy of the list has been supplied to the person served with this Order, and he or she has been given a reasonable opportunity to check the same.

(4) Save to the extent that this is impracticable, the premises shall not be searched, or any document or articles removed, except in the presence of an officer of the Defendant(s), or a person being, or appearing to be, a suitably responsible employee of the Defendant(s).

3 THAT the Defendant(s) do disclose forthwith to the Plaintiff's solicitor:

(1) the whereabouts of all specified items which are in his/her/its/their possession custody or power; and [10.15.3]

(2) to the best of the Defendant(s)'(s) knowledge and belief

    (a) the names and addresses of all persons to whom he/she/it/they has/have supplied or offered to supply any specified items; and

    (b) the names and addresses of all persons to whom he/she/it they has/have supplied or offered to supply and specified items; and

    (c) full details of the dates and quantities of each offer to supply and supply referred to in (a) and (b) above.

4 THAT the Defendant(s) do forthwith deliver to the Plaintiff(s)'(s) solicitor all specified items in his/her/its/their possession custody or power. [10.15.4]

5 THAT if any such item exists in computer readable form only the Defendant(s) shall cause it forthwith to be printed out and shall deliver the print out to the Plaintiff's Solicitors or (failing a printer) shall cause it forthwith to be displayed to the Plaintiff's solicitors in a readable form. [10.15.5]

6 That the Defendant(s) (and each of them) be restrained until after [date] 199 or further Order in the meantime from (in the case of the (first) Defendant whether itself or by its officers or employees or agents or otherwise howsoever and as regards the (second) Defendant whether himself/herself or by his/her employees or agents or otherwise howsoever) directly or indirectly informing any person company or firm of the existence of these proceedings or of the provisions of this Order or otherwise warning any person company or firm that proceedings may be brought against him/her/it/them [10.15.6]

by the Plaintiff(s) otherwise than for the purpose of such Defendant obtaining legal advice from his/her/its/ their lawyers.

Mareva Injunction

[9.11.2(a)] 7 The Defendants be restrained and an injunction be granted restraining them until trial or further order in the case of the [   ] Defendant whether by its directors or by its servants or agents or any of them or otherwise howsoever and as regards the [   ] Defendant whether by himself, his servants or agents or otherwise howsoever, from removing from the jurisdiction, disposing of, mortgaging, assigning, charging or otherwise dealing with any of its/their [respective or joint] assets within the jurisdiction, including, but not limited to:

[9.11.2(b)] [here set out any particular accounts or other assets which it is intended should be specifically covered by the injunction, eg:]

(i) the freehold property known as [name] or (if the same has been sold) the net proceeds of sale thereof after discharge of any subsisting mortgage or charge

(ii) the property and assets of the business known as [name] carried on by the Defendant(s) from premises at [address] or (if and in so far as the same have been sold) the proceeds of sale thereof

(iii) any moneys in [any] account(s) [numbered] at [bank's name] at [bank's address] and without prejudice to the foregoing pledging charging or otherwise parting with title to or possession of such assets

[9.12.1(a)] save in so far as the unencumbered value of those assets exceeds £....

8 Notwithstanding paragraph 1 hereof, the Defendants shall be entitled to draw and expend from a bank account or other source the identity of which shall first be notified by them to the Plaintiffs' solicitors:

[9.12.1(b)] (a) A sum not exceeding £.... per week for ordinary living expenses;

[9.12.1(c)] [(b) A sum not exceeding £.... per week for ordinary business expenses]

[(c) A sum not exceeding £.... per week for reasonable legal expenses]

(d) Such further sum or sums, if any, as the Plaintiffs' solicitors may from time to time agree in writing.

Provided, however, that nothing in sub-paragraph (a), (b), (c) or (d) of this paragraph shall impose any obligation on any third party to enquire into the purpose or purposes for which any sum or sums drawn by the Defendants thereunder are in fact required or used.

9   Nothing in this Order shall prevent any bank from exercising any rights of set-off it may have in respect of facilities afforded by such bank prior to the date of this Order. [9.12.1(d)]

10 The Defendant(s) [and each of them] do forthwith disclose the full value of his/her/its/their [respective and joint] assets within the jurisdiction of this Court identifying with full particularity the nature of all such assets and their whereabouts and whether the same be held of his/her/its/their own names or by nominees or otherwise on his/her/its/their behalf and the sums standing in such accounts such disclosures to be verified by affidavit(s) to be made by the Defendant(s) [and in the case of the [   ] Defendants by its/their proper officer] and served on the Plaintiffs' solicitors within [insert] days of service of this Order or notice thereof being given. [9.13.1]

[11 The Plaintiffs have leave to issue and serve the Writ on the Defendants at [address] or elsewhere in [country]. The time for acknowledgment of service shall be .... days.]

12 THE Defendant(s) is/are to be at liberty to apply to discharge or vary this Order upon giving to the solicitors for the Plaintiff [   ] hours' notice of his/her/its/their intention to do so.

DATED THIS   day of [month] 199

If you, the within-named [name(s)] disobey those parts of this order which forbid you from doing acts, or if you neglect to obey the parts of this order which require you to do acts, you may be held to be in contempt of Court and liable to imprisonment.

[OR adapt as in precedent 1A in the case of a body corporate]

THE SCHEDULE

The Premises

The Specified Items

11.4 PRECEDENT OF A WORLDWIDE MAREVA INJUNCTION (CHANCERY DIVISION)

IN THE HIGH COURT OF JUSTICE   199 Ch No
CHANCERY DIVISION
MR JUSTICE   the day of 199

IN THE MATTER OF AN INTENDED ACTION

BETWEEN:

                           Intended Plaintiff
         and

    (1)
    (2)
    (3)   Intended Defendants

UPON MOTION made by Counsel for the Intended Plaintiff ('the Plaintiff')

AND UPON READING the draft Affidavits of
and

AND the Plaintiff by his Counsel undertaking

(1) Forthwith to issue a Writ of Summons in the form of   [9.10.1]
the draft produced to the Court and initialled by the
Judge and to serve the same on the Intended
Defendants ('the Defendants') as soon as is reasonably practicable thereafter.

(2) Forthwith to swear and file an Affidavit(s) [in the form   [9.10.2]
of the draft initialled by the Judge] [covering the
additional information given to the Court].

(3) Forthwith to give notice of the terms of this Order to   [9.10.3]
the Defendants by [means] and of the telephone
number of a representative of the Plaintiff's solicitors
to whom any notice of an application to set aside or
vary this Order may be given out of office hours.

(4) Forthwith to serve upon the Defendants a copy of the
said affidavit and the copiable exhibits thereto and
Notice of Motion for [insert date]

[9.10.5]   (5) To abide by any order which the Court may make as to damages in case this Court is hereafter of the opinion that the Defendants or any other person served with notice of this Order have suffered any by reason of this Order which the Plaintiffs ought to pay.

[9.10.6]   (6) (a) To indemnify any third party in respect of any costs, expenses, fees or liabilities reasonably incurred, from the time when this Order first adversely affected such third party, as a result of the making of this Order;

         (b) to pay the reasonable costs and expenses incurred by any third party to whom notice of the terms of this Order has been given, in ascertaining whether any assets to which this Order applies are within their control and in complying with this Order and to indemnify any such person against all liabilities which may flow from such compliance.

    (7) To serve a copy of this Order upon any third party to whom the Plaintiffs have given notice of this Order.

[9.10.7]   (8) To notify the Defendants and any third party to whom notice of this Order is given by the Plaintiffs or their solicitors of their right to apply to the Court on notice to carry or set aside this Order in so far as it may affect them.

IT IS ORDERED THAT:

1   The Defendants be restrained and an injunction be granted restraining them until trial or further order in the case of the [   ] Defendant whether by its directors or by its servants or agents or any of them or otherwise howsoever and as regards the [   ] Defendant whether by himself, his servants or agents or otherwise howsoever, from

    (a) removing from the jurisdiction of this Court, disposing of, mortgaging, assigning, charging or otherwise dealing with any of its/their [respective or joint] assets within the jurisdiction, including, but not limited to:
    [here set out any particular accounts or other assets which it is intended should be specifically

covered by the injunction, eg as suggested in [9.11.2(b)]
precedent 1A.]

(b) disposing of, transferring, charging, assigning,
diminishing or dealing in any way whatsoever
with any such assets wheresoever the same may be
situated (whether within or without the jurisdiction of this Court)

save in so far as the unencumbered value of those [9.12.1(a)]
assets exceeds £....

2   Notwithstanding paragraph 1 hereof, the Defendants
shall be entitled to draw and expend from a bank
account or other source the identity of which shall first
be notified by them to the Plaintiffs' solicitors:

(a) A sum not exceeding £.... per week for ordinary [9.12.1(b)]
living expenses;

[(b) A sum not exceeding £.... per week for ordinary [9.12.1(c)]
business expenses]

[(c) A sum not exceeding £.... per week for reasonable
legal expenses]

(d) Such further sum or sums, if any, as the Plaintiffs'
solicitors may from time to time agree in writing.

Provided, however, that nothing in sub-paragraph (a),
(b), (c) or (d) of this paragraph shall impose any obligation on any third party to enquire into the purpose or
purposes for which any sum or sums drawn by the
Defendants thereunder are in fact required or used.

3   Nothing in this Order shall prevent any Bank from [9.12.1(d)]
exercising any rights of set-off it may have in respect of
facilities afforded by such Bank prior to the date of this
Order.

4   PROVIDED that, in so far as this order purports to have
any extraterritorial effect, no person shall be affected
thereby or concerned with the terms therof until it shall
be declared enforceable or be enforced by a foreign court
and then it shall only affect them to the extent of such
declaration or enforcement UNLESS they are:

(a) a person to whom this order is addressed or an
officer of or an agent appointed by a power of
attorney of such a person, or

    (b) persons who are subject to the jurisdiction of this court and who
      (i) have been given written notice of this order at their residence or place of business within the jurisdiction, and
      (ii) are able to prevent acts or omissions outside the jurisdiction of this court which assist in the breach of the terms of this order.

[9.13.1]   5   The Defendant(s) [and each of them] do forthwith disclose the full value of his/her/its/their [respective and joint] assets within and without the jurisdiction of this Court identifying with full particularity the nature of all such assets and their whereabouts and whether the same be held of his/her/its/their own names or by nominees or otherwise on his/her/its/their behalf and the sums standing in such accounts such disclosures to be verified by affidavit(s) to be made by the Defendant(s) [and in the case of the [   ] Defendants by its/their proper officer] and served on the Plaintiffs' solicitors within [insert] days of service of this Order or notice thereof being given.

[9.14.1]   6   The Defendant(s) [and each of them] do forthwith upon the service of this Order deliver up or cause to be delivered up into the custody of the Plaintiffs' solicitors the items specified in the Schedule hereto.

       [7   The Plaintiffs have leave to issue and serve the Writ on the Defendants at [address] or elsewhere in [country]. The time for acknowledgment of service shall be .... days.]

       8   The Plaintiff is at liberty to serve Short Notice for [date].

       9   The Defendant(s) is/are to be at liberty to apply to discharge this Order upon giving to the Plaintiff's solicitors [24/48] hours' notice of their intention to do so.

DATED this   day of   199

If you, the within-named [name(s)] disobey paragraph 1 of this order, or if you neglect to obey paragraphs 4 and 5 of this order by the time stated, you may be held to be in contempt of Court and liable to imprisonment.

[*OR, in the case of a body corporate:*
If you, the within-named X Ltd, disobey paragraph 1 of this order, or if you neglgect to obey paragraphs 4 and 5 of this order by the time stated, you may be held in contempt of court and liable to sequestration of your assets.

OR, in the case of a body corporate where the plaintiff may wish to take enforcement proceedings against a director or other officer of the company:

If X Ltd disobey paragraph 1 of this order, or if X Ltd neglects to obey paragraphs 4 and 5 of this order by the time stated, you, Uriah Heep (a director or officer of the said X Ltd) may be held in contempt of Court and liable to imprisonment.][1]

THE SCHEDULE

The Specified Items

1   See RSC Ord 45, r 7(4) and note 45/7/6 at page 752 of volume 1 of the *Supreme Court Practice 1993.*

Appendix A

SUPREME COURT ACT 1981, SECTIONS 37(1)-(3), 72

37. Powers of High Court with respect to injunctions and receivers
(1) The High Court may by order (whether interlocutory or final) grant an injunction or appoint a receiver in all cases in which it appears to the court to be just and convenient to do so.

(2) Any such order may be made either unconditionally or on such terms and conditions as the court thinks just.

(3) The power of the High Court under subsection (1) to grant an interlocutory injunction restraining a party to any proceedings from removing from the jurisdiction of the High Court, or otherwise dealing with, assets located within that jurisdiction shall be exercisable in cases where that party is, as well as in cases where he is not, domiciled, resident or present within that jurisdiction.

Other provisions

72. Withdrawal of privilege against incrimination of self or spouse in certain proceedings
(1) In any proceedings to which this subsection applies a person shall not be excused, by reason that to do so would tend to expose that person, or his or her spouse, to proceedings for a related offence or for the recovery of a related penalty –
- (a) from answering any question put to that person in the firstmentioned proceedings; or
- (b) from complying with any order made in those proceedings.

(2) Subsection (1) applies to the following civil proceedings in the High Court, namely –
- (a) proceedings for infringement of rights pertaining to any intellectual property or for passing off;
- (b) proceedings brought to obtain disclosure of information relating to any infringement of such rights or to any passing off; and

    (c) proceedings brought to prevent any apprehended infringement of such rights or any apprehended passing off.

(3) Subject to subsection (4), no statement or admission made by a person –

    (a) in answering a question put to him in any proceedings to which subsection (1) applies; or

    (b) in complying with any order made in any such proceedings, shall, in proceedings for any related offence or for the recovery of any related penalty, be admissible in evidence against that person or (unless they married after the making of the statement or admission) against the spouse of that person.

(4) Nothing in subsection (3) shall render any statement or admission made by a person as there mentioned inadmissible in evidence against that person in proceedings for perjury or contempt of court.

(5) In this section –

    'intellectual property' means any patent, trade mark, copyright, registered design, technical or commercial information or other intellectual property;

    'related offence', in relation to any proceedings to which subsection (1) applies, means –

    (a) in the case of proceedings within subsection (2)(a) or (b) –

        (i) any offence committed by or in the course of the infringement or passing off to which those proceedings relate; or

        (ii) any offence not within sub-paragraph (i) committed in connection with that infringement or passing off, being an offence involving fraud or dishonesty;

    (b) in the case of proceedings within subsection (2)(c), any offence revealed by the facts on which the plaintiff relies in those proceedings;

    'related penalty', in relation to any proceedings to which subsection (1) applies means –

    (a) in the case of proceedings within subsection (2)(a) or (b), any penalty incurred in respect of anything done or omitted in connection with the infringement or passing off to which those proceedings relate;

    (b) in the case of proceedings within subsection (2)(c), any penalty incurred in respect of any act or omission revealed by the facts on which the plaintiff relies in those proceedings.

(6) Any reference in this section to civil proceedings in the High Court of any description includes a reference to proceedings on appeal arising out of civil proceedings in the High Court of that description.

Appendix B

STATE IMMUNITY ACT 1978, SECTIONS 2–14

Exceptions from immunity

2. Submission to jurisdiction

(1) A State is not immune as respects proceedings in respect of which it has submitted to the jurisdiction of the courts of the United Kingdom.

(2) A State may submit after the dispute giving rise to the proceedings has arisen or by a prior written agreement; but a provision in any agreement that it is to be governed by the law of the United Kingdom is not to be regarded as a submission.

(3) A State is deemed to have submitted –

    (a) if it has instituted the proceedings; or

    (b) subject to subsections (4) and (5) below, if it has intervened or taken any step in the proceedings.

(4) Subsection (3)(b) above does not apply to intervention or for any step taken for the purpose only of –

    (a) claiming immunity; or

    (b) asserting an interest in property in circumstances such that the State would have been entitled to immunity if the proceedings had been brought against it.

(5) Subsection (3)(b) above does not apply to any step taken by the State in ignorance of the facts entitling it to immunity if those facts could not reasonably have been ascertained and immunity is claimed as soon as reasonably practicable.

(6) A submission in respect of any proceedings extends to any appeal but not to any counter-claim unless it arises out of the same legal relationship or facts as the claim.

(7) The head of a State's diplomatic mission in the United Kingdom, or the person for the time being performing his functions, shall be deemed to have authority to submit on behalf of the State in respect of any proceedings; and any person who has entered into a contract on behalf of and with the authority of a State shall be deemed to have

authority to submit on its behalf in respect of proceedings arising out of the contract.

3. Commercial transactions and contracts to be performed in United Kingdom

(1) A State is not immune as respects proceedings relating to –
    (a) a commercial transaction entered into by the State; or
    (b) an obligation of the State which by virtue of a contract (whether a commercial transaction or not) falls to be performed wholly or partly in the United Kingdom.

(2) This section does not apply if the parties to the dispute are States or have otherwise agreed in writing; and subsection (1)(b) above does not apply if the contract (not being a commercial transaction) was made in the territory of the State concerned and the obligation in question is governed by its administrative law.

(3) In this section 'commercial transaction' means –
    (a) any contract for the supply of goods or services;
    (b) any loan or other transaction for the provision of finance and any guarantee or indemnity in respect of any such transaction or of any other financial obligation; and
    (c) any other transaction or activity (whether of a commercial, industrial, financial, professional or other similar character) into which a State enters or in which it engages otherwise than in the exercise of sovereign authority; but neither paragraph of subsection (1) above applies to a contract of employment between a State and an individual.

4. Contracts of employment

(1) A State is not immune as respects proceedings relating to a contract of employment between the State and an individual where the contract was made in the United Kingdom or the work is to be wholly or partly performed there.

(2) Subject to subsections (3) and (4) below, this section does not apply if –
    (a) at the time when the proceedings are brought the individual is a national of the State concerned; or
    (b) at the time when the contract was made the individual was neither a national of the United Kingdom nor habitually resident there; or
    (c) the parties to the contract have otherwise agreed in writing.

(3) Where the work is for an office, agency or establishment maintained by the State in the United Kingdom for commercial purposes, subsection (2)(a) and (b) above do not exclude the application

of this section unless the individual was, at the time when the contract was made, habitually resident in that State.

(4) Subsection (2)(c) above does not exclude the application of this section where the law of the United Kingdom requires the proceedings to be brought before a court of the United Kingdom.

(5) In subsection (2)(b) above 'national of the United Kingdom' means a citizen of the United Kingdom and Colonies, a person who is a British subject by virtue of section 2, 13 or 16 of the British Nationality Act 1948 or by virtue of the British Nationality Act 1965, a British protected person within the meaning of the said Act of 1948 or a citizen of Southern Rhodesia.

(6) In this section 'proceedings relating to a contract of employment' includes proceedings between the parties to such a contract in respect of any statutory rights or duties to which they are entitled or subject as employer or employee.

5. Personal injuries and damage to property

A State is not immune as respects proceedings in respect of –
  (a) death or personal injury; or
  (b) damage or loss of tangible property, caused by an act or omission in the United Kingdom.

6. Ownership, possession and use of property

(1) A State is not immune as respects proceedings relating to –
  (a) any interest of the State in, or its possession or use of, immovable property in the United Kingdom; or
  (b) any obligation of the State arising out of its interest in, or its possession or use of, any such property.

(2) A State is not immune as respects proceedings relating to any interest of the State in movable or immovable property, being an interest arising by way of succession, gift or bona vacantia.

(3) The fact that a State has or claims an interest in any property shall not preclude any court from exercising in respect of it any jurisdiction relating to the estates of deceased persons or persons of unsound mind or to insolvency, the winding up of companies or the administration of trusts.

(4) A court may entertain proceedings against a person other than a State notwithstanding that the proceedings relate to property –
  (a) which is in the possession of a State; or
  (b) in which a State claims an interest, if the State would not have been immune had the proceedings been brought against it or, in a case within paragraph (b) above, if the claim is neither admitted nor supported by prima facie evidence.

7. Patents, trade-marks etc
A State is not immune as respects proceedings relating to –
- (a) any patent, trade-mark, design or plant breeders' rights belonging to the State and registered or protected in the United Kingdom or for which the State has applied in the United Kingdom;
- (b) an alleged infringement by the State in the United Kingdom of any patent, trade-mark, design, plant breeders' rights or copyright; or
- (c) the right to use a trade or business name in the United Kingdom.

8. Membership of bodies corporate etc
(1) A State is not immune as respects proceedings relating to its membership of a body corporate, an unincorporated body or a partnership which –
- (a) has members other than States; and
- (b) is incorporated or constituted under the law of the United Kingdom or is controlled from or has its principal place of business in the United Kingdom, being proceedings arising between the State and the body or its other members or, as the case may be, between the State and the other partners.

(2) This section does not apply if provision to the contrary has been made by an agreement in writing between the parties to the dispute or by the constitution or other instrument establishing or regulating the body or partnership in question.

9. Arbitrations
(1) Where a State has agreed in writing to submit a dispute which has arisen, or may arise, to arbitration, the State is not immune as respects proceedings in the courts of the United Kingdom which relate to the arbitration.

(2) This section has the effect subject to any contrary provision in the arbitration agreement and does not apply to any arbitration agreement between States.

10. Ships used for commercial purposes
(1) This section applies to –
- (a) Admiralty proceedings; and
- (b) proceedings on any claim which could be made the subject of Admiralty proceedings.

(2) A State is not immune as respects –
- (a) an action in rem against a ship belonging to that State; or
- (b) an action in personam for enforcing a claim in connection with such a ship, if, at the time when the cause of action

arose, the ship was in use or intended for use for commercial purposes.

(3) Where an action in rem is brought against a ship belonging to a State for enforcing a claim in connection with another ship belonging to that State, subsection (2)(a) above does not apply as respects the first-mentioned ship unless, at the time when the cause of action relating to the other ship arose, both ships were in use or intended for use for commercial purposes.

(4) A State is not immune as respects –

    (a) an action in rem against a cargo belonging to that State if both the cargo and the ship carrying it were, at the time when the cause of action arose, in use or intended for use for commercial purposes; or

    (b) an action in personam for enforcing a claim in connection with such a cargo if the ship carrying it was then in use or intended for use as aforesaid.

(5) In the foregoing provisions references to a ship or cargo belonging to a State include references to a ship or cargo in its possession or control or in which it claims an interest; and, subject to subsection (4) above, subsection (2) above applies to property other than a ship as it applies to a ship.

(6) Sections 3 to 5 above do not apply to proceedings of the kind described in subsection (1) above if the State in question is a party to the Brussels Convention and the claim relates to the operation of a ship owned or operated by that State, the carriage of cargo or passengers on any such ship or the carriage of cargo owned by that State on any other ship.

11. Value added tax, customs duties etc
A State is not immune as respects proceedings relating to its liability for –

    (a) value added tax, any duty of customs or excise or any agricultural levy; or

    (b) rates in respect of premises occupied by it for commercial purposes.

Procedure

12. Service of process and judgments in default of appearance
(1) Any writ or other document required to be served for instituting proceedings against a State shall be served by being transmitted through the Foreign and Commonwealth Office to the Ministry of Foreign Affairs of the State and service shall be deemed to have been effected when the writ or document is received at the Ministry.

(2) Any time for entering an appearance (whether prescribed by rules of court or otherwise) shall begin to run two months after the date on which the writ or document is received as aforesaid.

(3) A State which appears in proceedings cannot thereafter object that subsection (1) above has not been complied with in the case of those proceedings.

(4) No judgment in default of appearance shall be given against a State except on proof that subsection (1) above has been complied with and that the time for entering an appearance as extended by subsection (2) above has expired.

(5) A copy of any judgment given against a State in default of appearance shall be transmitted through the Foreign and Common-wealth Office to the Ministry of Foreign Affairs of that State and any time for applying to have the judgment set aside (whether prescribed by rules of court or otherwise) shall begin to run two months after the date on which the copy of the judgment is received at the Ministry.

(6) Subsection (1) above does not prevent the service of a writ or other document in any manner to which the State has agreed and subsections (2) and (4) above do not apply where service is effected in any such manner.

(7) This section shall not be construed as applying to proceedings against a State by way of counter-claim or to an action in rem; and subsection (1) above shall not be construed as affecting any rules of court whereby leave is required for the service of process outside the jurisdiction.

13. Other procedural privileges

(1) No penalty by way of committal or fine shall be imposed in respect of any failure or refusal by or on behalf of a State to disclose or produce any document or other information for the purposes of proceedings to which it is a party.

(2) Subject to subsections (3) and (4) below –
   (a) relief shall not be given against a State by way of injunction or order for specific performance or for the recovery of land or other property; and
   (b) the property of a State shall not be subject to any process for the enforcement of a judgment or arbitration award or, in an action in rem, for its arrest, detention or sale.

(3) Subsection (2) above does not prevent the giving of any relief or the issue of any process with the written consent of the State concerned; and any such consent (which may be contained in a prior agreement) may be expressed so as to apply to a limited extent or generally; but a provision merely submitting to the jurisdiction of the courts is not to be regarded as a consent for the purposes of this subsection.

(4) Subsection (2)(b) above does not prevent the issue of any process in respect of property which is for the time being in use or intended for use for commercial purposes; but, in a case not falling within section 10 above, this subsection applies to property of a State party to the European Convention on State Immunity only if –

    (a) the process is for enforcing a judgment which is final within the meaning of section 18(1)(b) below and the State has made a declaration under Article 24 of the Convention; or

    (b) the process is for enforcing an arbitration award.

(5) The head of a State's diplomatic mission in the United Kingdom, or the person for the time being performing his functions, shall be deemed to have authority to give on behalf of the State any such consent as is mentioned in subsection (3) above and, for the purposes of subsection (4) above, his certificate to the effect that any property is not in use or intended for use by or on behalf of the State for commercial purposes shall be accepted as sufficient evidence of that fact unless the contrary is proved.

(6) *(Applies to Scotland.)*

Supplementary provisions

14. States entitled to immunities and privileges

(1) The immunities and privileges conferred by this Part of this Act apply to any foreign or commonwealth State other than the United Kingdom; and references to a State include references to –

    (a) the sovereign or other head of that State in his public capacity;

    (b) the government of that State; and

    (c) any department of that government, but not to any entity (hereafter referred to as a 'separate entity') which is distinct from the executive organs of the government of the State and capable of suing or being sued.

(2) A separate entity is immune from the jurisdiction of the courts of the United Kingdom if, and only if –

    (a) the proceedings relate to anything done by it in the exercise of sovereign authority; and

    (b) the circumstances are such that a State (or, in the case of proceedings to which section 10 above applies, a State which is not a party to the Brussels Convention) would have been so immune.

(3) If a separate entity (not being a State's central bank or other monetary authority) submits to the jurisdiction in respect of proceedings in the case of which it is entitled to immunity by virtue of subsection (2) above, subsections (1) to (4) of section 13 above shall

apply to it in respect of those proceedings as if references to a State were references to that entity.

(4) Property of a State's central bank or other monetary authority shall not be regarded for the purposes of subsection (4) of section 13 above as in use or intended for use for commercial purposes; and where any such bank or authority is a separate entity subsections (1) to (3) of that section shall apply to it as if references to a State were references to the bank or authority.

(5) Section 12 above applies to proceedings against the constituent territories of a federal State; and Her Majesty may by Order in Council provide for the other provisions of this Part of this Act to apply to any such constituent territory specified in the Order as they apply to a State.

(6) Where the provisions of this Part of this Act do not apply to a constituent territory by virtue of any such Order subsections (2) and (3) above shall apply to it as if it were a separate entity.

Appendix C

CIVIL JURISDICTION AND JUDGMENTS ACT 1982,
SECTIONS 24, 25 AND SCHEDULE 1 ARTICLE 1

PART IV
MISCELLANEOUS PROVISIONS

Provisions relating to jurisdiction

24. Interim relief and protective measures in cases of doubtful jurisdiction

(1) Any power of a court in England and Wales or Northern Ireland to grant interim relief pending trial or pending the determination of an appeal shall extend to a case where –

    (a) the issue to be tried, or which is the subject of the appeal, relates to the jurisdiction of the court to entertain the proceedings; or

    (b) the proceedings involve the reference of any matter to the European Court under the 1971 Protocol.

(2) *(Applies to Scotland only.)*

(3) Subsections (1) and (2) shall not be construed as restricting any power to grant interim relief or protective measures which a court may have apart from this section.

25. Interim relief in England and Wales and Northern Ireland in the absence of substantive proceedings

(1) The High Court in England and Wales or Northern Ireland shall have power to grant interim relief where –

    (a) proceedings have been or are to be commenced in a Contracting State other than the United Kingdom or in a part of the United Kingdom other than that in which the High Court in question exercises jurisdiction; and

(b) there are or will be proceedings whose subject-matter is within the scope of the 1968 Convention as determined by Article 1 (whether or not the Convention has effect in relation to the proceedings).

(2) On an application for any interim relief under subsection (1) the court may refuse to grant that relief if, in the opinion of the court, the fact that the court has no jurisdiction apart from this section in relation to the subject-matter of the proceedings in question makes it inexpedient for the court to grant it.

(3) Her Majesty may by Order in Council extend the power to grant interim relief conferred by subsection (1) so as to make it exercisable in relation to proceedings of any of the following descriptions, namely –

(a) proceedings commenced or to be commenced otherwise than in a Contracting State;

(b) proceedings whose subject matter is not within the scope of the 1968 Convention as determined by Article 1;

(c) arbitration proceedings.

(4) An Order in Council under subsection (3) –

(a) may confer power to grant only specified descriptions of interim relief;

(b) may make different provision for different classes of proceedings, for proceedings pending in different countries or courts outside the United Kingdom or in different parts of the United Kingdom, and for other different circumstances; and

(c) may impose conditions or restrictions on the exercise of any power conferred by the Order.

(5) An Order in Council under subsection (3) which confers power to grant interim relief in relation to arbitration proceedings may provide for the repeal of any provision of section 12(6) of the Arbitration Act 1950 or section 21(1) of the Arbitration Act (Northern Ireland) 1937 to the extent that it is superseded by the provisions of the Order.

(6) Any Order in Council under subsection (3) shall be be subject to annulment in pursuance of a resolution of either House of Parliament.

(7) In this section 'interim relief', in relation to the High Court in England and Wales or Northern Ireland, means interim relief of any kind which that court has power to grant in proceedings relating to matters within its jurisdiction, other than –

(a) a warrant for the arrest of property; or

(b) provision for obtaining evidence.

SCHEDULE 1
TITLE 1
SCOPE
ARTICLE 1

This Convention shall apply in civil and commercial matters whatever the nature of the court or tribunal. It shall not extend, in particular, to revenue, customs or administrative matters. The Convention shall not apply to:

(1) the status or legal capacity of natural persons, rights in property arising out of a matrimonial relationship, wills and succession;

(2) bankruptcy, proceedings relating to the winding-up of insolvent companies or other legal persons, judicial arrangements, compositions and analogous proceedings;

(3) social security;

(4) arbitration.

Appendix D

TORTS (INTERFERENCE WITH GOODS) ACT 1977,
SECTION 4

4. Interlocutory relief where goods are detained

(1) In this section 'proceedings' means proceedings for wrongful interference.

(2) On the application of any person in accordance with rules of court, the High Court shall, in such circumstances as may be specified in the rules, have power to make an order providing for the delivery up of any goods which are or may become the subject matter of subsequent proceedings in the court, or as to which any question may arise in proceedings.

(3) Delivery shall be, as the order may provide, to the claimant or to a person appointed by the court for the purpose, and shall be on such terms and conditions as may be specified in the order.

(4) The power to make rules of court under section 99 of the Supreme Court of Judicature (Consolidation) Act 1925 or under section 7 of the Northern Ireland Act 1962 shall include power to make rules of court as to the manner in which an application for such an order can be made, and as to the circumstances in which such an order can be made; and any such rules may include such incidental, supplementary and consequential provisions as the authority making the rules may consider necessary or expedient.

(5) The preceding provisions of this section shall have effect in relation to county courts as they have effect in relation to the High Court, and as if in those provisions references to rules of court and to section 99 of the said Act of 1925 or section 7 of the Northern Ireland Act 1962 included references to county court rules and to section 102 of the County Courts Act 1959 or section 146 of the County Courts Act (Northern Ireland) 1959.

Appendix E

RULES OF THE SUPREME COURT 1965, ORDER 24 RULE 14A,
ORDER 29 RULES 1, 1A, 2, 2A, 3, ORDER 30 RULE 1,
ORDER 41 RULES 5(2), 9, ORDER 45, RULE 7,
ORDER 72 RULE 1

ORDER 24 RULE 14A

Use of documents
14A. Any undertaking, whether express or implied, not to use a document for any purposes other than those of the proceedings in which it is disclosed shall cease to apply to such document after it has been read to or by the Court, or referred to, in open Court, unless the Court for special reasons has otherwise ordered on the application of a party or of the person to whom the document belongs.

ORDER 29

Interlocutory injunctions, interim preservation
of property, interim payments etc

Interlocutory injunctions, interim preservation of property, etc

Application for an injunction
1.—(1) An application for the grant of an injunction may be made by any party to a cause or matter before or after the trial of the cause or matter, whether or not a claim for the injunction was included in that party's writ, originating summons, counterclaim or third party notice, as the case may be.

(2) Where the applicant is the plaintiff and the case is one of urgency such application may be made ex parte on affidavit but, except as aforesaid, such application must be made by motion or summons.

(3) The plaintiff may not make such an application before the issue of the writ or originating summons by which the cause or matter is to be begun except where the case is one of urgency, and in that case the injunction applied for may be granted on terms providing for the issue of the writ or summons and such other terms, if any, as the Court thinks fit.

Cross-examination on assets disclosure affidavit

1A.—(1) Where –
- (a) the Court has made an order restraining any party from removing from the jurisdiction of the High Court, or otherwise dealing with, any assets,
- (b) that party has in compliance with the order, or any order made in connection with it, filed affidavit evidence as to his or any other assets, and
- (c) the Court has ordered that that party shall be cross-examined on his affidavit,

the Court may order that the cross-examination shall be conducted otherwise than before a judge, in which case the cross-examination shall take place before a master or, if a master so orders, before an examiner of the Court.

(2) The following provisions of Order 68 shall apply to a cross-examination of a kind referred to in paragraph (1)(c) as if it were a trial with witnesses in the Queen's Bench or Chancery Division and as if the person presiding were the judge –
- (a) rule 1(1) (except the words 'unless the judge otherwise directs'); and
- (b) rules 2(2) and (3) and 8.

(3) A cross-examination of a kind referred to in paragraph (1)(c) shall take place in chambers and no transcript or other record of it may be used by any person other than the party being cross-examined for any purpose other than the purpose of the proceedings in which the order for the cross-examination was made, unless and to the extent that that party consents or the Court gives leave.

Detention, preservation, etc, of subject-matter of cause or matter

2.—(1) On the application of any party to a cause or matter the Court may make an order for the detention, custody or preservation of any property which is the subject-matter of the cause or matter, or as to which any question may arise therein, or for the inspection of any such property in the possession of a party to the cause or matter.

(2) For the purpose of enabling any order under paragraph (1) to be carried out the Court may by the order authorise any person to enter upon any land or building in the possession of any party to the cause or matter.

(3) Where the right of any party to a specific fund is in dispute in a cause or matter, the Court may, on the application of a party to the cause or matter, order the fund to be paid into court or otherwise secured.

(4) An order under this rule may be made on such terms, if any, as the Court thinks just.

(5) An application for an order under this rule must be made by summons or by notice under Order 25, rule 7.

(6) Unless the Court otherwise directs, an application by a defendant for such an order may not be made before he acknowledges service of the writ or originating summons by which the cause or matter was begun.

Delivery up of goods under section 4 of Torts Interference with Goods) Act 1977

2A.—(1) Without prejudice to rule 2, the Court may, on the application of any party to a cause or matter, make an order under section 4 of the Torts (Interference with Goods) Act 1977 for the delivery up of any goods which are the subject-matter of the cause or matter or as to which any question may arise therein.

(2) Paragraphs (2) and (3) of rule 1 shall have effect in relation to an application for such an order as they have effect in relation to an application for the grant of an injunction.

Power to order samples to be taken, etc

3.—(1) Where it considers it necessary or expedient for the purpose of obtaining full information or evidence in any cause or matter, the Court may, on the application of a party to the cause or matter, and on such terms, if any, as it thinks just, by order authorise or require any sample to be taken of any property which is the subject-matter of the cause or matter or as to which any question may arise therein, any observation to be made on such property or any experiment to be tried on or with such property.

(2) For the purpose of enabling any order under paragraph (1) to be carried out the Court may by the order authorise any person to enter upon any land or building in the possession of any party to the cause or matter.

(3) Rule 2(5) and (6) shall apply in relation to an application for an order under this rule as they apply in relation to an application for an order under that rule.

ORDER 30, RULE 1

Receivers

Application for receiver and injunction
1.—(1) An application for the appointment of a receiver may be made by summons or motion.

(2) An application for an injunction ancillary or incidental to an order appointing a receiver may be joined with the application for such order.

(3) Where the applicant wishes to apply for the immediate grant of such an injunction, he must do so ex parte on affidavit.

(4) The Court hearing an application under paragraph (3) may grant an injunction restraining the party beneficially entitled to any interest in the property of which a receiver is sought from assigning, charging or otherwise dealing with that property until after the hearing of a summons for the appointment of the receiver and may require such a summons returnable on such date as the Court may direct, to be issued.

ORDER 41, RULES 5(2), 9

Affidavits

Contents of affidavit
5.—(2) An affidavit sworn for the purpose of being used in interlocutory proceedings may contain statements of information or belief with the sources and grounds thereof.

Filing of affidavits
9.—(1) Every affidavit used in a cause or matter proceeding in a district registry must be filed in that registry.

(2) Every affidavit used in an Admiralty cause or matter must, subject to paragraph (1) be filed in the Admiralty Registry.

(3) Every affidavit used in a cause or matter proceeding in the principal registry of the Family Division must be filed in that registry.

(3A) Every affidavit used in a cause or matter proceeding in the Chancery Division must, subject to paragraph (1), be filed in Chancery Chambers.

(4) Except as otherwise provided by these rules, every affidavit must be filed in the Central Office.

(5) Every affidavit must be indorsed with a note showing on whose behalf it is filed and the dates of swearing and filing, and an affidavit which is not so indorsed may not be filed or used without the leave of the Court.

ORDER 45, RULE 7

Service of copy of judgment, etc, prerequisite to enforcement under r 5

7.—(1) In this rule references to an order shall be constructed as including references to a judgment.

(2) Subject to Order 24, rule 16(3), Order 26, rule 6(3), and paragraphs (6) and (7) of this rule, an order shall not be enforced under rule 5 unless –

  (a) a copy of the order has been served personally on the person required to do or abstain from doing the act in question, and

  (b) in the case of an order requiring a person to do an act, the copy has been so served before the expiration of the time within which he was required to do the act.

(3) Subject as aforesaid, an order requiring a body corporate to do or abstain from doing an act shall not be enforced as mentioned in rule 5(1)(ii) or (iii) unless –

  (a) a copy of the order has also been served personally on the officer against whose property leave is sought to issue a writ of sequestration or against whom an order of committal is sought, and

  (b) in the case of an order requiring the body corporate to do an act, the copy has been so served before the expiration of the time within which the body was required to do the act.

(4) There must be prominently displayed on the front of the copy of an order served under this rule a warning to the person on whom the copy is served that disobedience to the order would be a contempt of court punishable by imprisonment, or (in the case of an order requiring a body corporate to do or abstain from doing an act) punishable by sequestration of the assets of the body corporate and by imprisonment of any individual responsible.

(5) With the copy of an order required to be served under this rule, being an order requiring a person to do an act, there must also be served a copy of any order made under Order 3, rule 5, extending or abridging the time for doing the act and, where the first-mentioned order was made under rule 5(3) or 6 of this Order, a copy of the previous order requiring the act to be done.

(6) An order requiring a person to abstain from doing an act may be enforced under rule 5 notwithstanding that service of a copy of the order has not been effected in accordance with this rule if the Court is satisfied that pending such service, the person against whom or against whose property is sought to enforce the order has had notice thereof either –

  (a) by being present when the order was made, or

  (b) by being notified of the terms of the order, whether by telephone, telegram or otherwise.

(7) Without prejudice to its powers under Order 65, rule 4, the Court may dispense with service of a copy of an order under this rule if it thinks it just to do so. -

ORDER 72, RULE 1

Commercial actions

Application and interpretation

1.—(1) This Order applies to commercial actions in the Queen's Bench Division, and the other provisions of these Rules apply to those actions subject to the provisions of this Order.

(2) In this Order 'commercial action' includes any cause arising out of the ordinary transactions of merchants and traders and, without prejudice to the generality of the foregoing words, any cause relating to the construction of a mercantile document, the export or import of merchandise, affreightment, insurance, banking, mercantile agency and mercantile usage.

Appendix F

COUNTY COURT REMEDIES REGULATIONS 1991 (SI 1991/1222)

1. These Regulations may be cited as the County Court Remedies Regulations 1991 and shall come into force on 1 July 1991.

2. In these Regulations, 'prescribed relief' means relief of any of the following kinds:–
   (a) an order requiring a party to admit any other party to premises for the purpose of inspecting or removing documents or articles which may provide evidence in any proceedings, whether or not the proceedings have been commenced;
   (b) an interlocutory injunction –
       (i) restraining a party from removing from the jurisdiction of the High Court assets located within that jurisdiction; or
       (ii) restraining a party from dealing with assets whether located within the jurisdiction of the High Court or not.

3. (1) Subject to the following provisions of this regulation a county court shall not grant prescribed relief or vary or revoke any order made by the High Court granting such relief.

(2) Paragraph (1) shall not apply to –
   (a) any county court held by a judge of the Court of Appeal or judge of the High Court sitting as a judge for any county court district;
   (b) a patents county court held by a person nominated under section 291 of the Copyright, Designs and Patents Act 1988 to sit as a judge of that court.

(3) A county court may grant relief of any kind referred to in regulation 2(b) –
   (a) when exercising jurisdiction in a family proceedings within the meaning of Part V of the Matrimonial and Family Proceedings Act 1984;
   (b) for the purpose of making an order for the preservation, custody or detention of property which forms or may form the subject matter of proceedings;

(c)   in aid of execution of a judgment or order made in proceedings in a county court to preserve assets until execution can be levied upon them.

(4) Paragraph (1) shall not –

(a)   affect or modify powers expressly conferred on a county court by or under any enactment other than section 38 of the County Courts Act 1984; or

(b)   prevent a county court from varying an order granting prescribed relief where all the parties are agreed on the terms of the variation.

4. An application to the High Court for relief of a kind referred to in regulation 2(a) in county court proceedings shall be deemed to include an application for transfer of the proceedings to the High Court.

5. (1) After an application for the prescribed relief has been disposed of by the High Court, the proceedings shall, unless the High Court orders otherwise, be transferred to a county court if –

(a)   they were transferred to the High Court; or

(b)   apart from these Regulations, they should have been commenced in a county court.

(2) Where an order is made on an ex parte application the application shall not be treated as disposed of for the purposes of paragraph (1) until any application to set the order aside or vary the order has been heard, or until the expiry of 28 days (or such other period as the Court may specify) during which no such application has been made.

Appendix G

PRACTICE DIRECTION (JUDGE IN CHAMBERS: PROCEDURE)
[1983] 1 WLR 433 AS AMENDED BY *PRACTICE DIRECTION
(JUDGE IN CHAMBERS: AMENDED PROCEDURE)* [1989]
1 WLR 359

A: Queen's Bench judge in chambers: special appointments.

1. All inter partes applications and appeals to the Queen's Bench judge in chambers will initially be entered in a general list. They will be listed for hearing in room 98[1] or some other room at the Royal Courts of Justice on Tuesdays or Thursdays.

Whenever it appears or is agreed that any application or appeal is likely to last more than 30 minutes it will immediately and automatically be transferred to either (1) the chambers appeals list or (2) for all cases other than appeals to the special appointments list.

2. Cases in the special appointments list will usually be heard on a date fixed after application to fix has been made by the parties.

The application to fix must be accompanied by an estimate of the length of the hearing signed by the applicant's counsel or solicitor who is to appear on the application.

3. Cases in the chambers appeals list will be listed in the Daily Cause List. This will be done by the Clerk of the Lists when he prepares the following day's list at 2pm. They may be listed on any day of the week but particularly on Fridays when there is often a need for short cases. They may be listed 'Floaters' when, because no experts or other witnesses are involved, they seem particularly well suited as such. Fixtures will only be given in exceptional circumstances.

4. In order to ensure that a complete set of papers in proper order is available for perusal by the judge before hearing such applications and

1 Now Room E101.

appeals, the parties must in advance of the hearing lodge in room 119 a bundle properly paged in order of date and indexed, containing copies of the following documents: (i) the notice of appeal or, as the case may be, the application; (ii) the pleadings (if any); (iii) copies of all affidavits (together with exhibits thereto) upon which any party intends to rely; and (iv) any relevant order made in the action. The bundle should be agreed. The originals of all affidavits intended to be relied on should be bespoken or produced at the hearing and all exhibits thereto should be available.

Where a date for hearing has been fixed (which will normally be the case for special appointments) the bundle must be lodged *not later than five clear days before the fixed date.*

For appeals and other cases where there is no fixed date for hearing the bundle must be lodged not later than 48 hours after the parties have been notified that the case is to appear in the warned list.

Except with leave of the judge, no document may be adduced in evidence or relied on unless a copy of it has been lodged and the original bespoken as aforesaid.

In cases of complexity a skeleton argument, or, where that would be helpful, a chronology should be lodged in room 119 at the same time as the bundle.

B. Queen's Bench judge in chambers: ex parte applications

A large increase in the number of applications made ex parte to the Queen's Bench judge in chambers makes it necessary to introduce a new and clearly understood procedure, which will be strictly followed.

1. The standard procedure, suitable for all ordinary ex parte applications will be: (1) that the applicant shall lodge with the clerk to the judge in chambers by 3.00pm on the day before the application is to be made, papers which should include (a) the writ (b) the affidavit in support, and (c) a draft minute of the order sought; (2) that the judge in chambers will hear the application at 10.00am on the following morning before embarking on his published list.

2. There will be some cases where the 3.00pm deadline specified in paragraph 1(1) cannot be met and where the urgency is too great to permit up to 24 hours' delay. Such applications should be dealt with in one or another of the three following ways. (1) The applicant's advisers shall attend on the clerk to the judge in chambers at 9.50am and lodge with him the papers listed in paragraph 1(1) and also a certificate signed by counsel (or solicitor if counsel is not instructed) that the application is of extreme urgency. The application will be heard by the

judge in chambers at 10.00am. (2) The applicant's advisers shall lodge the papers to include all those specified in paragraph 1(1) and attend on the clerk at 1.50pm. The application will be heard at 2.00pm. (3) In the very rare case where the application is of such urgency as to preclude either of the foregoing procedures the applicant's advisers may give notice to the clerk to the judge in chambers and the judge in chambers will hear the application at once, interrupting his list if necessary. In such a case the applicant's counsel or solicitor must be prepared to justify taking this exceptional course.

3. (1) Attention is drawn to the provisions of RSC Ord 29, r 1 which ordinarily requires the issue of a writ or originating summons and the swearing of an affidavit in support of an ex parte application for an injunction before it is made. (2) The affidavit in support should contain a clear and concise statement: (a) of the facts giving rise to the claim against the defendant in the proceedings; (b) of the facts giving rise to the claim for interlocutory relief; (c) of the facts relied on as justifying the application ex parte, including details of any notice given to the defendant or, if none has been given, the reasons for giving none; (d) of any answer asserted by the defendant (or which he is thought likely to assert) either to the claim in the action or to the claim for interlocutory relief; (e) of any facts known to the applicant which might lead the court not to grant relief ex parte; (f) of the precise relief sought. (3) Applicants for ex parte relief should prepare and lodge with the papers relating to the application a draft minute of the order sought. Such minute should specify the precise relief which the court is asked to grant. While the undertakings required of an applicant will vary widely from case to case, he will usually be required: (a) to give an undertaking in damages; (b) to notify the defendant of the terms of the order forthwith, by cable or telex if he is abroad; (c) in an application of Mareva type, to pay the reasonable costs and expenses incurred in complying with the order by any third party to whom notice of the order is given; (d) in the exceptional case where proceedings have not been issued, to issue the same forthwith; (e) in the exceptional case where a draft affidavit has not been sworn, or where the facts have been placed before the court orally, to procure the swearing of the affidavit or the verification on affidavit of the facts outlined orally to the court.

The order should as a general rule contain provisions for the defendant to apply on notice for discharge or variation of the order and for costs to be reserved.

Appendix H

GUIDELINES FOR THE MAKING OF ORDERS FOR THE DELIVERY UP OF CHATTELS, FROM *CBS (UK) V LAMBERT* [1983] CH 37, PER LAWTON LJ AT 44

'First, there should be clear evidence that the defendant is likely, unless restrained by order, to dispose of or otherwise deal with his chattels in order to deprive the plaintiff of the fruits of any judgment he may obtain. Moreover, the court should be slow to order the delivery up of property belonging to the defendant unless there is some evidence or inference that the property has been acquired by the defendant as a result of his alleged wrong-doing. In the present case, for example, the inference is that the motor vehicles which the defendants own could only have been purchased out of the proceeds of sale by the defendants of articles which infringe the plaintiffs' copyright. The inference is also that, if the defendants are forewarned or left in possession of the motor vehicles, those vehicles will be sold and the proceeds of sale dissipated or hidden so that the plaintiffs would be deprived not only of damages but also of the proceeds of sale of infringing articles which belong to the plaintiffs.

Secondly, no order should be made for the delivery up of a defendant's wearing apparel, bedding, furnishings, tools of his trade, farm implements, live stock or any machines (including motor vehicles) or other goods such as materials or stock in trade, which it is likely he uses for the purposes of a lawful business. Sometimes furnishings may consist of objets d'art of great value. If the evidence is clear that such objects were bought for the purposes of frustrating judgment creditors they could be included in an order.

Thirdly, all orders should specify as clearly as possible what chattels or classes of chattels are to be delivered up. A plaintiff's inability to identify what he wants delivered up and why is an indication that no order should be made.

Fourthly, the order must not authorise the plaintiff to enter on the defendant's premises or to seize the defendant's property save by permission of the defendant. In *Anton Piller KG v Manufacturing Processes Ltd* [1976] Ch 55 Lord Denning MR emphasised that the order in that case, at p 60:

> ". . . does not authorise the plaintiffs' solicitors or anyone else to enter the defendants' premises against their will . . . It only authorises entry and inspection by the permission of the defendants. The plaintiffs must get the defendants' permission. But it does do this: It brings pressure on the defendants to give permission. It does more. It actually orders them to give permission – with, I suppose, the result that if they do not give permission, they are guilty of contempt of court."

The order in the present case was in the same form.

Fifthly, no order should be made for delivery up to anyone other than the plaintiff's solicitor or a receiver appointed by the High Court. The court should appoint a receiver to take possession of the chattels unless satisfied that the plaintiff's solicitor has, or can arrange, suitable safe custody for what is delivered to him.

Sixthly, the court should follow the guidelines set out in *Z Ltd v A-Z and AA-LL* [1982] QB 558 in so far as they are applicable to chattels in the possession, custody or control of third parties.

Finally, provision should always be made for liberty to apply to stay, vary or discharge the order.

Guidelines are guidelines; they are not rules of court and the spirit of them and not the letter should be kept in mind.'

Appendix I

GUIDELINES RELATING TO MATERIAL SEIZED IN
EXECUTION OF ANTON PILLER ORDERS, FROM *COLUMBIA
PICTURE INDUSTRIES INC V ROBINSON* [1987] CH 38 AT 76–77

(a) Once the plaintiff's solicitors have satisfied themselves what material exists and have had an opportunity to take copies thereof, the material ought to be returned to its owner. The material need be retained no more than a relatively short period of time for that purpose. The order should be so drafted.

(b) It is essential that a detailed record of the material taken should always be required to be made by the solicitors who execute the order before the material is removed from the respondent's premises. So far as possible, disputes as to what material was taken, the resolution of which depends on the oral testimony and credibility of the solicitors on the one hand and the respondent on the other hand, ought to be avoided. In the absence of any corroboration of a respondent's allegation that particular material (for instance, divorce papers) was taken, a solicitor's sworn and apparently credible denial is likely always to be preferred. This state of affairs is unfair to respondents.

(c) No material should be taken from the respondent's premises by the executing solicitor unless it is clearly covered by the terms of the order. In particular, stated Scott J, it is wholly unacceptable that a practice has grown up whereby the respondent to the order is procured by the executing solicitor to give consent to additional material being removed: Scott J stated that he would not be prepared to accept that an apparent consent by a respondent had been freely and effectively given unless the respondent's solicitor had been present to confirm and ensure that the consent was a free and informed one.

(d) It is inappropriate that seized material, the ownership of which is in dispute, should be retained by the plaintiff's solicitors pending the trial. If the proper administration of justice requires that material taken under an Anton Piller order from the defendant should, pending trial, be kept from the defendant then those responsible for the administration of justice might reasonably be expected to provide a neutral officer of the court charged with the custody of the material. In lieu of such officer, and there is none at present, the plaintiff's solicitor ought, as soon as solicitors for the defendant are on the record, be required to deliver the material to the defendant's solicitors on their undertaking for its safe custody and production, if required, in court.

(e) The nature of the Anton Piller orders requires that affidavits in support of applications for them ought to err on the side of excessive disclosure. In the case of material falling into the grey area of possible relevance, the judge, not the plaintiff's solicitors, should be the judge of relevance.

Appendix J

GUIDELINES RELATING TO EXECUTION OF ANTON PILLER ORDERS, FROM *UNIVERSAL THERMOSENSORS LTD V HIBBEN* [1992] 1 WLR 840 PER SIR DONALD NICHOLLS V-C AT 860–861

'But arising out of the history of what occurred in the present case, the following points may be noted.

(1) Anton Piller orders normally contain a term that before complying with the order the defendant may obtain legal advice, provided this is done forthwith. This is an important safeguard for defendants, not least because Anton Piller orders tend to be long and complicated, and many defendants cannot be expected to understand much of what they are told by the solicitor serving the order. But such a term, if it is to be of use, requires that in general Anton Piller orders should be permitted to be executed only on working days in office hours, when a solicitor can be expected to be available. In the present case Mrs Hibben was alone in the house, with her children in bed. She was brought to the door in her night attire at 7.15am, and told by a stranger knocking on the door that he had a court order requiring her to permit him to enter, that she could take legal advice forthwith, but otherwise she was not permitted to speak to anyone else at all. But how could she get legal advice at that time in the morning? She rang her solicitor's office but, predictably, there was no response.

(2) There is a further feature of the situation to which I have just alluded which must never be allowed to occur again. If the order is to be executed at a private house, and it is at all likely that a woman may be in the house alone, the solicitor serving the order must be, or must be

accompanied by, a woman. A woman should not be subjected to the alarm of being confronted without warning by a solitary strange man, with no recognisable means of identification, waving some unfamiliar papers and claiming an entitlement to enter her house and, what is more, telling her she is not allowed to get in touch with anyone (except a lawyer) about what is happening.

(3) In the present case a dispute arose about what documents were taken away, and from which of the premises visited. Understandably, those who execute these orders are concerned to search and seize and then get away as quickly as possible so as to minimise the risk of confrontation and physical violence. Nevertheless, in general Anton Piller orders should expressly provide that, unless this is seriously impracticable, a detailed list of the items being removed should be prepared at the premises before they are removed, and that the defendant should be given an opportunity to check this list at the time.

(4) Anton Piller orders frequently contain an injunction restraining those on whom they are served from informing others of the existence of the order for a limited period. This is to prevent one defendant from alerting others to what is happening. There is an exception for communication with a lawyer for the purpose of seeking legal advice. In the present case that injunction was expressed to last for a whole week. That is far too long. I suspect something want awry with the drafting of the order in this case.

(5) In the present case there was no officer or employee of TPL or Emco present when their offices and workshops were searched and documents and components taken away. This is intolerable. Orders should provide that, unless there is a good reason for doing otherwise, the order should not be executed at business premises save in the presence of a responsible officer or representative of the company or trader in question.

(6) The making of an Anton Piller order in this case can be seen to be justified by what was discovered. But it is important not to lose sight of the fact that one thing which happened was that Mr James carried out a thorough search of all the documents of a competitor company. This is most unsatisfactory. When Anton Piller

orders are made in this type of case consideration should be given to devising some means, appropriate to the facts of the case, by which this situation can be avoided.

(7)   Anton Piller orders invariably provide for service to be effected by a solicitor. The court relies heavily on the solicitor, as an officer of the court, to see that the order is properly executed. Unhappily, the history in the present case, and what has happened in other cases, show that this safeguard is inadequate. The solicitor may be young and have little or no experience of Anton Piller orders. Frequently he is the solicitor acting for the plaintiff in the action, and however diligent and fair minded he may be, he is not the right person to be given a task which to some extent involves protecting the interest of the defendant. I think there is a force in some of the criticisms set out in the invaluable article by Professor Dockray and Mr Hugh Laddie QC on 'Piller Problems' (1990) 106 LQR 601. It seems to me that the way ahead here, pursuing one of the suggestions made in that article, is that when making Anton Piller orders judges should give serious consideration to the desirability of providing, by suitable undertakings and otherwise, (a) that the order should be served, and its execution should be supervised, by a solicitor other than a member of the firm of solicitors acting for the plaintiff in the action; (b) that he or she should be an experienced solicitor having some familiarity with the workings of Anton Piller orders, and with the judicial observations on this subject (eg as summarised in the notes in *The Supreme Court Practice 1991* to RSC Ord 29, r 3); (c) that the solicitor should prepare a written report on what occurred when the order was executed; (d) that a copy of the report should be served on the defendants; and (e) that in any event and within the next few days the plaintiff must return to the court and present that report at an inter partes hearing, preferably to the judge who made the order. As to (b), I can see advantages in the plaintiff being required to include in his evidence, put to the judge in support of his application for an Anton Piller order, details of the name of the solicitor and of his experience.

Of course this procedure would add considerably to the cost of executing an Anton Piller order. The Plaintiff would have to be responsible for paying the fees of the solicitor in question, without prejudice to a decision by the court on whether ultimately those costs should be borne in whole or in part by the defendant. But it must be appreciated, and certainly it is my view, that in *suitable and strictly limited cases*, Anton Piller orders furnish courts with a valuable aid in their efforts to do justice between two parties. Especially is this so in blatant cases of fraud. It is important therefore that these orders should not be allowed to fall into disrepute. If further steps are necessary to prevent this happening, they should be taken. If plaintiffs wish to take advantage of this truly draconian type of order, they must be prepared to pay for the safeguards experience has shown are necessary if the interests of defendants are fairly to be protected.'

Index